Organisational Learning and Effectiveness

Learning is increasingly seen as crucial to the success of organisations but many studies of the subject offer very little empirical evidence to substantiate this. Based upon in-depth research, including over seventy interviews with managers and employees, *Organisational Learning and Effectiveness* is an original and comprehensive analysis of learning organisations. Contents include:

- detailed case studies of five major international companies: Coca-Cola and Schweppes Beverages, 3M, Siebe, Mayflower and Morgan Crucible;
- the intellectual origins of organisational learning;
- best practice in organisational learning;
- the importance of leadership roles and skills;
- a critical examination of the usefulness and relevance of organisational learning and effectiveness.

Integrating management theory and practice, this volume is an extremely valuable resource for all those with an interest in organisational behaviour and human resource development.

John Denton has a PhD from the School of Management, Royal Holloway, University of London. He now works as a consultant for KPMG's HR Consulting Group.

Organisational Learning and Effectiveness

John Denton

London and New York

First published 1998
by Routledge
11 New Fetter Lane, London EC4P 4EE

Simultaneously published in the USA and Canada
by Routledge
29 West 35th Street, New York, NY 10001

© 1998 John Denton

Typeset in Perpetua by Routledge
Printed and bound in Great Britain by Creative Print and Design
(Wales), Ebbw Vale

British Library Cataloguing in Publication Data
A catalogue record for this book is available from the British
Library

Library of Congress Cataloging in Publication Data
A catalogue record for this book has been requested

ISBN 0–415–19214–5 (hbk)
ISBN 0–415–19215–3 (pbk)

Contents

Illustrations

Acknowledgements

Numerous people have contributed in a variety of ways to the realisation of this work. However, two people made contributions without which the project would have been impossible. Professor Charles Harvey, of Royal Holloway, University of London, was the wellspring of many of the conceptual insights in this book and my earlier PhD thesis. He was, despite a formidably full schedule, generous with his time and advice. He had the annoying ability of always being right, especially when I ignored his advice. Nevertheless, Professor Harvey's encouragement, support and advice are greatly appreciated. More than anything he gave me numerous ad hoc lessons in how to achieve things.

Alec Reed not only provided the financial support which made this research possible, but was also an invaluable source of ideas, inspiration, imagination, invention and often pure intuition. Despite his role as Chairman of Reed Executive plc, Mr Reed always found time to listen to my thoughts and ideas. He frequently took these ideas, remoulded them and returned them with a new, improved insight. In short, without the assistance of Messrs Reed and Harvey, this book would have been unlikely ever to see the light of day.

Dr Christian De Cock added a new level of complexity to the analysis with his knowledge and understanding of issues previously beyond the conceptualisation of the author. More than anything else he raised my understanding of methodological issues to a level hitherto unobtainable. Dr Paul Pal, a truly world-class expert in his field, guided me superbly through the collection and analysis of survey data. It is to his great credit that such valuable results accrued from the questionnaires.

As will become obvious to the reader, I am deeply indebted to managers in the five case companies, who generously allowed me to learn from their experience. Special mention goes to those who were kind (or foolish) enough to endure more than one interview: Ken Jackson and John Mueller at 3M; Keith Dennis at CCSB; Mike Fell at Mayflower; and Andy McIntosh at Morgan Crucible. Interviews with these men often managed to excite my enthusiasm just when spirits were beginning to flag.

The following individuals read and commented on early drafts of individual chapters or offered valuable ideas: Anita Criddle, Michael Gold, Peter Holt, Mairi McLean, Chris Rowley and David Skyrme. Denise Elliott saved me literally hundreds of hours of work by conscientiously typing many of the interview transcripts.

Two of my colleagues deserve special mention here: Ali Al-Shamali taught me how to win friends and influence people, while Jutta Howard listened to my problems and boosted my ego on the rare occasion that it flagged. I am pleased to include them both among my friends. Finally, a special thought here goes to my mother, who always believed in me and helped me to believe in myself.

1   Introduction

This book stems from the realisation that there remains a vital need to integrate managerial theory and practice. The search for a general theory of management has failed because the more comprehensive and inclusive any such theory becomes, the greater the barriers to its implementation. As Argyris suggests, 'no managerial theory, no matter how comprehensive, is likely to cover the complexity of the context in which the implementation is occurring' (Argyris, 1996: 1). Organisational learning, by emphasising change, adaptability and the utilisation of new knowledge, can offer a way of detecting and filling the gaps between theory and effective practice.

Almost all scholars would agree with the assertion that organisations must be able to learn. For example, in her wide-ranging review of the literature on organisational learning, Dixon concludes that learning is 'the critical competency of the 1990s' (Dixon, 1992). It is more open to question, although still widely accepted, that learning can be a source of competitive advantage. However, the actions that organisations should take to learn, and to use what they learn as a source of competitive advantage, are unclear. We are therefore in a situation where the need to learn at an organisational level is widely accepted, yet there is little or no agreement as to how organisations should achieve this. What is clear, however, is that both practitioner-oriented and academic authors have begun to acknowledge that people and knowledge are key determinants of organisational effectiveness. This realisation came to greatest prominence through the work of Peters and Waterman (1982), who championed customer service, corporate culture, vision and productivity through people as the means by which to achieve 'excellence'. This increasing focus on behavioural issues – rather than industry analysis and structure or competitive positioning – as sources of competitive advantage has been one of the dominant themes in management thinking during the 1980s and 1990s.

The particular element of organisational behaviour under most scrutiny has changed on a number of occasions during this period – vision, customer service, decentralisation, culture, teamworking, empowerment, learning – but the legacy has been an acceptance of the need to inspire commitment and participation from all quarters of the organisation.

It is in this climate that the concept of a learning organisation has arisen to meet a clear need. In Chapter 2 the trend towards the creation of learning organisations is seen as the result of a confluence of circumstances in which a set of antecedents have come together to create the environment where becoming a learning organisation is almost an imperative. Jones and Hendry explain that 'as an idea [the learning organisation] encapsulates a number of concerns and developments in the HRM field for bringing out the best in organizations and individuals' (Jones and Hendry, 1994: 153). Dibella *et al.* believe that 'theorists who advocate learning organisations have done a great service by envisioning the latest, if not the most critical state in an organisation's development' (Dibella *et al.*, 1996: 361). Senge argues, in the introduction to his best-selling book *The Fifth Discipline*, that 'the organizations that will truly excel in the future will be the organizations that discover how to tap people's commitment and capacity to learn at *all* levels in an organization' (Senge, 1990a: 4). It was Senge's work that really brought the notion of the learning organisation to the fore, and it spawned a rash of follow-ups, including one from Senge himself (see Senge *et al.*, 1994). However, organisational learning actually pre-dates Senge, particularly within the academic community. In Chapter 2 we will look at the work of authors such as Cyert and March (1963), Argyris and Schön (1978) and Pettigrew (1975, 1985), which laid the foundations for much of the later work on the learning organisation.

The learning organisation is an important concept in that it has attracted widespread interest from within both the academic and business communities. As we will see in Chapter 2, academics and practitioners have often taken markedly different approaches. Practitioners typically take a positive view of organisational learning, seeing it as an important route to sustainable competitive advantage. Academics, on the other hand, generally take a much more sceptical view of organisational learning, in many cases questioning whether it is anything more than a fashionable management fad with little or no real substance. One of our research goals is to assess these competing views critically and to mediate between them.

At this point it is apposite to offer a definition of a learning organisation, although we will consider this more fully in the next chapter. Returning to Senge's work, he describes learning organisations as places where 'people continually expand their capacity to create the results they truly desire, where new and expansive patterns of thinking are nurtured, where collective aspiration is set free, and where people are continually learning how to learn together' (Senge, 1990a: 3). Fiol and Lyles offer a simpler, yet more compelling, definition: 'organisational learning means the process of improving actions through better knowledge and understanding' (Fiol and Lyles, 1985: 803).

Organisational learning and the learning organisation

In this section we explain how the terms 'organisational learning' and 'learning organisation' are used in this book. Many previous works have used the terms organisational learning and learning organisation interchangeably. We will follow this convention here. Thus we are saying, in effect, that a learning organisation can be defined as an organisation that practices organisational learning. Conversely, organisational learning is the distinctive organisational behaviour that is practised in a learning organisation. Thus the two terms are effectively synonyms, but there are differences of nuance that should be pointed out. A learning organisation is an entity, while organisational learning is a process, a set of actions: organisational learning is something the organisation does; a learning organisation is something the organisation is.

Questions in organisational learning

The need for research into organisational learning should be evident from the above, and this view is borne out both by interest from the business community and by calls for further study from academics. Kilmann notes that 'many academics and practitioners are currently optimistic about the prospects for organizational learning – as a theoretical concept and a social technology' (Kilmann, 1996: 203). He goes on to point out that 'as this timely convergence of active interest rarely happens across these two (mostly separate) communities it seems important to seize the opportunity to produce useful knowledge for organizations' (*ibid.*). From a more traditionally academic standpoint, Dodgson (1993) argues that for a more complete understanding of the complexity of organisational learning a multidisciplinary approach would be required. Similarly, Miner and Mezias note that 'the ratio of systemic, empirical learning research to learning theories is far too low' (Miner and Mezias, 1996: 95). They go on to state: 'we believe that the current popularity of learning as a practical vision for managers increases rather than decreases the need for rigorous systematic research' (*ibid.*).

The interest of the business community in organisational learning is demonstrated by the excellent response to the questionnaire survey that forms an important part of this research and by the co-operation offered by the case-study companies. The questionnaire survey received a 40 per cent response rate, exceptionally high for a postal survey. Business interest in becoming learning organisations stems from the belief that this can be a valuable source of competitive advantage. For example, Andy McIntosh, Director of Group Personnel at Morgan Crucible, says: 'I think the organisation that sets out to be a learning organisation is one which inevitably has a competitive advantage.' In a similar vein, Ken Jackson, Director of Human Resources at 3M, believes that 'a learning organisation is a successful organisation'.

On the academic side, interest in organisational learning stems from a recognition of the appeal of the concept and the academic challenge involved in testing the main propositions put forward by populist writers. As Moingeon and Edmondson note: 'in recent popular management literature, learning is presented as a source of competitive advantage, but definitions and mechanisms involved in achieving this advantage are not specified' (Moingeon and Edmondson, 1996: 12). They also note the lack of empirical evidence to link learning with competitive advantage, while at the same time recognising the need to 'inspire further work in this promising new area of inquiry' (*ibid.*).

Ghoshal (1987) has argued that learning as a strategic objective (and particularly as part of a global strategy) has not been given adequate attention in the literature. Similarly, Inkpen asserts that: 'despite the logical notion that learning by organizations is essential to their success, there is a lack of synthesis and cumulative work in the area of organizational learning' (Inkpen, 1995: 48). Jones and Hendry offer an 'agenda for further research', including a call for studies to determine 'whether and how a learning organization gains a leading edge across its activities' (Jones and Hendry, 1994: 160–1). They also call for further research to establish whether 'there are specific advantages for organizations if they concentrate, over time, on creating and developing attitude change linked to learning, and how this manifests itself in terms of an expanding human resource strategy' (Jones and Hendry, 1994: 160).

A recurring theme among these calls for further research is the lack of an established link between organisational learning, on the one hand, and organisational effectiveness or competitive advantage, on the other. This is best expressed by Beer *et al.* (1996), who lament the lack of knowledge about the relationship between the substantive issues of business strategy and organisational learning.

It is these limitations in the current state of knowledge that are addressed in this book. The relationship between organisational learning and strategy is explicitly investigated, and the role of organisational learning as a source of competitive advantage is comprehensively examined. The main purpose of the research is to evaluate organisational learning as a means of building competitive advantage. The putative link between organisational learning and competitive advantage is a leitmotif of this book.

Major organisational learning research issues

In order to achieve the main aim noted above – the evaluation of organisational learning as a source of competitive advantage – a number of research goals were developed. The first research issues to be considered were the questions of why organisational learning is seen as important and why it has risen to prominence in recent years. In order to address this issue the following research goal was formulated: to explore the factors which have spurred the development of the learning organisation.

There was, and remains, a readily apparent need to establish exactly what a learning organisation is and how it differs from a 'standard' or 'non-learning' organisation. The best way of addressing this need is through the development of a model which enunciates the main characteristics of organisational learning. We will also consider which of these characteristics are considered most important by the case companies and why. Alternative definitions and views of the learning organisation are considered in the process.

Once we have addressed the characteristics of organisational learning, the next important issue is how these characteristics have been developed and applied in different organisational settings. A specific goal is the identification of best practice in organisational learning. Allied to this is the question of how businesses can become learning organisations. It is proposed that leadership has a vital role in creating a learning strategy, a clear vision and commitment throughout the organisation to the idea of organisational learning. An important, albeit secondary, goal is to assess the role that top management plays in creating learning organisations.

The final, and arguably most important, issues that this book addresses are the usefulness and relevance of the concept of organisational learning. These pertain directly to our main goal of evaluating organisational learning as a source of competitive advantage. There are a number of important issues. The first of these is the usefulness of organisational learning as a means of building competitive advantage. The second is the appropriateness of the learning organisation concept as a response to changes in the business environment. We will also look at the relevance of organisational learning to managers and ask whether it amounts to anything more than a disparate group of fairly standard management practices. A related issue is the relevance of organisational learning in different settings and situations. We consider the possibility that organisational learning may be exceedingly useful and highly relevant to certain groups in certain situations, but of little or no use and relevance to other groups in other situations. Overall, we shall see that the study provides interesting and original answers to a wide range of research questions. The book thus makes an original contribution to work in the field of organisational learning. It is particularly useful for its evaluation of the links between organisational learning, strategy, leadership and competitive advantage. Table 1.1 lists the research goals developed for this book and shows in which chapter or chapters they are addressed.

Research sources and methods

This section will describe the research methods chosen and the sources of data used for this book. An in-depth discussion of research methodology is beyond the scope of the book, and so we will confine ourselves to an explanation of what was done during the course of this research and why.

In the initial stage an exploratory questionnaire was sent to 400 medium-sized and large firms in the South-east of England, selected on a random basis, yielding 160 usable responses. The results confirmed that the majority of firms were familiar with the organisational learning concept and that active steps were being taken to promote the learning ideal. The companies that participated in the questionnaire are listed in Appendix 2.

The questionnaire was useful in highlighting the extent of familiarity with the organisational learning concept and the emphasis given in the literature to such things as teamworking and cross-functional working. It also served as a 'jumping-off' point for deeper qualitative research into the motivational and experiential aspects of organisational learning through the identification of potential research partners. Ultimately, five companies agreed to grant access

Table 1.1 Goals of the book

Goal	Chapter
To explore the factors which have spurred the development of the learning organisation	2: The antecedents of organisational learning
To develop a model of the characteristics of organisational learning and how they interrelate	3: Organisational learning practice in the five case companies 4: Best practice in organisational learning
To assess which of these characteristics are considered important by the case companies and why	3: Organisational learning practice in the five case companies 4: Best practice in organisational learning
To examine current best practice in organisational learning	3: Organisational learning practice in the five case companies 4: Best practice in organisational learning
To investigate how businesses can become learning organisations	4: Best practice in organisational learning 5: Organisational learning and leadership
To evaluate the role of top management in creating learning organisations	5: Organisational learning and leadership
To assess the usefulness of organisational learning as a means of achieving organisational effectiveness	6: The usefulness and relevance of organisational learning
To determine whether organisational learning is an appropriate and realistic response to changes in the business environment	6: The usefulness and relevance of organisational learning
To analyse whether organisational learning has any relevance for managers other than as an umbrella term for a disparate group of standard management practices	6: The usefulness and relevance of organisational learning
To assess the relevance of organisational learning for different groups and in different settings	6: The usefulness and relevance of organisational learning

to their management team, and to provide information in documentary form over and above that gathered through interviews. The five companies – 3M, Coca-Cola Schweppes Beverages (CCSB), Mayflower, Morgan Crucible and Siebe – all met the criteria for selection: they were involved in large-scale manufacturing operations; were UK-based (although not necessarily UK-owned); and were implementing, or about to implement, organisational learning initiatives across the company. Initially the organisation as a whole was considered; then we looked more closely at the use that the organisation makes of organisational learning as a source of competitive advantage.

The complex nature of this research made it clear that interviewing was the most suitable technique for gathering the sort of in-depth qualitative data required. The companies were comfortable with this approach and senior managers were in general happy to be interviewed. Most interviewees were open and quite willing to offer their opinions on a wide range of issues.

Appendix 1 lists the names of the interviewees at the five case companies, together with their position and the date of the interview. In total, sixty-six semi-structured interviews were carried out. Initially contact was made with a senior member of the human resource (HR) department (or equivalent department) in each company. HR directors were considered likely to be interested in the subject and also to have the necessary contacts within the organisation to facilitate the necessary interviews. For this reason, these senior managers were interviewed on more than one occasion in order to offer progress reports and maintain their support as key gatekeepers in the organisation. This also had the advantage of introducing a longitudinal element, as they could provide information on changes that had taken place since the previous interview. Interviews were requested with the chief executive or managing director of each organisation. Also high on the list of potential interviewees were people directly involved with organisational learning. In addition to this, suggestions were often made by the HR directors: 'You should go and talk to . . . he/she has been working on a very interesting project concerning . . . .' In this way the list of participants in the initial round of interviews was built up. Often these interviewees would suggest someone else who might be able to provide interesting information. This snowballing technique allowed interesting lines of research to be followed that might otherwise have stopped after one interview.

The approach to interviewing was semi-structured. Open-ended discursive questions and prompts were interspersed with direct questions put to all interviewees. This was considered to be the best way of encouraging individual managers to reveal how they thought and felt about organisational learning, how they had come across the idea, how they might capitalise upon it and how they assessed its potential. Instead of mirroring the official discourse, we aimed by this means to gain an understanding of the logic underlying the rise to prominence of the organisational learning concept.

The interview data were analysed using the conceptually clustered matrix technique. This involved an iterative search for recurring themes and issues in the data to codify response patterns as a prelude to the identification of similarities and differences between the five case companies. A particular strength of this technique is that it accommodates ambiguity, uncertainty and equivocation as legitimate qualifiers rather than compressing the data into predetermined categories. Meaning and generalisation are thus derived, not imposed.

In summary, the key research methods employed were to build a complex web of interviews on a strong foundation of survey research. The five case companies offered high-level access to managers who dealt regularly with organisational learning issues. The results of the fruitful interviews with these managers form the core of this book.

Outline of the book

In this section we outline the structure of the book. This may assist readers in selecting those parts of most interest. Chapter 2, 'The antecedents of organisational learning', focuses on those factors which have formed the driving forces behind the increased prominence and perceived significance of organisational learning. It thus addresses the first of the research goals presented in Table 1.1, the exploration of the factors which have spurred the widespread acceptance of organisational learning. The chapter begins by defining organisational learning and discussing its origins in the literature. The six antecedents of organisational learning are then discussed in detail. They are the shift in the relative importance of the factors of production away from capital towards labour, particularly intellectual labour; the increasing acceptance of knowledge as a prime source of competitive advantage; the increasingly rapid pace of change in the business environment; increasing dissatisfaction with the traditional command-and-control management paradigm; the increasingly competitive nature of global business; and the greater demands being placed on all businesses by customers. The driving forces, or antecedents, form the context in which organisational learning must be placed for it to be properly evaluated. The discussion of these antecedents is followed by an explanation of the filters through which knowledge regarding organisational learning is communicated to senior managers.

Figure 1.1 describes the author's model of the creation of a learning organisation. It shows the role of the six antecedents in creating first the opportunity and then the desire for organisational learning. This model is used as a basis for much of the book, with sections of the model reproduced

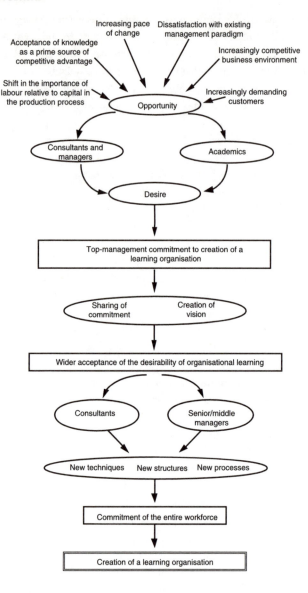

Figure 1.1 The creation of a learning organisation

in Chapters 2 and 5. Chapter 2 discusses how top management commitment to the creation of a learning organisation develops, while Chapter 5 looks at the steps through which top management might create a learning organisation. Other chapters also consider individual aspects of the model, with sharing of commitment and creation of vision both emphasised in the case studies in Chapter 3. New techniques, structures and processes are discussed in Chapter 4.

Chapter 3, 'Organisational learning practice in the five case companies', describes and assesses the way in which each of the five participating organisations approaches organisational learning. Each case study is considered in terms of three dimensions: strategy, structure and culture. This chapter introduces entirely new information, drawn from interviews with managers and employees in the case companies. The information is used to create a comprehensive picture of the way in which organisational learning is practised. It shows that there are significant differences between the approaches adopted by each company. This suggests that organisational learning is best viewed as a fairly loose construct.

The case studies in Chapter 3 are used as the foundation for much of Chapter 4, 'Best practice in organisational learning'. Chapter 4 is divided into two main parts: 'The characteristics of organisational learning' and 'The five case companies and best practice in comparative perspective'. In the first part a model will be developed showing the key characteristics of organisational learning. This part also outlines 'ideal' behaviour in terms of each characteristic. The second part places the five case companies in comparative perspective and assesses their respective attempts to achieve best practice. Comparative analysis of the key characteristics of organisational learning is followed by an integrative section comparing and contrasting the companies' approaches to organisational learning practice as a whole.

Chapter 5, 'Organisational learning and leadership', addresses a key management topic, and one which plays a vital role in the creation of a learning organisation. The chapter presents case studies of leadership and strategy in four of the case companies. The latest trends in leadership – such as self-managing teams, transformational leadership, corporate clusters and delayering – are discussed, and their implications for learning organisations are considered. Attention then turns to the leadership roles required to assist in the creation of learning organisations, including the leader as designer, as steward and as teacher. The chapter concludes by arguing that leadership roles have changed significantly and will continue to do so. Leaders must fulfil new roles to create shared vision and commitment, and to design a team-based organisation, the two foundations on which a learning organisation can be built.

Chapter 6, 'The usefulness and relevance of organisational learning', directly addresses our main theme of organisational learning as a source of competitive advantage. The usefulness of organisational learning refers to its ability to create meaningful benefits for companies which become learning organisations, while the relevance of organisational learning depends on its applicability in a variety of organisational settings.

In the first section, on usefulness, businesses which have applied the concept of organisational learning are examined to determine whether they have gained meaningful benefits. The chapter looks first at individual learning and then at the conversion of individual learning into organisational learning. The importance of achieving new behaviours as a result of learning is noted, as are the barriers which often prevent or delay change. Finally, we question whether the changed behaviour is necessarily superior, and whether changes can be measured or compared to what would otherwise have occurred. We show that it is difficult to attribute specific benefits to organisational learning but that it is probable that benefits do exist.

In a section on the relevance of organisational learning, we question the implicit assumption made by many writers that organisational learning is equally applicable to all organisations. Organisational learning is considered in different situations, in large and small organisations, in different industries, in the public sector and in different countries. We also discuss the prescience of organisational learning and argue that organisational learning is a timely counterpoint to the continuing trends in downsizing, delayering and outsourcing. The conclusion to this chapter outlines the view that the usefulness and relevance of organisational learning depend on how it is defined and on who is doing the defining. Managers tend to view organisational learning in terms of the group of management practices that it represents, which means it has limited, but still significant, usefulness as a guiding principle. Academics tend to define organisational learning far more tightly, making it valuable when explaining certain types of organisational behaviour, but limiting its value by narrowing the field of vision.

Chapter 7, 'Organisational learning and organisational effectiveness: myth and reality', provides an opportunity to review the previous chapters and draw out their significance. It is argued that organisational learning is an attractive concept, particularly to managers, despite readily apparent problems of definition and application. Notwithstanding the breadth, even vagueness, of the concept, it is likely that learning will become an important aspect of the strategies of many more companies. It is difficult to establish definitively a causal link between organisational learning and competitive advantage. However, it is clear that knowledge, and more specifically the application of knowledge, is a key source of competitive advantage, as are the people within an organisation. Organisational learning prioritises the creation and acquisition of new knowledge, and emphasises the role of people in the creation and utilisation of that knowledge. In this way, organisational learning represents an important route to competitive advantage.

2 The antecedents of organisational learning

Introduction

In this chapter we focus on the factors which have raised to prominence the notion of organisational learning. We attempt to answer the first of the research questions raised in the introduction: what factors have spurred the development of the learning organisation? We then turn to look at the various filters through which these driving forces are communicated to senior managers. The driving forces, or antecedents, form the context in which organisational learning must be placed before it may be explored effectively. Six antecedents of organisational learning have been identified as a result of both an extensive literature survey and discussions with managers from the case companies. The factors we consider include the shift in the relative importance of the factors of production away from capital towards labour, particularly intellectual labour; the increasing acceptance of knowledge as a prime source of competitive advantage; the increasingly rapid pace of change in the business environment; increasing dissatisfaction among managers and employees with the traditional, command-and-control management paradigm; the increasingly competitive nature of global business; and the greater demands being placed on all businesses by their customers. The discussion of these antecedents draws extensively on the existing literature in a number of areas, but this will be combined with new research from both the case companies and the questionnaire survey.

As Figure 2.1 shows, these antecedents do not on their own combine to create learning organisations; they merely create an environment in which the learning organisation is a possible route to competitive advantage. In other words, the driving forces create only the opportunity for organisations to become learning organisations. Some commentators would go further, arguing that the goal of becoming a learning organisation is necessary to survival. Stata, for example, argues that 'the rate at which individuals and organizations learn may become the only sustainable competitive advantage' (Stata, 1989: 64). Schein concurs, stating that 'current circumstances tell us that learning is no longer a choice but a necessity' (Schein, 1993: 85). It is not necessary to examine this debate too closely here, but it is clear that the antecedents combine to make organisational learning a desirable goal, if not a necessity.

Before an organisation is in a position to attempt to embark on becoming a learning organisation, desire must be added to opportunity. If a company's top management is to be committed to organisational learning, a prerequisite for its creation, then consultants and academics have a key role to play. They are required to disseminate and, in effect, sell the organisational learning concept to managers. Once the idea has penetrated the organisation it can be

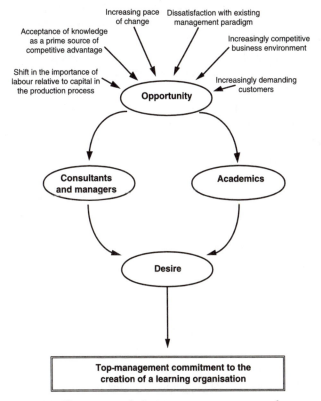

Figure 2.1 The creation of a learning organisation: antecedents to top-management commitment

communicated internally, but there is undoubtedly an initial step in which an outside agency must play a part. In the final part of this chapter we briefly look at these two filters, through one of which the idea of organisational learning is almost certain to pass before it can be implemented.

Before delving too deeply into either the antecedents of organisational learning or the relevant literature, it is necessary to ask, and answer, two other questions: first, what is meant by organisational learning and how can it be defined and, second, what are the origins of the concept?

Organisational learning defined

A variety of definitions of organisational learning have been put forward. These range from the technical – 'an entity learns if, through its processing of information, the range of its potential behaviours is changed' (Huber, 1991: 89) – to the simplistic – 'organizational learning is a process of detecting and correcting error' (Argyris, 1977: 116). Perhaps the most readily comprehensible and commonsense definition is that of Fiol and Lyles: 'organizational learning means the process of improving actions through better knowledge and understanding' (Fiol and Lyles, 1985: 803). A narrower definition is given by Levitt and March, who state that 'organizations are seen as learning by encoding inferences from history into routines that guide behaviour' (Levitt and March, 1988: 319). Pedler *et al.* describe a learning company as 'an organisation which facilitates the learning of all its members and continuously transforms itself' (Pedler *et al.*, 1988).

This range of definitions demonstrates that there is no widespread agreement about what organisational learning is or what constitutes a learning organisation. However, the definitions do allow some limited conclusions to be drawn about the nature of a learning organisation. Clearly, an organisation which has any claim to be a learning organisation must be able to generate new ideas, to propose new, untried solutions to its problems and, in general, to be 'creative'. Creativity, however, is not sufficient for an organisation to be a true learning organisation. A learning organisation must be able to act on the ideas it generates and to evaluate its ideas, rejecting those which are unsuitable. The organisations which are likely to be able to do this are those which are the most outward-looking and the most willing to change their behaviour. In short, generating ideas only makes becoming a learning organisation a possibility; it is the process of evaluating, selecting and implementing those ideas which characterises a learning organisation.

In the case companies examined in this research a number of different definitions of a learning organisation emerged. Morgan Crucible's Director of Group Personnel, Andy McIntosh, defined a learning organisation as 'an organisation that is constantly responding to the environment in which it operates'. At Siebe the Vice-President, Human Resources, Richard Bradford, defined organisational learning thus: 'individuals in the organisation may look at themselves internally and may benchmark against the outside and try to pick up knowledge by a process of either benchmarking or knowing what's going on in other industries'. 3M's Human Resources Director, Ken Jackson, defined a learning organisation as 'a company that's open-minded from top to bottom, to continually assess what it's doing, look outside, i.e. benchmark, and see where the best practice is outside'. He goes on to define organisational learning as 'clearly defined processes operating to enable the organisation to completely refresh and rethink its approaches to strategy and the way it operates'. The Personnel Director at CCSB, Keith Dennis, defines a learning organisation as an organisation 'that responds to the environment and recognises the changes that are taking place and that would continually adapt and change the way it behaves in order to stay relevant'. These definitions all emphasise the need to change and adapt, the need to look outside the organisation and, most importantly, stress that learning must not just take place for its own sake, but must result in a change in the organisation's behaviour or 'action patterns'.

Origins of organisational learning in the literature

The earliest reference to the term 'learning organisation' in the literature is probably from 1978, when Argyris and Schön published *Organizational Learning: A Theory in Action Perspective*. Another early reference to the learning organisation was included in Peters and Waterman's *In Search of Excellence: Lessons from America's Best-run Companies* (1982: 110). Probably the first publication with the phrase 'learning organisation' in the title was Hayes, Wheelwright and Clark's *Dynamic Manufacturing: Creating the Learning Organization* (1988), although there are many references to 'organisational learning' which pre-date this. The term 'learning organisation' was popularised by Peter Senge in his best-selling 1990 book on the subject, *The Fifth Discipline: The Art and Practice of the Learning Organization*, and it is now in widespread use among managers. As was explained in the introduction, the terms 'organisational learning' and 'learning organisation' are used interchangeably in this research. However, to some authors, notably Jones and Hendry (1994), the concepts are quite distinct. In fact, they argue that 'the emphasis within "organisational learning" on HRM [human resource management], training, and knowledge and skills acquisition tends to obscure the real issues behind the learning organisation' (Jones and Hendry, 1994: 154). Far from obscuring the real issues, I would argue that knowledge acquisition, for example, *is* one of the real issues behind the learning organisation. The distinction that can be created between 'organisational learning' and the 'learning organisation' is both unhelpful and unnecessary. As we have seen, there is already a great deal of debate about what is meant by organisational learning, and to create a further, artificial, distinction will only create further confusion. Managers, who are often the best judges of whether a term has any meaning, certainly use both terms interchangeably. Authors such as Wittgenstein (1990) have suggested that the meaning of a term is defined by its usage and location in particular social contexts. Thus from this viewpoint the terms 'learning organisation' and 'organisational learning' can be used interchangeably, since managers use them to represent the same aspect of organisational reality in terms of both meaning and content. For example, when asked what he understands by the term organisational learning, 3M's Director of Human Resources offers his definition, but then points out that 'I would have answered the same way to the question: what do I see as a learning organisation?' At CCSB the synonymous nature of the two terms is even more apparent. When faced with the same question about his understanding of the term 'organisational learning', the Director of Personnel replied, not by defining organisational learning, but by explaining what he saw as the attributes of a learning organisation. In these circumstances it would be perverse to create an artificial difference between the two terms when it is apparent not only that they are regularly used interchangeably but that this can be done without any loss of meaning.

The work on organisational learning stems, in part, from Cyert and March's (1963) observation that organisations adapt over time, a behaviour pattern that they term organisational learning. Their work has influenced a large number of other writers who have different ways of defining and describing learning. Argyris and Schön (1978) were particularly important in developing the work on learning as new insights or new knowledge, building on their distinction between single-loop and double-loop learning. By 1982 Chakravarthy was arguing that organisational learning was really about the process of adaptation and that adaptation is a key part of strategic decision-making. The work of Pettigrew (1975, 1985) widened the scope of organisational learning and brought it more into the mainstream. He also made important contributions in the areas of corporate culture, strategy and

HRM, which were, and are, complementary to his work on organisational learning.

Despite the existence of an increasing body of academic work on organisational learning, the concepts of organisational learning and the learning organisation, as conceived by managers today, are founded equally on the work of consultants. In many ways the notion of the learning organisation really arose as a more academic and philosophic development of the work on excellence, success and achievement in organisations. This body of work, typified by Peters and Waterman (1982), Gervitz (1984), Kanter (1989a) and Pascale (1990), tended to provide examples of best practice from successful, or not so successful, organisations. These books encouraged managers to work in ways compatible with the concept of a learning organisation, albeit without describing it as such.

This work on 'excellence' and the 'excellent organisation' was followed, and complemented, by Porter's (1985) work on competitive strategies and the creation of competitive advantages. In turn, the work of Hamel and Prahalad (1994) on core competencies goes beyond the Porterian perspective. Mintzberg (1994) and Kay (1993) have both written in the same spirit as Hamel and Prahalad. In *The Rise and Fall of Strategic Planning* (1994) Mintzberg is, as one would expect from the title of his book, fiercely critical of planning approaches to strategy. Hamel and Prahalad (1994) argue that strategic planning is no longer radical enough and is not sufficiently long term. This is due to the typically incremental nature of its goals. To overcome these problems they advocate the creation of strategic architecture. This is an altogether more radical approach, based on the complete redesign of an industry and thus the creation of an entirely new industry, in which the firm has a unique advantage. These theories have cross-fertilised much of the work on organisational learning and helped to push organisational learning to the forefront of managers' agendas.

The six antecedents of organisational learning

Senge (1990a) argues that organisations must learn (which he defines as finding ways to expand employees' capacity to create and produce results) if they want to succeed in the 1990s and beyond. He goes on to outline why the model used by most organisations is flawed and thus why they must become learning organisations. He states that the old, bureaucratic command-and-control model will not be good enough for the challenges ahead:

- It will not be fast enough to meet the new product development time of foreign competitors or to spot new market opportunities.
- It will not be wise enough to deliver the high levels of service customers will increasingly demand.
- It will not be smart enough to manage a diverse workforce or to motivate its smartest employees.

These three challenges touch on a number of the antecedents of organisational learning, but from a close look at the literature and careful attention to managers' views additional factors have been identified. In total, six main antecedents of organisational learning have been identified; they are:

1   The shift in the relative importance of the factors of production away from capital towards labour, particularly intellectual labour.
2   The increasing acceptance of knowledge as a prime source of competitive advantage.
3   The increasingly rapid pace of change in the business environment.
4   Increasing dissatisfaction among managers and employees with the traditional command-and-control management paradigm.
5   The increasingly competitive nature of the global business environment.
6   The greater demands being placed on all businesses by their customers.

In the next sections we will examine each of these antecedents in turn, drawing on both the existing literature and the research carried out in the case companies to explain their importance and their role in the emergence of organisational learning.

The shifting importance of factors of production

There is now a general consensus among informed commentators that a significant shift has taken place in the relative importance of the factors of production: the inputs or resources used in the production of goods or services. The three main factors of production are traditionally said to be land, labour and capital, with entrepreneurship often cited as the fourth factor. The dramatic shift that has taken place since the end of the Second World War has seen a greatly diminished role for land and capital. On the other hand, labour, and in particular intellectual labour, has become a much more powerful influence on production. Part of the reason for this shift has been the increasing importance of the tertiary sector of the economy relative to the secondary sector and, even more markedly, relative to the primary sector. More important, however, has been the easy availability of capital that has characterised business since 1945. In the introduction to her report *The Learning Organisation*, Graham writes that 'for several decades the world's most prescient observers of societal change have predicted the emergence of a new economy in which brainpower, not machine power, is the critical resource' (Graham, 1996: 1). Of these 'prescient observers of societal change' the most prominent is Peter Drucker, considered by many to be the most influential management thinker of the twentieth century. He dominates the work on both the shifting relative importance of the factors of production and the closely related topic of the increasing importance of knowledge, to which we will turn next. With regard to factors of production, Drucker (1992a) has suggested that capitalism is effectively dead. While this may be going a little too far, the assumption implicit in his statement – that capital is no longer the dominant factor of production – is more readily acceptable. Charles Handy (1989) has been another 'prescient observer of societal change', and he has argued consistently that people are now the core assets of organisations.

If Drucker has been the prophet bringing news of the end of capitalism, then Peters has been the champion of the factor of production that has replaced it – labour, or rather people. In all his books people are identified as a key source of success. The longest chapter of *In Search of Excellence* is devoted to 'Productivity Through People' (Peters and Waterman, 1982: 235–78), while in *A Passion for Excellence* one of the three 'secrets of long term excellence' is to make 'full use of the abilities of every company employee' (Peters and Austin, 1985: back cover). This theme of people as a key factor of production, as a critical success factor and a key source of sustainable competitive advantage, is revisited in Peters's later books. In *Liberation Management* (1992) he argues that the ability of individuals must be liberated and that, while strategy, organisation and processes are all important, it is people who are the key driving forces in a company.

Although individual learning is clearly different from organisational learning, the need to demonstrate a commitment to having a highly educated workforce may be an important reason for the movement towards organisational learning. The emphasis many organisations now place on education is exemplified by British Airways, which Heller (1992) describes as the Flying Business School because of its commitment to learning in general and management education in particular.

During the research carried out for this book, a number of managers touched on the importance of people, as opposed to capital, land, strategy or structure. At 3M the Chairman and Chief Executive states that:

> they [3M] have been very good to me, and very good to a lot of people, and I think that's one of the hallmarks of the company, and I think it's also one of the success criteria; that 3M, for at least as long as I've been with the company, and certainly our history suggests that we pay a great deal of attention to people, and I think that is a great assist to providing a proper environment for innovation and corporate renewal.
>
> (John Mueller, Chairman and Chief Executive, 3M UK)

Equally, 3M's Management Development Manager, Jeff Skinner, affirms his belief in 'some of the issues around "people are your only source of competitive advantage"'. At Morgan Crucible the Director of Group Personnel believes that:

> as an organisation we recognise that we're only ever going to be as good as the people that we have within the organisation, so I think over the last ten years we have made incredible step changes to our commitment to the development of our people.
>
> (Andy McIntosh, Director of Group Personnel)

The evidence from interviews in the five case companies is strongly supported here by evidence from the questionnaire survey. When asked to say what, if anything, makes their company distinctive, 47 (out of 160) respondents gave replies that could be interpreted as referring to the human resources (HR) in the organisation. This made HR the most popular answer, with quality second, with 36 replies. Answers referred to 'our people', 'the expertise of our staff' and 'enthusiastic, conscientious employees'. Clearly, the business community in general, as well as the case companies, has captured the idea that the people are vital to the success of organisations.

Given that the relative importance of the factors of production has shifted away from capital towards labour, we must examine the implications for organisational learning. What evidence is there to support the idea that this is one of the driving forces behind the emergence of organisational learning? When capital was the most powerful factor of production, bureaucratic command-and-control mechanisms were seen as the most effective management tools. The increasing importance of people has gradually forced companies to reduce levels of bureaucracy and create cultures which allow their employees greater freedom. Organisational learning is clearly a people-oriented philosophy, and so many organisations have come to see organisational learning as a way of managing the transition from focusing on mechanisms to focusing on people.

Knowledge as a source of competitive advantage

The second antecedent of organisational learning is the increasing importance of knowledge as a source of competitive advantage. It was Francis Bacon (1597) who first described knowledge as power, and this has never been more true than in today's information age. The original Latin phrase *nam et ipsa scientia potestas est* literally translates as 'for also knowledge itself is power'. With knowledge becoming ever more important, organisations which have the ability to learn, or the ability to create and gain knowledge, will have a clear source of power. Again, Drucker has been at the forefront in documenting the elevation of knowledge to the central position it occupies in business today, saying: 'knowledge is *the* primary resource for individuals and the economy overall' (Drucker, 1992a: 95). Since he coined the term 'knowledge work' in the 1960s it has been a recurring theme of his work. In *The Age of Discontinuity* (1969) he describes the United States as a 'knowledge economy'. In *Managing for the Future* he suggests that: 'from now on the key is knowledge' (Drucker, 1992b: 267), while in *Post-capitalist Society* Drucker writes: 'wealth-creating activities will be neither the allocation of capital to productive uses, nor "labour" . . . value is now created by "productivity" and "innovation", both applications of knowledge work' (Drucker, 1993: 7).

From a more rigorous and academic standpoint than Drucker's books, the work of von Krogh and Roos (1995, 1996) has been particularly influential in establishing the importance of knowledge as a source of competitive advantage. In *Managing Knowledge: Perspectives on Cooperation and Competition*, they argue that 'as we move from the industrial age to the information age, knowledge is becoming increasingly critical for the competitive success of firms' (von Krogh and Roos, 1996: 1) and 'the key to success in today's business is the application and development of specialised knowledge and competencies' (*ibid.*). They use epistemology to explain a range of organisational activities including globalisation, restructuring and strategic change. Frohman supports the importance of new knowledge in achieving change. He reports that, in every instance of change he studied, the change initiators had to learn something new: 'they grew in knowledge, experience, and skill as a result of bringing about the change' (Frohman, 1997). Boisot (1995) demonstrates his belief in the importance of knowledge as a factor of production by highlighting the need for a satisfactory economic theory to help manage the production and exchange of intangible objects like knowledge.

Another important writer in the field of knowledge and its importance to business is the Japanese academic, Ikujiro Nonaka. He introduces the concept of knowledge-creating companies, which are organisations where 'inventing new knowledge is not a specialised activity . . . it is a way of behaving, indeed a way of being, in which everyone is a knowledge worker' (Nonaka, 1991: 97). Describing knowledge-creating as a way of being and everyone as a knowledge worker may be more than a little extreme, but the general principle holds true: learning is a mode of behaviour, not a narrow, mechanical activity. In looking at the creation and transference of knowledge it is important to distinguish between tacit knowledge and explicit knowledge. Nonaka characterises tacit knowledge as highly personal, hard to formalise and therefore difficult to pass on to others. It is typified by the technical skills of a craftsman, which can only be learnt by years of training. However, the technical skills are only part of the tacit skills; an equally important part is played by the models, beliefs and perspectives of the craftsman.

Explicit knowledge, by contrast, is information which can be communicated relatively easily. By articulating tacit knowledge that has been assimilated it may be possible to create explicit knowledge. Following on from the distinction between tacit and explicit knowledge, Nonaka suggests four basic ways in which knowledge may be created in any organisation:

- from tacit to tacit;
- from explicit to explicit;
- from tacit to explicit;
- from explicit to tacit.

Tacit knowledge is created from tacit knowledge when one individual shares his own knowledge with another person. This occurs when one person learns directly from another, for example an apprentice learning directly from a skilled craftsman. The problem with the creation of tacit knowledge is that it cannot easily be taken advantage of by the organisation.

The creation of explicit knowledge from explicit knowledge occurs when an individual or an organisation puts existing, explicit pieces of information together and creates a new whole. Nonaka gives the example of a financial report, which is created by bringing together existing information but is new knowledge in the sense that it synthesises the information. The problem is, however, that the report does not really extend the organisation's knowledge base.

Tacit knowledge is converted into explicit knowledge through its articulation. If the craftsman can effectively communicate and explain his skills, then the knowledge becomes explicit. This is very important for the organisation because the knowledge is now much more easily exploited.

Explicit knowledge is converted into tacit knowledge if it is internalised by individuals. This often occurs when new knowledge is shared in the organisation; it often becomes part of the background information required for the job and it is taken for granted.

Nonaka goes on to suggest that in the knowledge-creating company 'all four of these patterns exist in dynamic interaction, a kind of spiral of knowledge' (Nonaka, 1991: 99). He suggests that articulation and internalisation are the critical steps in the spiral of knowledge, and that this is because of the active individual involvement needed. This need for articulation, internalisation and personal involvement means that the tools for managing a knowledge-creating company are very different from those found in many organisations at present. Nonaka suggests a number of tools for managing knowledge-creating companies:

- the use of metaphors, models and analogies;
- redundancy, i.e. the conscious overlapping of activities, information and responsibilities;
- teamwork and autonomy.

Nonaka suggests that the 'store of figurative language and symbolism that managers can draw from to articulate their intuitions and insights' (Nonaka, 1991: 99–100) is a very powerful tool for converting tacit knowledge into explicit knowledge. However, he complains that this is often overlooked by Western managers, while Japanese managers often use 'evocative and sometimes extremely poetic language' (*ibid.*: 100), especially in product development.

Turning to the concept of redundancy, Nonaka suggests that 'building a redundant organization is the first step in managing the knowledge-creating company' (Nonaka, 1991: 102). He shrugs off fears of unnecessary duplication and waste, and says that organisational design should have the specific goal of causing overlaps in company information, business activities and managerial responsibilities. Redundancy encourages frequent dialogue and communication, and thus it facilitates the transfer of tacit knowledge.

Looking at the importance of teamwork and autonomy, Nonaka says that 'teams play a central role in the knowledge-creating company' (Nonaka, 1991: 104). They provide an opportunity for individuals to interact and to create new perspectives through dialogue and discussion. The team pools the information of its members and then creates a new perspective from the sum of that knowledge.

Nonaka's concept of a knowledge-creating company undoubtedly has important implications for learning organisations. His distinction between tacit and explicit knowledge offers a useful model for looking at the different ways in which knowledge is created. Above all, he emphasises the importance of knowledge as a source of competitive advantage and as a driving force behind changes in organisational behaviour, structure and strategy.

Another key author in this area is James Brian Quinn, whose book *Intelligent Enterprise* (1992) is subtitled *A New Paradigm for a New Era: How Knowledge and Service Based Systems are Revolutionizing the Economy, All Industry Structures, and the Very Nature of Strategy and Organization.* This title might be somewhat long-winded, but it accurately conveys the flavour of the book, where Quinn prophesies that 'intelligent enterprises will derive sustainable competitive advantage from knowledge and service based activities that leverage intellectual assets' (Quinn, 1992). One of the most important points he makes concerns the way in which many of the traditional sources of competitive advantage – the largest raw materials resource, the most modern manufacturing plant or the best equipment – are now relatively easy to replicate. Knowledge, by contrast, is far more difficult to replicate, and so he predicts a move away from 'ephemerally superior products' to 'a few highly developed knowledge and service based "core competencies"' (*ibid.*).

The concept of knowledge as a key source of competitive advantage is not as apparent in the findings of this research as some of the other antecedents of organisational learning, but it is by no means absent. One manager who made particular reference to Drucker's concept of knowledge work was Siebe's Vice-President of Human Resources, who described the company's management development programme as 'majoring on what we call the knowledge worker'. 3M has a long and distinguished record of creating both new products and new knowledge. Its UK Technical Director, John Howells, explains that 'the one thing we are good at is converting technologies, capitalising, getting the return on investment from the technologies we have'. The technologies 3M possesses echo the knowledge-based core competencies to which Quinn refers, and they certainly represent a source of competitive advantage that is difficult to replicate.

The connection between the prominence of organisational learning and the increasing importance of knowledge as a source of competitive advantage should be readily apparent. If organisational learning means anything it must mean improving the ability of the organisation to create knowledge, to transfer knowledge, to use knowledge as a source of competitive advantage. If knowledge is truly becoming more important, then so must organisational learning. Thus the increasing importance of knowledge is a key antecedent of organisational learning. This idea is supported by Shoshana Zuboff, who notes that an organisation may need to become:

> [a] learning institution, since one of its principal purposes will have to be the expansion of knowledge – not knowledge for its own sake (as in academic pursuit), but knowledge that comes to reside at the core of what it means to be productive.
>
> (Zuboff, 1988: 395)

The increasingly rapid pace of change in the business environment

Change has probably generated as much interest as any management issue in the 1980s and 1990s. Certainly numerous academic articles have been written, and companies have devoted millions of personnel hours (and millions of pounds) to initiating change, managing change and trying to benefit from change. Perhaps most impressively, following a survey of approximately 12,000 managers from twenty-five countries for the *Harvard Business Review* World Leadership Survey, Kanter (1991) concluded that change is now an integral and accepted part of corporate life.

In any discussion of change it is important to distinguish between short-term or cyclical changes and long-term fundamental changes. Short-term changes might be fluctuating exchange, interest or inflation rates. The appropriate response in these cases is likely to be relatively limited. However, there is a danger that by 'fire-fighting' in response to problems managers fail to recognise longer-term underlying trends. Senge (1990a: 22) uses the parable of the boiled frog to illustrate this paradox. A frog placed in a pot of boiling water will immediately jump out. However, a frog placed in a pot of water which is at room temperature will stay put. If the water is then gradually heated the frog will happily sit in the water until it boils. The frog's ability to sense danger can pick up sudden changes in its environment, but not gradual changes which are equally threatening. In management some of the most important changes that take place are so gradual that they escape the notice of all but the most observant.

Long-term fundamental changes in the business environment inevitably call for major changes in a company's strategic direction. These may be as a result of economic changes, such as the globalisation of markets; technological changes, such as advances in information technology; political changes, such as privatisation; or social changes, such as increasing concern for the environment. There is no doubt that these changes have gathered pace in recent years and that new terminology has been developed to describe the changes. Sadler uses the word 'turbulent' to describe 'an environment characterised both by several changes occurring rapidly and simultaneously and by a situation such that only the most optimistic see the possibility of a return to a more stable environment in the foreseeable future' (Sadler, 1995: 21).

In a similar vein, Vaill refers to 'a world of permanent white water' (Vaill, 1989: 2), while Morgan conceives of 'riding the waves of change' (Morgan, 1988). Interestingly, both these authors use analogies that liken change to the movement of water. Peters (1987, 1992) stresses the importance of succeeding as a result, talking about *Thriving on Chaos* and *Necessary Disorganization for the Nanosecond Nineties*. In *Competing for the Future* Hamel and Prahalad (1994) point out that the increasing rate of change inevitably means that some companies will fail to keep pace. They argue that 'the painful upheavals in so many companies in recent years reflect the failure of one-time industry leaders to keep up with the accelerating pace of industry change' (*ibid.*: 5). They cite IBM, Philips, TWA, Texas Instruments, Xerox, Boeing, Daimler-Benz, Salomon Brothers, Citicorp, Bank of America, Sears and Pan Am among their list of companies which 'saw their success eroded or destroyed by the tides of technological, demographic, and regulatory change and order-of-magnitude productivity and quality gains made by non-traditional competitors' (*ibid.*: 6).

The idea that change is occurring at an ever-increasing rate is not confined to academic debate, however. It is a concept that has been accepted by most, if not all, managers who were interviewed for this research. At CCSB the Managing Director, Derek Williams, expressed his view of the pace and size of change thus: 'thinking about the future is probably going to be a redundant exercise because this massive reality is going to change in a massive way fairly shortly. It's always bloody changing.' Following Vaill's (1989) terminology, the Chairman and Chief Executive of 3M describes the 'ability to prosper in a period of permanent whitewater' as 'one of management's principle challenges of the next decade or so'.

The idea that a learning organisation can cope more effectively with rapid

Table 2.1 Conscious learning strategy and readiness for change

		Readiness for changes (relative to competitors)			
		Much lower / Slightly lower / About the same	Slightly higher	Much higher	Total
Conscious learning strategy	No	27 (17.1%)	21 (13.3%)	11 (7.0%)	59 (37.3%)
	Yes	19 (12.0%)	52 (32.9%)	28 (17.7%)	99 (62.7%)
	Total	46 (29.1%)	73 (46.2%)	39 (24.7%)	158 (100%)

Notes:
Chi-square value = 12.65014
DF = 2
Significance = 0.00179

change is supported by evidence from the questionnaire survey. One of the questions that respondents were asked was whether their organisation had a conscious learning strategy. In a separate question, respondents were asked to rate the readiness of their organisation for changes in the business environment. The answers to these two questions were cross-tabulated. As Table 2.1 shows, this produced a statistically significant result. Companies with a conscious learning strategy were found to be, in their opinion, more ready for changes in the business environment (see Figure 2.2).

Another interesting point is that, when asked to say what, if anything, makes their company distinctive, 24 (out of 160) respondents gave replies that could be interpreted as referring to the organisation's ability to manage change. Clearly, the business community has grasped the idea that increasing rates of change make the ability to manage change a key attribute of a successful organisation.

The most salient point about change from an organisational learning

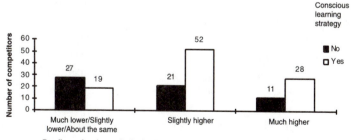

Figure 2.2 Conscious learning strategy and readiness for change

perspective is the impetus that it provides for organisations to find new information about their customers, their markets, their competitors, their
suppliers and themselves. The faster the world changes, the more there will
be to learn, and the more time, effort and money will be needed to keep pace
with all the changes. Becoming a learning organisation may be one way to
reduce the costs of learning by making learning a core competence which the
organisation can do effectively as part of its everyday activities.

Dissatisfaction with the existing paradigm

In 1970 Alvin Toffler presaged the dissatisfaction, uncertainty and worry felt
by many business people today. He coined the phrase 'future shock', which he
describes as 'the shattering stress and disorientation that we induce in individuals by subjecting them to too much change in too short a time' (Toffler,
1970: 12). He also defines future shock as 'the dizzying disorientation
brought on by the premature arrival of the future' (*ibid.*: 19–20). It has
become increasingly apparent in recent years that managers as well as
employees are suffering from future shock, i.e. they are dissatisfied with the
existing management paradigm and its inability to cope with the changes that
have already taken place, never mind the changes we can expect in the future.
This dissatisfaction is one of the key drivers of the development of the
learning organisation. The traditional bureaucratic command-and-control
model is increasingly felt to be outmoded, and many believe that it is time for
a change. The man who has articulated this dissatisfaction most thoroughly is
Handy. Crainer believes that 'Handy's increasingly bleak perspectives on the
nature of work and organisations are essential reading' (Crainer, 1996: 236).
In *The Age of Unreason* Handy is troubled that 'a world where the individual is
left even more to his or her own devices, as more of work and life moves
outside the institutions of society, could be a world designed for selfishness'
(Handy, 1989: 202). While much of the book is about change and the idea that
'the only prediction that will hold true is that no prediction will hold true'
(*ibid.*: 4), Handy repeatedly returns to the detrimental effect of the changes
that are now occurring for both organisations and individuals. In *The Empty
Raincoat* (1994) he argues that organisational life is increasingly dominated by
a series of paradoxes. Indeed the book was called *The Age of Paradox* in the
USA. Foremost among these paradoxes is the way in which information technology, despite promises to the contrary, has singularly failed to improve the
quality of people's lives. Handy believes that 'if economic progress means that
we become anonymous cogs in some great machine, then progress is an

empty promise' (Handy, 1994: x). Handy sees himself as the person with the opportunity to articulate the concerns and problems of many people, although he doesn't claim to be able to offer any solutions. Peters (1992) recognises many of the same problems as Handy, but he goes further, offering a vast range of potential solutions from which the reader is free to pick those that are relevant to him or her.

One of the reasons that Senge (1990a) gives for the increasing importance of organisational learning is the inability of the traditional command-and-control management system to motivate 'smart' employees. The traditional bureaucratic system may stifle the talents of the organisation's best people, encouraging them to fit in with the company profile, discouraging risk-taking and valuing experience more than results. By contrast, effective learning organisations recognise their employees as valuable assets, encouraging them to take risks and rewarding their successes. Probably more importantly, learning organisations trust their employees: managers and employees have a common set of values, information on the organisation's performance is widely circulated and rewards are equitably distributed.

Dissatisfaction with the traditional management paradigm was less apparent in the interviews, perhaps because of the desire of many managers to present an idealised vision of their organisation. However, dissatisfaction did surface on a number of occasions. At 3M the Chairman and Chief Executive touched on this dissatisfaction, saying:

> you have to work on how you make people comfortable in an environment that is always changing. You're fighting against some very basic tenets of the human creature; people like structure, they like to know how things work around here, and how to things get done, and their role in it. If you say, 'I can't tell you because it's always going to vacillate', then they get real uncomfortable.
>
> (John Mueller, Chairman and Chief Executive, 3M UK)

He goes on to point out that if the organisation abrogates its responsibility to tell them what's what 'they will always fill it in with the worst possible outcomes – Murphy's Law'. Mike Fell recognises the same problem and expresses similar sentiments:

> what I want to try to do, because it'll be much more powerful if we can get these people [middle managers] feeling comfortable, is to give them

a role which makes them important, so you take away the 'what's happening to my job?'
(Mike Fell, Human Resource Director, Automotive Division, Mayflower)

The clear dissatisfaction that exists in some parts of the business community is a very powerful force behind the rise of the learning organisation. Dissatisfaction with the existing paradigm creates a void, and organisational learning is one of the ideas competing to fill this void. The learning organisation is one of the most attractive of these ideas because it effectively meets many of the concerns that have led to the traditional paradigm being discredited. A study by Graham (1996) suggests a number of negative aspects of the status quo that may be addressed by organisational learning. These include lack of time and 'fire-fighting' (cited by 63 per cent of respondents), inability to gain access to information perceived to be privileged (47 per cent) and company politics (46 per cent).

The increasingly competitive nature of the business environment

Increasingly fierce competition has become a way of life for many businesses and a recurring theme of the management literature. In *When Giants Learn to Dance* Kanter says that winning in the new 'Corporate Olympics' requires:

> faster action, more creative manoeuvring, more flexibility, and closer partnerships with employees and customers than was typical in the traditional corporate bureaucracy. It requires more agile, limber management that pursues opportunity without being bogged down by cumbersome structures or weighty procedures that impede action. Corporate giants, in short, must learn to dance.
>
> (Kanter, 1989a: 20)

Could organisational learning be one way for companies to learn to dance? A learning organisation would certainly be likely to possess some of the characteristics that Kanter describes: the creative manoeuvring, the flexibility and the partnerships with employees. Kanter's thesis has proved compelling for many business leaders, including interviewees for this research, because it resonates so strongly with their own experience.

One of the key reasons for the increasingly competitive nature of the business environment is the increasing globalisation of business. This is not the place for an extended debate about the extent of globalisation, or an explanation of the causes of globalisation. However, its effects are to increase first the number and second the variety of competitors that a company faces. Companies now have to compete not just with their local or regional peers, but also with their global peers. This naturally leads to a more competitive environment, especially for those companies that previously enjoyed considerable market power in their home country or region.

Increased levels of competition, for whatever reason, mean that companies must be more aware of what their competitors are doing. In addition, more competitors now exist about which to be concerned. This means that more extensive competitor and environmental analyses are required. These are two key aspects of organisational learning: learning from competitors and learning from the environment.

Managers in the case companies were well aware of the increasingly competitive nature of the business environment. At CCSB the Managing Director emphasised that it is not just his company that is facing increased competition; his customers are too: 'the customer has changed over ten or twelve years. The customer is under a great deal more pressure to perform. His competition has gone up.' In this particular case much more is at stake than just increasingly fierce competition; the whole nature of the competitive playing field has changed. CCSB's customer is now its competitor: 'The major competitor for soft drinks in Sainsbury's is Sainsbury's. They have a 65 per cent share of soft drinks in Sainsbury's, because they own the company, own the stores, own the shelves and own their own brands.'

At Morgan Crucible the Managing Director, Bruce Farmer, emphasises the importance of globalisation, saying: 'if you don't become global, forget it' and 'global positioning is the key. Putting bases down in the key trading blocks around the world and then also developing the materials technology so we have a very wide range of markets that we go in.'

This increasingly competitive business environment is thus a powerful driving force behind the growth of the learning organisation. It is becoming more and more important for organisations to be manoeuvrable, fast-acting, aware of their competitors' actions. As this trend continues, the idea of becoming a learning organisation is made ever more attractive.

Increasingly demanding consumers

The rising power of consumers and the increasing demands they are making on companies constitute the final antecedent of organisational learning. As with the increasingly competitive business environment, globalisation has been a key factor in intensifying consumer pressure. In this case, however, it is the globalisation of markets rather than the globalisation of individual companies that has been a prime cause.

Key writers on this topic include Albrecht (1992) and Whiteley (1991), who both address the need for businesses to focus upon the demands of their customers. They both advocate making customers the focus of a company's strategy. Numerous other authors have expanded on the customer-focus theme, emphasising in particular the need to ensure that all interactions between company and customer are of a consistently high quality (Davis, 1994; Heller, 1992; Peters, 1987). It has been suggested, and is widely accepted by managers, that organisations need to improve both their understanding of customer requirements (Barabba and Zaltman, 1991; Zeithaml *et al.*, 1990) and their ability to meet those needs quickly and effectively (Meyer, 1993; Stalk and Hout, 1990).

Heller (1992) offers a classic example of the way in which companies have been forced to respond to the increasing demands of their customers. He cites rapid product development and, equally importantly, the ability to spot market opportunities as crucial to the success of Sony and many other Japanese high-tech companies. This is especially true when a comparison is made with European electronics companies like Philips. Despite producing the first video cassetter recorder (VCR) (and one which was clearly superior to its subsequent competitors) Philips failed to launch its Philips 2000 system until rival formats were well established. Not surprisingly, the launch failed and Philips was left lagging hopelessly behind Sony and JVC, who had both created successful business systems. These dynamic business systems contrasted markedly with Philips's slow, bureaucratic approach.

The importance of good service and the increasingly determined methods of many companies to provide this are well documented. It should be self-evident that only by learning what customers want (from the customers themselves) can an organisation have a realistic chance of providing an excellent service. Heller suggests that since 'the object of the exercise [redesigning the organisation] is to satisfy customers better and faster, customer information is the basic tool – along with information in general' (Heller, 1992). Echoing Garvin (1993), he suggests that information should not be generated by specialists, but by the people who will use it.

The pressing need to address the demands of the company's customers has been recognised and articulated by many of the interviewees in the case companies. 3M's Chairman and Chief Executive describes one of the company's features as 'its sensitivity to the customer' and he explains that, although 'this is certainly in vogue in all of the marketing press today, 3M's been practising it since the twenties'. He goes further, saying that 'the area we're really working on now, that is simply taking the whole capability forward, is to do a better job of what we call discovering unarticulated needs'. By this he means that although customers are often better able to anticipate their future needs they are often unable to articulate those needs effectively.

Organisational learning can allow organisations more effectively to address the increasing demands of their customers in two ways. First, learning organisations should be better equipped to understand exactly what it is that their customers want (Haines and McCoy, 1995). This knowledge can be acquired only by a constant effort to understand customers and learn from them. Second, having obtained the information, learning organisations should be well placed to respond rapidly to the needs of their customers. Responsiveness, both in terms of speed and quality of response, was commonly understood by managers in the case companies to be a crucial factor in determining whether business was won or lost.

The six antecedents: some conclusions

It should be clear from the above that the six antecedents are powerful driving forces, which, when working together, have led to the increased prominence and importance of organisational learning. Learning organisations thus result, in this analysis, from a confluence of circumstances, from the interaction of all the above antecedents. It is easy to see that the antecedents are related in a number of ways. In fact, they can be divided, with a reasonably high degree of order and common sense, into three pairs.

The increasing importance of knowledge as a source of competitive advantage is closely related to the shift in importance of the factors of production away from capital and towards labour. This increasing importance of intellectual labour, in particular, and its unique ability, the ability to apply knowledge, have clearly been an important reason for organisations to have the capacity to learn. As learning and knowledge have become more important, so have the people in the organisation, for it is only through these people that the organisation can acquire and apply that knowledge.

The dissatisfaction felt with the existing management paradigm is, as Senge (1990a) suggests, closely related to its inability to deal with the rapid pace of change that is prevalent today. Toffler makes this point clearly, with 'future shock', the very shock that managers and employees are now experiencing, being solely the result of 'too much change in too short a time' (Toffler, 1970:

12). It is clear that much of the dissatisfaction is a result of change, and thus a concept that allows change to be managed more effectively will also reduce the level of dissatisfaction.

The final pair of antecedents are the increasingly competitive nature of the business environment and the greater demands that customers are placing on all companies. The relationship between these two factors is not immediately apparent, but it is present nevertheless. The fact that customers are placing greater demands is a result, in large part, of the increasing choices that are available. The advent of global markets means that customers can now choose from goods and services provided by many more companies, operating from many more countries. This, in turn, means that customers are able to make greater demands on their current suppliers, purely because they now have the option of going elsewhere.

These are the six main antecedents that have driven the trend toward organisational learning, but there are other factors that have played a part. These include environmental pressures, which have forced companies to seek new ways of alleviating public concerns and meeting new demands; advances in information technology, which have placed it at the core of almost all organisations; and changes in society, which have led to a boom in temporary employment, outsourcing and flexible working. These factors have played a relatively small role, but some organisations may see organisational learning as a relevant response to some or all of these changes.

In summary, we can see that the emergence of organisational learning is not the result of any one factor, but rather the result of a confluence of circumstances. These circumstances, each of which by itself suggests that organisational learning may be a suitable way to proceed, have conspired to make organisational learning highly attractive to organisations faced with the long-term prospect of dealing with the combined problems resulting from the antecedents discussed above. This underlines why organisational learning represents a good opportunity for many organisations. However, to complete the picture we must also consider how the concept is communicated to organisations in general and to individual managers in particular. It is only after the concept and its potential benefits have been successfully communicated and the desire to become a learning organisation is established that organisational learning can become a reality.

Organisational learning filters

Huczynski (1993) argues that there are three main conduits through which management ideas can reach practising managers: academic gurus, consultant gurus and hero managers. To illustrate his taxonomy he classifies Philip Kotler, Michael Porter and Rosabeth Moss Kanter as academic gurus; Peter Drucker, Tom Peters and W. Edwards Deming as consultant gurus; and Lee Iacocca, John Harvey-Jones and Akio Morita as hero managers.

When one looks at the way in which ideas on organisational learning are communicated from a similar perspective, a clear dichotomy becomes apparent in the literature. Rather than the trichotomy that Huczynski creates, it is clear that there are effectively only two main groups of writers on organisational learning. As the learning organisation is a relatively new concept, certainly compared to the long-standing ideas Huczynski considers, there are, as yet, very few hero managers giving the world the benefit of their experiences in building learning organisations. For this reason, managers and consultants can be grouped together, especially as they write from a broadly similar perspective and make generally similar observations. This means that on one side of the divide are management consultants, for example Tobin (1993) and Wick and Leon (1993), senior managers, for example Stata (1989) and De Geus (1988), and a small number of academics, for example Garvin (1993) and Marquardt and Reynolds (1994); while on the other side of the divide is the majority of academics, for example Watkins and Marsick (1993) and Huber (1991). We will refer to these two groups as the consultancy school and the academic school, respectively. The difference between the two schools is apparent in the target audience for their works. On the consultancy side the books are written almost exclusively for the management market, while on the academic side the target market is students and other academics, as well as managers. The consultancy books are typically written in a highly prescriptive manner, extrapolating from case-study research in order to establish best practice. The authors then use their various models of best practice to make recommendations and provide solutions for a range of managerial problems. The academic works inevitably follow a more theoretical, analytical approach. They examine the factors influencing changes in organisational behaviour, and seek to explain, rather than merely describe, prevailing systems and practices. There is surprisingly little crossover between these two – in many ways opposing – schools. The only book to gain real credibility with the academic community while also selling to managers in large numbers is Senge's *The Fifth Discipline:The Art and Practice of the Learning Organization* (1990a). The importance of this book is shown in the discussion of the ways in which managers in the case companies learnt about organisational learning; this is presented later in this chapter.

Table 2.2 summarises the differences between the two schools in terms of a number of different criteria and outlines the different characteristics of each school. We then move on to look at each characteristic in detail.

The authors: consultants, managers and academics

On one side of the organisational learning dichotomy stand management consultants, senior managers and a small number of academics. On the other side is the majority of the academic community. It is interesting at this point to

Table 2.2 Organisational learning: consultancy school and academic school

Characteristic	Consultancy school	Academic school
Type of authors	Consultants	Academics
	Senior managers	
	Some academics	
Key writers	Calhoun Wick	C. Marlene Fiol
	Lu Stanton Leon	George Huber
	Michael Marquardt	Marjorie Lyles
	Angus Reynolds	Victoria Marsick
	David Garvin	Peter Vaill
	Michael Pearn	Karen Watkins
	Daniel Tobin	
Target audience	Managers	Academics
	Consultants	Students
Perspective	Best practice	Analytical
	Seek to make recommendations	Theoretical
View of organisational learning	Positive	Neutral
Terminology	Learning organisation	Organisational learning
Sources of information	Case studies	Empirical research
		Case studies
Type of publication	Books	Academic journals
	Harvard Business Review	Some books
	Training and personnel journals	

examine the motives of each group for writing about learning organisations. Management consultants typically write for one of two reasons: to promote their consultancy business or to sell large numbers of books. Both these motives encourage the authorship of particular types of books. For them to promote their consultancy businesses, organisational learning must be seen as a 'good thing' which any right-thinking manager would want to create. The manager should then, the logic runs, turn to the management consultant for (highly lucrative) advice on how to build a learning organisation. Equally, to sell large numbers of books the writer must make the concept appear attractive. However, if this is the motive he or she must go further and make the book interesting, entertaining, perhaps even controversial.

Academics, by contrast, typically write books for entirely different reasons. One key reason is to make a name for themselves in their chosen field. To do this they must be seen as educated, erudite, learned – in short, as academic. Naturally this desire colours the books written by academics; they are likely to be theoretical, with many references and abstract, theoretical arguments. Another motive for academics to publish books or articles on organisational learning is the very pressure to publish itself. Clearly, then, there are important differences between the two groups of authors, and we will reflect further on the consequences of these differences in what follows.

Key writers

In this section we will look at a number of the key authors on organisational learning and attempt to determine to which school they belong. Table 2.3 shows a number of leading authors in the field, an example of their work, their academic role (if any) and their professional role (if any). This information, together with an analysis of their work, is used to determine the final column, the school to which they belong.

Target audience

There is a marked contrast between the target audiences for each school and this is reflected in the content of the works. The consultancy school's books sell mainly to managers, with a significant number also being sold to consultants and academics. Managers clearly represent a much larger market for a successful book than academics, but ideally an author would wish to sell to both markets. Books written by members of the academic school are more likely to be purchased by academics and, in some cases, by students.

Table 2.3 Leading writers, their roles and schools

Name	Key work	Academic role	Professional role	School
Chris Argyris	*Organizational Learning: A Theory of Action Perspective* (with D. A. Schön)	Professor, Harvard Business School	Some consulting activities	Academic
Barbara Braham	*Creating a Learning Organisation*	None	Writer and speaker	Consultancy
Lu Stanton Leon	*The Learning Edge: How Smart Managers and Smart Companies Stay Ahead* (with C. W. Wick)	None	Journalist	Consultancy
James March	'Exploration and exploitation in organizational learning', *Organization Science*	Professor, Stanford University	None	Academic
Michael Marquardt	*Building the Learning Organisation: A Systems Approach to Quantum Improvement and Global Success*	Professor, George Washington University	President, Global Learning Associates (consultancy firm)	Consultancy
Victoria Marsick	*Sculpting the Learning Organization: Lessons in the Art and Science of Systemic Change* (with K. E. Watkins)	Associate Professor, Columbia University	Former Head of Training, UNICEF	Academic
Michael Pearn	*Learning Organizations in Practice* (with C. Roderick and C. Mulrooney)	None	Member (with his co-authors), Pearn Kandola Occupational Psychologists	Consultancy
Angus Reynolds	*The Global Learning Organisation: Gaining Competitive Advantage through Continuous Learning* (with M. J. Marquardt)	Former Professor, New York Institute of Technology	Instructional Technologist, EG&G Energy Measurements	Consultancy
Peter Senge	*The Fifth Discipline: The Art and Practice of the Learning Organization*	Director of Systems Thinking and Organisational Learning Program, MIT	Founding Partner, Innovation Associates (consulting firm)	Both
Ray Stata	'Organisational learning: the key to management innovation', *Sloan Management Review*	None	CEO, Analog Devices	Consultancy
Daniel Tobin	*Re-educating the Corporation: Foundations for the Learning Organisation*	None	Independent consultant	Consultancy
Peter Vaill	*Learning as a Way of Being: Strategies for Survival in a World of Permanent White Water*	Professor, George Washington University	None	Academic
Karen Watkins	*Sculpting the Learning Organization: Lessons in the Art and Science of Systemic Change* (with V. J. Marsick)	Associate Professor, University of Georgia	None	Academic
Calhoun Wick	*The Learning Edge: How Smart Managers and Smart Companies Stay Ahead* (with L. S. Leon)	Alfred Sloan Fellow, Sloan School of Management	Founder and President, Wick & Co. (consulting firm)	Consultancy

Note: These descriptions are taken from the relevant book or article. The individuals concerned may now hold different positions.

Perspective

Members of the consultancy school typically take a three-stage approach to writing about organisational learning. First, they seek to identify organisations that practice organisational learning. These learning organisations are then used to determine best practice. This best practice is then distilled into a series of recommendations for any organisation seeking to become a learning organisation. This approach has its advantages in its obvious appeal to managers wishing to create learning organisations. However, members of the academic school would argue that a more analytical approach is necessary. Thus works from this school use a more theoretical approach and attempt to assess critically the concept of the learning organisation. Recurring themes are the question of what is meant by learning, the difference between individual and organisational learning, and the principles and processes involved in developing a learning organisation. Clearly, however, these perspectives are quite different, and this is invariably a reflection of the target audience for the book.

Positive or negative view of organisational learning

We have already touched on the two schools' contrasting views of organisational learning, but it is instructive to examine this in more detail as the prevailing viewpoint raises important questions concerning the validity of the two schools' ideas. Those belonging to the consultancy school almost invariably have a very positive view of the potential benefits of organisational learning. Some seem to go so far as to regard organisational learning as a panacea for companies of any size, in any industry. One academic author who is particularly critical of the views of some consultants and their ignorance of the importance of issues such as power and politics is John Coopey (1996). Similarly, Mayo and Lank argue that 'Most writing on the learning organisation describes "ideal" cultural states where power agendas, politics and short-term thinking are subsumed under the greater issue of encouraging learning' (Mayo and Lank, 1995: 26).

Other authors of the consultancy school are more careful, acknowledging the undoubted problems that have occurred in many companies which have tried to create learning organisations. Academic writers, by contrast, adopt a much more critical stance. This is not to say that their view of organisational learning is automatically negative; rather, that they are more concerned with the relative costs and benefits of creating a learning organisation. The key point of difference here is in the two schools' treatment of learning. The consultancy school regards learning as a 'good thing' and seems to see no reason to question whether or not learning necessarily leads to improved organisational effectiveness. There are many examples of the consultants' positive views of organisational learning and there is room here only to list a few:

> In order for any organization to compete globally, it *must* foster constant learning. International businesses *must* become global learning organizations!
>
> (Marquardt and Reynolds, 1994: 19)

> Creating a learning organization is the way to move successfully from the old world to the new, from age-old business practices to a new set of procedures that will enable your company to thrive in the coming century.
>
> (Tobin, 1993)

> The most successful corporation of the 1990s will be something called a learning organization, a consummately adaptive enterprise with workers freed to think for themselves, to identify problems and opportunities, and to go after them.
>
> (Dumaine, 1989: 24)

As we have argued, the academic school takes a much more critical view of organisational learning. There is far less willingness to accept unquestioningly that learning automatically leads to benefits. Huber writes that: 'learning does not always increase the learner's effectiveness, or even potential effectiveness' (Huber, 1991). Friedlander (1983) goes further than this, pointing out that even if learning does result in a change in behaviour this might not be visible. He says that 'learning may result in new and significant insights and awareness that dictate no behavioural change' (*ibid.*: 194). If this is the case, then an individual or an organisation only learns if the range of potential behaviours is changed. This is a point that is overlooked in the consultancy school's desire, for various reasons, to present the creation of a learning organisation as a positive target that all organisations should be striving to achieve. This leaves the question of how to create a learning organisation as the remaining problem, and one that the consultants claim to be able to answer. We will consider the various answers to this question shortly, but first we must consider the sources of information that each school utilises.

Terminology: organisational learning or the learning organisation

One of the many distinctions we can make between the two schools is in the choice between the terms 'organisational learning' and 'learning organisation'. Academic writers tend to use the phrase 'organisational learning', while members of the consultancy school tend to write about 'learning organisations'. While this distinction does not hold true in all cases, it is sufficiently strong for a clear difference of emphasis to emerge. Many works in the field have used the phrases 'organisational learning' and 'learning organisation' interchangeably, but the choice of title, in particular, is a good indicator of target market and the school to which the work belongs. Of the two terms, 'learning organisation' is slightly softer, and perhaps its use allows members of the consultancy school to present a more favourable view.

Sources of information

This is one area in which there is a relatively high degree of uniformity in the literature. The vast majority of research on organisational learning, from academics and from consultants, takes the form of case studies. These typically involve the detailed analysis of a small number of companies. Each case is then written up in one of two ways. The first way is to write each case up separately to form a description of the way in which a particular company practices organisational learning. Alternatively, examples can be taken from each of the cases to illustrate more general points about organisational learning. Each of the two methods has its advantages, but the key point to make here is that the two schools both make extensive use of case studies when writing about organisational learning. This is taken to its extreme in the books that do not claim to be anything other than consultancy reports. An excellent example of this is Graham's *The Learning Organisation: Managing Knowledge for Business Success* (1996). This report contains a total of twenty case studies, and more of the report is taken up with these case studies than with all the other sections put together. While academic works also make use of case studies to examine current practice in organisations, there is a tendency in the consultancy school to overuse this technique. The academic school takes more care to examine whether the results it sees in one case are generalisable to other companies. Another problem with the consultant's approach is that there is a possibility that the writer will merely describe structures and processes in the case company, rather than seeking to explain the organisation's behaviour.

Type of publication

As we have already seen, writers from the consultancy school are most likely to publish their work as a book, while academics tend to favour articles in academic journals. As with all aspects of this analysis, there are, of course, a number of exceptions. Some members of the consultancy school have chosen to publish their work in the *Harvard Business Review*, other practitioner-oriented journals or even academic journals. Equally, an increasing number of academics have chosen to publish their work in book form, seemingly often in an attempt to widen their appeal to include managers.

Case companies' sources of information on organisational learning

During the sixty-six interviews with managers and employees from the case companies, each interviewee was asked whether he or she had heard of the concept of organisational learning. Those who had heard of the concept were then asked the source of their knowledge. The responses to this question are presented in Table 2.4. The following categories were derived using an iterative procedure: Senge's *The Fifth Discipline* (1990a); the *Harvard Business Review*; other publications; consultants; colleagues or other managers. All responses then fell into the most appropriate of these.

Managers' responses demonstrate the influential nature of Senge's work on organisational learning. Other important sources of information are the *Harvard Business Review*, other publications and conversations with other managers. Consultants were relatively unimportant as a source of information on organisational learning, with academics not featuring among the responses.

Table 2.4 Sources of information on organisational learning

Source of information	Number of responses
Senge's *Fifth Discipline*	7
Harvard Business Review	8
Other publications	12
Consultants	5
Colleagues/other managers	19
Total	51

Interestingly, however, total responses numbered fifty-one, the remaining fifteen interviewees being either previously unaware of the concept of organisational learning or unable to recall the source of their knowledge. This suggests that these fifteen managers or employees first came across organisational learning as an integrated set of management ideas in the interview with the author.

The intuitive appeal of organisational learning as a response to the changes that many managers know are taking place in the business environment means that it is an idea that can win acceptance even by word of mouth. This explains the importance of colleagues and other managers as a source of information. Organisational learning is, on one level at least, a simple, attractive idea and thus can be readily communicated by one manager to his or her colleagues. This is unlikely to be true of more complicated or less appealing management ideas.

Overall, the main originating sources of information are likely to be from the consultancy school. Practitioner-oriented works are, unsurprisingly, much more popular than academic works as a source of information for managers. This suggests that managers in the case companies are likely to have a positive view of organisational learning, reflecting the view of the consultancy school as a whole. This is something that will be confirmed in subsequent chapters when managers from the case companies describe their views of organisational learning.

Organisational learning filters: some conclusions

The clear difference in approach and outcome between the two schools means that anyone interested in organisational learning should be aware of the existence of both schools. An individual manager's view of organisational learning may well depend, more than any other factor, on which school he has been exposed to. Managers exposed to the consultancy school are likely to see organisational learning as a positive goal to aspire to, although there is of course the danger that the consultant will be seen as merely selling the latest fad. Managers exposed to the academic school are likely to see organisational learning in a different light, perhaps as a theoretical concept that has little relevance to their business. They are likely to be more critical of what the concept can or cannot achieve, although this may be a positive thing if it allows them to evaluate accurately the potential of organisational learning. The fact remains, however, that the concept of organisational learning has to pass through one of these two filters before it can become a reality in any organisation.

The antecedents of organisational learning: a restatement

The key objective of this chapter has been to answer the question of what factors have spurred the development of the learning organisation. We have seen that there are six main factors, or antecedents, which have combined to spur the development of the learning organisation. They are the shift in the relative importance of the factors of production towards labour; the importance of knowledge as a source of competitive advantage; the rapid pace of change; dissatisfaction with the existing paradigm; increasing competition; and increasingly demanding consumers. These factors, taken individually, represent a partial explanation of the emergence of the concept of the learning organisation. Taken together, they represent a very powerful spur for the development of the learning organisation.

We have seen the way that the learning organisation is presented as a potential solution to some or all of the problems created by these antecedents. Writers on organisational learning fall into two schools, each of which provides a different way of looking at organisational learning. These differing insights influence the way organisational learning is perceived by managers.

Overall, we must conclude that a very powerful set of factors has spurred the development of the learning organisation. These antecedents represent a powerful case for a change in the traditional management paradigm, and organisational learning has been presented as a suitable alternative. We will next look in more detail at the characteristics of organisational learning, before turning to assess its relevance, its usefulness and whether indeed it is a genuine alternative.

3 Organisational learning practice in the five case companies

Introduction

This chapter examines the ways in which each of the five organisations participating in this study approaches organisational learning. Each case looks at the organisation in terms of three levels or dimensions: strategy, structure and culture. The main objective is to introduce entirely new information, drawn largely from interviews with managers and employees in the case companies. This information is of value in creating a clearer picture of the ways in which organisational learning is practised.

Thus, rather than merely providing a summary of each company from published information, the chapter offers rich, fresh, detailed insights about dominant structures, processes and cultures. This chapter is complemented by Chapter 4, which places the cases in comparative perspective and develops a realistic model of best practice.

The practice of organisational learning: the case of 3M

3M is the preferred name of the Minnesota Mining and Manufacturing Company. It is a company that between 1985 and 1995 gave its investors a solid 15.5 per cent annual return. Between 1985 and 1996 it scored in the top ten on *Fortune*'s list of Most Admired Corporations ten times (Stewart, 1996). 3M is widely regarded as one of the world's most innovative companies. The *International Directory of Company Histories* notes that 'observers and outsiders frequently describe Minnesota Mining and Manufacturing in terms approaching awe' (Derdak, 1988: 499).

The keys to understanding organisational learning within 3M are its structure and its culture – the two strongest elements of its organisational identity.

These elements combine to give 3M its most distinctive attribute: its ability to innovate. However, this is not to say that strategy does not play an important role within 3M, and certainly the vision element of its strategy is an important source of strength for the company. 3M's impressive diversity of products is unique among the case companies – and, arguably, among companies at large.

The strategic dimension

It could be argued that 3M has failed to create a strategy of conscious learning. However, its strategy consciously embraces innovation so thoroughly that this has to be considered a de facto learning strategy. No organisation can innovate unless it can learn. New products cannot be created unless new knowledge is also created. A key aspect of 3M's strategy is its well-publicised commitment to produce 30 per cent of revenue each year from products introduced in the last four years (*3M Annual Report*, 1994). This objective is regularly met or exceeded, both by the company as a whole and by the individual businesses within 3M. This approach has now been extended to include a further goal, with the current Chairman and Chief Executive, Livio DeSimone, declaring in 1994 that he wanted 10 per cent of revenues to come from products less than a year old. 3M's other key financial objectives are earnings-per-share growth of 10 per cent or better a year, on average; return on capital employed of 20 per cent or better; and return on equity of between 20 and 25 per cent. These are three very ambitious objectives, yet are similar to those of many other companies. By contrast, a target for creating new products is unusual, or at least it has been until recently. This objective represents a clear target throughout the company:

> the 30 per cent rule is a corporate objective, so it starts right at the top of the company, and by being a corporate objective every manager in the company, particularly the business and R&D [research and development] managers, recognise that it is part of their objectives as well.
>
> (John Howells, Technical Director, 3M UK)

In addition to its corporate objectives, 3M has a number of what it calls principles for, amongst other areas, human resource management and corporate citizenship. These can appear at first sight to be rather vague, for example: '3M management recognises that 3M's business operations have broad societal impact' and 'it will endeavour to be sensitive to public attitudes and social concerns' (see 3M's Web page at www.mmm.com/profile/looking/goals.html). However, they do have real impact on policy decisions. For example, the company is currently refusing to sell products (such as printed Post-it Notes) which are used to promote the sale of tobacco products. Overall, 3M's goals appear to be consistent with the creation of a learning organisation, even if the company does not have this as a stated policy.

A key strategic focus at 3M is listening to the ideas, suggestions and requirements of customers. Again and again, interviewees at all levels emphasised the importance of understanding and meeting customer needs. This allows 3M more accurately to predict changes that may take place and then plan accordingly. However, this depends on customers knowing what will happen, when in fact they may be equally lacking in foresight. Inevitably, customers do not know precisely what will happen, but they can make valuable suggestions. The company aims to observe the current and potential problems of its customers and endeavour to solve them. One example of 3M's strategy affecting its external business environment is its Pollution Prevention Pays policy. 3M has gone from being routinely criticised about its environmental record to being seen as a champion of green issues, and at the same time it has created important new markets: 'many of us have begun to realise that the world's recognition of the importance of the planet we live on represents a significant business opportunity' (John Mueller, Chairman and Chief Executive, 3M UK). One of 3M's major businesses, Occupational Safety and Health, has benefited enormously from increased concern for the environment. 3M's recent announcement of its intention to spin off or close a number of businesses is an example of the company carefully choosing to target a specific market. 3M has decided that one of the areas it operates in at present, its audio- and video-tape business, does not represent a good long-term investment. It is closing this business so that it can concentrate on other, more profitable markets. This is an excellent example of a company undertaking strategic planning by deliberately setting out to choose the most favourable target markets.

An important aspect of 3M's strategy is benchmarking, and more specifically the choosing of benchmarking partners. In 3M benchmarking is seen as key in a number of areas, most notably human resources (HR). Other areas do not engage in formal benchmarking exercises, but do undertake broadly similar exercises, particularly in the form of partnerships. In HR benchmarking is 'very much built into our processes now', and the company benchmarks annually with twenty-five other companies. Each year the company will tell its employees how it compares to those twenty-five companies, and the best of the companies, in each area, present best practice to the others. In more technical areas 3M has a partnership scheme, involving Hewlett-Packard, Rolls-Royce, British Aerospace, Unilever, ICI and BP, among others. These companies are all considered world class in their respective fields. The scheme encompasses sharing information, continuous improvement and benchmarking. 3M's UK Chairman and Chief Executive, John Mueller, emphasises the importance of looking to seemingly entirely unrelated businesses for benchmarking partners. For example, when looking to become more effective and efficient in logistics, 3M used DHL and Federal Express as two exemplars of best practice. Another benchmarking partner is LL Bean, a US clothing manufacturer renowned for its high levels of customer service and excellence in mail-order distribution. It should be clear from the above that 3M places a high degree of importance on environmental scanning, particularly in terms of benchmarking and listening to customers.

3M is a company with a long and distinguished record of making the creation of new knowledge a strategic goal. John Howells, the Technical Director, goes so far as to claim that 'the one thing we are good at is converting technologies, capitalising, getting the return on investment from the technologies we have'. This is a clear indication of the importance with which 3M regards transferring knowledge within the company. One of the most important reasons for this is the attitude in the company that Howells describes thus: 'technologies are owned by the corporation but we encourage and expect our R&D people in all our businesses to capitalise and make use of them'. This means that even before a new technology has been launched in the marketplace other companies will be looking at it to see if the technology can usefully be incorporated into their business. All corporate scientists (a senior technical role) are given the responsibility of sharing their ideas within the company.

3M's Principles of Management and Corporate Objectives are a key statement of its strategic vision. Its three key principles of management are stated as follows:

> Our first principle is the promotion of entrepreneurship and insistence upon freedom in the work place to pursue innovative ideas. Policies, practices and organisational structure have been flexible and characterised by mutual trust and co-operation.
>
> Second is our adherence to uncompromising honesty and integrity. This is manifested in our commitment to the highest standards of ethics throughout our organisation and in all aspects of 3M's operations.

Third is our preservation of individual identity in an organizational structure which embraces widely diverse businesses and operates in different political and economic systems throughout the world. From this endeavour there has developed an identifiable 3M spirit and a sense of belonging to the 3M family.

(www.mmm.com)

It is on these three principles that 3M's four corporate objectives are founded. The corporate objectives are in the following four areas: profits and growth, products/customers, HR and citizenship. As an example, this is 3M's corporate objective in the area of products/customers:

It is 3M Management's objective to develop and sell unique products and services of high quality and reliability that are genuinely useful to customers and consumers. In this mission, 3M contributes to a better quality of life and a higher standard of living for its employees and the public generally.

(www.mmm.com)

Statements like the one above represent the detail of 3M's vision. The problem that the company has faced is the difficulty inherent in creating a single vision which is equally applicable to people in the many different parts of a diverse business. 3M's UK Director of Human Resources, Ken Jackson, says that 'a company like ours, which is pulling together many diversified businesses, has an enormous need for "glue" for the corporation, and I think that vision, goals and values are absolutely essential to pull together the many pieces'. In the words of 3M's UK Chairman and Chief Executive, 'it's only been in the last couple of years that 3M has really addressed the issue of a vision statement which is an umbrella for the whole company'. He continues: 'I think our present Chairman [Livio DeSimone, Chairman and Chief Executive of 3M worldwide] has really done a nice job in that he's come to two statements that I can certainly subscribe to, and I think over time will become more inculcated within all our people.' The two statements are, first, that 3M wants to be the supplier of choice to all the varied markets and constituencies that it serves; and, second, that 3M wants to be seen, by all the constituencies it serves, its shareholders, its customers and its employees, as the most innovative enterprise. 3M's UK Chairman and Chief Executive points out that:

innovation applies to all functions, not just R&D. That [the two state-ments], as you can see, is not the how. That's the goal, and how to get there is going to differ for each business and probably for each function.

(John Mueller, Chairman and Chief Executive, 3M UK)

It is evident that 3M has gone to considerable lengths to create a powerful, unifying vision. The key question, however, is still to be answered: is this vision shared throughout the organisation? 3M's senior managers certainly believe that communicating the vision is very important. 3M UK's Director of Human Resources says that '3M has clear goals and clear values, and I think, much more than average companies, they are clearly defined, well communicated, and they haven't changed regularly.' The Chairman and Chief Executive says:

the way that [the vision] gets inculcated is you just have to work at communicating why that's apt, why it's good for a particular constituency, employee, shareholder, customer, whatever. The best way to get at the how is to show an illustration of how parts of the company are making it happen.

(John Mueller, Chairman and Chief Executive, 3M UK)

At lower levels of the business it is clear that parts of 3M's vision have been successfully communicated. Employees at lower levels of the organisational hierarchy have generally given similar answers to questions, suggesting a strong, common set of ideas within the organisation. While the full set of 3M's Principles of Management might not be very meaningful or accessible to the average employee, the main vision statement, for example, regarding the importance of innovation, can be recited by the majority of employees.

The structural dimension

3M has a matrix structure, which its UK Chairman and Chief Executive describes as 'a very powerful management or organisational structure'. In matrix structures there are two lines of authority, one by functional depart-ment and one by product division. The Chairman and Chief Executive continues:

the 3M Matrix is not just businesses, and in the case of Europe, regions. It is also our drive toward functional excellence, and the fourth major influence on our matrix is our corporate imperatives, the goals of the company that emanate to us here from the States.

(John Mueller, Chairman and Chief Executive, 3M UK)

Many of the company's business centres are built around a technology base or a family of products, as opposed to the more fashionable market-based structures. This can be attributed to the way in which the success of the company has traditionally been based on its technological strength. However, it has now created a number of market-based structures, for example in Hospital Markets, Consumer and Office, and Electronics Markets.

3M is a very complex company and may sometimes lack a clear directive line. Peters and Waterman describe 3M as being marked by 'barely organized chaos surrounding its product champions' (Peters and Waterman, 1982: 15). If its current structure is anything to go on, little has changed since then. This complexity provides great strengths but may also lead to increased costs. The complexity of the company is a function of its diversity. This diversity takes many forms: in products, in markets, in technologies and in people (Jeff Skinner, Management Development Manager, 3M UK). As the law of requisite variety suggests, for a company to be able to adapt to its environment it must have variety. Without internal variety the organisation is less able to deal with change or complexity in the external environment (see Pascale, 1990). Put another way, the level of variety and complexity within the company must mirror the level of external variety and complexity.

An example of the way 3M has designed its structure to encourage organisational learning and innovation is the dual career ladder. This gives middle-ranking scientists and engineers the opportunity to climb up through the company while remaining in research and development areas rather than moving into management. In the words of 3M's UK Technical Director, John Howells: 'it is in our interest to keep the best on that side so we can continue to succeed and deliver new products'. Although this is by no means a unique scheme (Procter and Gamble, for example, have a similar scheme), it is one reason for 3M's undoubted success in creating new, innovative products. 3M has a structure that helps to facilitate, even stimulate, learning in general and new product development in particular. However, this structure is not without its costs in terms of managing such a complex organisation. Some of these problems were addressed by the spin-off of 3M's data-storage and imaging businesses into a separate company, together with the closure of its unprofitable audio- and video-tape businesses. This should allow Imation, the newly created data-storage and imaging company, which is competing in highly competitive, fast-moving markets, to be able to respond more flexibly (see Denton and De Cock, 1997).

3M's formal organisational structure bears relatively little relation to the real, underlying structure. As Stewart points out, 'that handsome pyramid [the organisation chart] has little or nothing to do with how the place runs' (Stewart, 1996). The real structure is based on the organisation's technologies and the businesses that grow out from these technologies. The formal structure also takes no account of the in-built redundancy on which 3M thrives. The company has over 8,000 scientists scattered around many different labs in many different countries. There is central R&D; there are labs for each of 3M's two big operating sectors, labs for each group, labs for businesses and eleven centres dedicated to particular technology platforms. As Stewart (*ibid.*) says, deliberate duplication abounds at 3M and the company thrives on it.

An important part of 3M's structure is the councils for technical people, for marketing people, for manufacturing people and for engineering people. Each of these councils is a regular forum in which members can exchange knowledge on their respective subjects. The councils examine best practice within 3M and bring in experts from outside to introduce new ideas. There are also ways for people to move between councils, thereby exchanging knowledge between various groups. Another method of transferring knowledge within 3M is the company database of information for R&D people. For example, people in the UK have ready access to information on projects that are taking place in St Paul, Minnesota. While there are a number of safeguards for security reasons, most people can access general information on specific projects, before securing approval to receive all the relevant information. The company also has a comprehensive e-mail system which the company's scientists and managers use to keep in touch with colleagues overseas and at different locations.

A good example of knowledge transfer within 3M is the development of DART (Door Aperture Resealing Tape). This product originated from a customer's idea which was given directly to a visiting salesman. The idea passed from 3M Belgium, first to 3M Germany and finally to 3M UK, which was considered the most suitable location for developing the concept. In summary, 3M's ability to create and transfer knowledge is undoubtedly first class, with many mechanisms, both formal and informal, available to stimulate and facilitate both the creation and transfer of knowledge.

In many of its operations, 3M makes extensive use of teams and networks as an integral part of its organisational structure. A good example of networking involves the improvements in distribution made by 3M. The critical success factor in this project was the multi-firm and cross-functional make-up of the team. The team comprised employees from three different companies (3M, Boots and Standard Photographic Supplies – SPS) and from many different functions (logistics, information technology, manufacturing, etc.). It was concerned with the following products, all of which were Boots' own-brand products manufactured by 3M or SPS: photographic films, video cassettes and healthcare products. The network was set up as the result of a request from Boots for an improvement in the supply process. As a result of this project 3M gained a significant advantage over other suppliers because of its improved supply system and its close links with Boots. Stock is now collected from SPS (where it is packaged) by a Boots lorry, in Boots 'rolling cages', and goes to Nottingham, where the lorries can 'jump the queue' at Boots' warehouse. On arrival, the cages are rolled straight into the loading bays to go to Boots' regional warehouses. This process has significantly reduced the total level of inventory in the system and eliminated the time spent by drivers waiting to unload at the warehouse. Paper has been eliminated from the system thanks to the use of electronic data interchange (EDI), creating savings in both time and expense. Looking more generally at 3M's processes, it is very common to find cross-functional teams undertaking important projects. There is 'a growing recognition of the need to solve certain problems with cross-functional teams – the idea of cross-functional teams has been grabbed' (Jeff Skinner, Management Development Manager, 3M UK).

One problem that 3M has in terms of creating a flexible structure that encourages organisational learning, despite the matrix structure of the company, is that cross-functional career moves are relatively rare. 3M's UK Management Development Manager, Jeff Skinner, says that 'our career development processes and our approach to careers in this company, by and large, is very functionally driven. We don't get a lot of movement across functions.' In particular, cross-functional career moves are not usual in the early parts of people's careers. So, although the company has come to make use of cross-functional teams, some of the advantages of this may be lost through the emphasis on functional development and the resultant lack of cross-functional understanding. Overall, 3M's structure seems to be quite effective in promoting organisational learning, although the high level of complexity means that the organisation can sometimes appear to move more slowly than would be ideal.

The cultural dimension

Turning to look at culture, it is evident that 3M places great value on both employees and customers. The company provides many incentives for innovation. The most obvious of these is the way in which many people, in managerial as well as technical areas, are promoted on the strength of their contribution to innovation. The 15 per cent 'bootlegging time' is another example of the way in which 3M tries to facilitate innovation and make it a 'habit' within the company. Bootlegging is the phrase used in 3M for the time which employees can use to work on projects of their own choosing. This practice has been a contributory factor in many new products, most famously the development of the Post-it Note. Of the new product development programmes examined in this study, bootlegging was identified as very important to the development of DART. The many ways in which 3M tries to stimulate innovation should leave the reader in little doubt that the company has a corporate culture ideally suited to encouraging learning. This is supported by the UK Chairman and Chief Executive, who claims that there is 'a sincere recognition that we have to foster and provide an environment that is conducive to learning and to changing, not just in the management ranks but throughout the organisation'.

Since the 1980s quality has increasingly been recognised as vital to business success. 3M's drive for quality emphasises the importance of a bottom-up approach, and the need to develop and maintain an appropriate 'quality culture'. Ron Neal, a 3M Quality Manager, explains that the company has a highly developed quality system which has evolved from Quality Circles to Continuous Quality. Within 3M's Treasurer's Group – which includes accounts receivable, cash management, payroll, insurance and pensions – 'quality' has progressed from being seen as a management responsibility in 1986, to Quality Circles (involving most people) in 1988, to Total Quality (involving everyone) in 1989, to 3M Quality Achievement Awards in 1990 and, finally, to Q90s in the 1990s. Q90s is described as being about '(1) uncompromising commitment to customer satisfaction; and (2) continuous improvement' (Ron Neal, 3M UK's Treasurer's Group). The Treasurer's Group believes that it has gained the following benefits from Q90s: increased customer focus (both internal and external customers); process involvement (awareness of business processes that flow upstream and downstream from the Treasurer's Group; supplier quality (monitor supplier performance, particularly where it has an impact on customer service); and better measurement. Measurement has moved from being productivity related, to the use of internal measures of performance, to (under Q90s) customer-satisfaction measures. 3M has won a number of quality awards, including the European Quality Award.

One of the most striking aspects of 3M's culture is the emphasis placed on the welfare of its employees, many of whom are impressed by the honesty and integrity of the company. More than this, however, the company devotes significant time and resources to the development of its employees. The Chairman and Chief Executive states that one of the most distinctive features of the company is its culture: 'this focus and value placed on the initiatives of the individual, the commitment to people, and the recognition that it's only through people that we get all things accomplished'. He continues: 'there's the commitment, the understanding that our single most valuable asset is truly the people that make up the organisation'. These are fine words, but the question is whether they are backed up by actions and opportunities. In 3M's case they clearly are; in the case of the UK Chairman and Chief Executive himself, the company paid for him to go to college for nine years. 3M's dual career ladder allows employees to develop in the direction that they wish and the 15 per cent 'bootlegging' time allows employees to pursue individual projects that they find interesting. These schemes allow employees to develop their productive capacity while still being productive.

Other strengths of 3M are its integrity and honesty. Jeff Skinner, Management Development Manager, says: 'some of the stuff in this corporation around integrity is an absolute given, more so than in any other company that I've ever seen, and it's one of the things that I like best about this company'. Indeed, one of the company's Principles of Management is its 'adherence to uncompromising honesty and integrity. This is manifested in our commitment to the highest standards of ethics throughout the organisation and in all aspects of 3M's operations.'

Another of 3M's principles deals with 'freedom in the workplace to pursue innovative ideas' and an organisational structure that is 'flexible and characterised by mutual trust and co-operation'. The final principle deals with the preservation of individual identity in the organisational structure, while encouraging the development of an identifiable 3M spirit and 'a sense of belonging to the 3M family'.

One way in which 3M employees are made to feel valuable and empowered is the 'Thank You Awards', which give employees the chance to reward their colleagues, in a small way, for their help. Importantly, these awards can be sent by employees, without their first having to fight their way through a bureaucratic system. Another example of the responsibility that 3M employees perceive themselves to have is the common saying within 3M that 'it is easier to ask for forgiveness than to ask for permission'. This suggests that people are not scared to make decisions for themselves, even though they know that their decision may be wrong and that they may have to justify it later. The Director of Human Resources admits that the company is 'not a quick-changing organisation, particularly in terms of our people processes'. He goes on: 'We think our employees like us the way we are with our principles and values, and we are reluctant to make dramatic swings from that point of view.' 3M's Management Development Manager develops a similar theme: 'the Human Resource Function . . . I don't believe has been at the forefront of running the corporation'. Even the UK Chairman and Chief Executive acknowledges that, 'while 3M has treasured and nurtured its work in what we call innovation, we have tended to tie that term inappropriately only to research and development . . . Innovation can be applied to any aspect of your business.'

Overall, we can conclude that 3M's strategy encompasses learning and, especially, innovation as goals; its structure provides an excellent platform on which to create new products and new knowledge; and its culture is geared towards encouraging learning and innovation.

The practice of organisational learning: the case of CCSB

For most of the period of the research underpinning this book Coca-Cola Schweppes Beverages Limited (CCSB) was a joint venture company, 51 per cent owned by Cadbury Schweppes plc and 49 per cent by the Coca-Cola Company (*Insight into the Foundations of Our Success*, internal publication). In July 1996 Cadbury Schweppes decided to sell its share of CCSB to Coca-Cola Enterprises, a subsidiary of the Coca-Cola Company (Oram, 1996).

CCSB is very different from the other case companies. Most significantly, it relies on one group of products, soft drinks, for all its revenue. The company was formed in 1987 by its two parent companies, the Coca-Cola Company and Cadbury Schweppes, to manufacture, distribute and sell their soft drink brands. The result of this deliberate 'company-building' is evident in CCSB's organisational structure and culture. The company is unusual among the five companies in that the creation of new products is not part of its *raison d'être*. The company's role as a manufacturer and distributor of its shareholders' brands means that it is reliant on these two companies for its new products, and so its overall focus, or even its *raison d'être*, is necessarily different.

The strategic dimension

CCSB is a very results-oriented company, and this is reflected both in the language of the company and in its strategy. The company measures its annual results in comparison to the previous year's in three areas: sales volume, sales revenue and market share. Hence in 1995 the company achieved 'record sales, record share and record volume' (Keith Dennis, Director of Personnel). The question is whether this focus on results detracts from or encourages the development of an effective learning strategy. The majority of evidence suggests that the company is very focused on learning. The Managing Director, Derek Williams, describes two ways in which CCSB is distinctive. The first of these is the company's results, which at one time were so successful that the company spent three years being examined by the Monopolies and Mergers Commission, something that he regards as a sign of exceptional performance. The second distinctive feature is that the company has:

> enough structure and control to enable us in a disciplined way to deliver those attributes that we value and prize highly, i.e. to be out of control, to go in a different direction, to change our minds, to increase the pace, to be an enabling organisation.
>
> (Derek Williams, Managing Director, CCSB)

Williams goes on to say that 'fresh perception is one of the key ingredients to organisational effectiveness'. Fresh perception is surely only a different way of expressing the concept of learning. So, if learning is highly valued at the top of the organisation, does this make it, de facto, a part of the organisation's strategy? To have a learning strategy the company needs to have made a conscious decision to place learning at the top of its list of priorities and to have put in place the necessary conditions for learning to occur. CCSB has undoubtedly made learning a priority, with its Lifetime Learning Links (LLLs) being a good example of this, and the company certainly has the necessary conditions for learning to occur. This suggests that CCSB has a conscious learning strategy, although of course its strategy also embraces other goals.

CCSB is very successful at evaluating its external environment. The company's understanding of marketing in general, and of the specific market in which it operates, is second to none. CCSB publishes annually a comprehensive analysis of the soft-drinks market called *Soft Drinks Market Profile*. This details the size and make-up of the market, as well as CCSB's performance. This knowledge of the market is a critical advantage in the strategic planning process.

However, one problem CCSB encounters when it seeks to influence its environment stems from the way in which the company was set up. The joint-venture status of the company means that CCSB's activities are constrained by its founding charter. For example, CCSB cannot compete with outside bottlers to produce private or own-label products. The Managing Director believes that without this constraint 'the majority of own-label cola would have been made by us'. The other key problem facing CCSB in this area is that its customers are now in many ways its major competitors. The growth of own-label products has left CCSB competing directly with the major stores which sell its products. What is more, the company believes that these competitors, the major retailers, are behaving unfairly, mainly in the way that they display CCSB's products relative to their own.

CCSB's approach to creating a shared vision differs significantly from the approaches of the other case companies. While the company does have a mission statement and vision, no real attempt is made to communicate these ideas in their entirety to the employees. However, the company has a simple statement, 'No. 1 and Pulling Ahead', which is used to express both the success of the company to date and the company's desired future. The obvious advantage is that the company's vision is easily communicated to the employees. While it does not have the detail of 3M's various statements, objectives and principles, it has the advantage of clarity in expressing where the company wishes to go. When new employees join the company they receive a comprehensive induction pack which begins to instil the company philosophy through, for example, a statement on video from the Managing Director. A further advantage CCSB's senior managers have in creating a shared vision is the recent founding of the company. This has enabled management to create a culture and vision of their own design. In addition to the company's youth, management has benefited from the opportunity to bring in new employees, many of whom did not have experience in the industry before joining CCSB. When CCSB's Wakefield factory (which is the largest soft-drinks bottling plant in Europe) opened in 1989 only five people on the site had drinks-making experience. This has meant that people have not brought with them preconceptions of how the company should work, making them more open to the company's culture and more willing to share in the company's vision.

The structural dimension

CCSB has what its Director of Personnel describes as a 'very pragmatic and opportunistic approach to the way we structure our people and the organisation'. Boursiquot (1996) notes that ad hoc projects are common in the company, particularly within the marketing and market research functions. Looking specifically at the personnel function, we note that it has switched completely from being organised on a functional-specialism basis to a generalist approach since the company was set up in 1987. When the organisation was founded there were separate departments for compensation and benefits, employee relations, training and development, and resourcing. This was considered appropriate for the first eighteen months of the organisation's life, particularly in the area of employee relations, where there was a need to change many of the agreements between management and employees. These agreements were carry-overs from CCSB's two parent companies, and the new management realised that they were likely to prove an impediment to the organisation they wished to create. In order to change these agreements a strong, centralised, personnel department was considered necessary.

The organisation has now created what are referred to as 'one-stop shops', with personnel managers organised by function. Thus one personnel team deals with distribution, one with manufacturing and one with marketing. Each team member is a generalist and a point of contact for all personnel in his or her part of the business. The advantage of this system is that the personnel department's customers are not driven from pillar to post in search of answers to their questions. The personnel manager may sometimes need to seek advice from the Remuneration and Benefits Manager or the Training and Development Manager, for example, but generally the flow of information is quicker and more consistent than previously. CCSB, although a far less diverse company than 3M (or any of the other cases), has already shown itself to be prepared to change structures when necessary. This has applied equally to structures the company inherited from Coca-Cola and Cadbury Schweppes, and to structures it created itself.

As we have seen, the creation of new products is not part of CCSB's remit. However, the company's organisational structure does help in creating new management knowledge. The transfer of knowledge is important at CCSB, with individual areas very keen to learn from successes elsewhere. For example, CCSB's state-of-the-art factory at Wakefield is used as a model for the other factories, while the success of Best Operator Practice (BOP), CCSB's quality and training programme, at Wakefield has been used as a model for its application in other functions. Richard Doyle, CCSB's Human Resource Manager for Distribution, who has introduced BOP throughout Distribution, emphasises the importance of the learning gained from the distribution site at Wakefield, although the mechanism for its introduction has been different in the rest of the company. CCSB has made a major investment in technology to facilitate the transfer of knowledge. The company has installed LLLs at almost all its sites. Each LLL is equipped with a wide range of learning technology for training purposes, including books, audio-tapes, open-learning packages, interactive discs, computer-based training packages and videos. Also provided are general-interest information in the form of books, audio-tapes and videos for language learning.

For training purposes, each LLL is equipped with:

1   TV monitor and video for viewing training-related videos.
2   Audio language lab.
3   Multimedia workstation. This is the equipment with which computer-based training and interactive video is used. The workstation comprises a PC unit, a laser-disc player, keyboard and mouse.

CCSB's *Catalogue and User Guide* explains that:

> multi-media training is interactive and PC based. The trainee is fully involved and can dictate the pace and direction of his or her training by responding to prompts and questions. Because of the individuality of responses, no two training sessions are the same and the training suits individual needs.
>
> (CCSB, *Catalogue and User Guide*)

LLLs provide interactive training in two forms:

1   CBT – computer-based training. This is a computer programme using a mixture of text, computer graphics and sound to create stimulating interactive training. It is particularly useful for learning PC applications.
2   IV – interactive video. This combines the benefits of two media types: video and CBT. Video scenarios are used to demonstrate situations and techniques. This simulation of real-life circumstances within an interactive PC-based training programme helps the trainee to learn faster and retain the training messages.

The above descriptions, adapted from CCSB's own publications, show the company's commitment to the use of technology. Technology is embedded in the company as part of its training structure. The question remains, however, of the extent to which the facilities are used. When asked how much the LLLs are used, interviewees usually reply that they use them themselves but that overall the facilities are underutilised. Usage is likely to follow a sine curve, with usage high at launch, followed by a gradual drop-off. The underuse is then recognised and the facility is promoted, leading to high usage for a short period. One problem with the LLLs is that some of the material and the technology has become dated. The problem is currently being addressed by equipping most of the centres with CD-ROMS, a more up-to-date technology. There is also an increasing recognition that the company will not give employees the opportunity to go on external courses, so they will have to learn in-house.

One way in which CCSB has made substantial use of technology to transfer knowledge is as part of the BOP programme in Distribution. For each warehouse worker and driver there is 'an hour of multimedia training, it's PC based, combining animation, sound, pictures, movement, and then interaction between the individual and the PC. Basically, it takes them through a series of assessments' (Richard Doyle, HR Manager – Distribution and Logistics, CCSB). This has two advantages over traditional training methods: first, it replicates what happens in the workplace, allowing the company to test people; and, second, it allows people to become familiar with the PC environment. This is becoming increasingly important, with many more people having to use PCs, even on forklift trucks. It is clear that CCSB is committed to the use of technology to transfer knowledge and has made some important steps forward. The company still needs to promote the use of its facilities within the organisation, and it faces a constant battle to keep pace with advances in technology. We can see that, although the creation of new knowledge is not a priority for CCSB in the same way as it is for 3M, the company can realistically claim both to create new knowledge and to transfer it successfully within the company. In particular, it makes great use of technology to aid learning and to encourage the transfer of knowledge to large numbers of employees.

Another key aspect of CCSB's structure is the emphasis placed on teams and, in particular, cross-functional teams. CCSB's Director of Personnel, Keith Dennis, says: 'we have an awful lot of cross-functional teams working on some of our process issues, whether that be supply chain management or manufacturing systems or whatever.' At Wakefield there is also a very strong emphasis on teams. Part of the BOP programme at Wakefield is a four-stage process which is seen as a journey from competent operators, through competent teams and achieving teams, to self-managing teams. This final stage is one in which teams have developed to the point where their members are 'people who are virtually business people, understand their kit, feel an ownership of this kit, understand the product, own the product, and are probably to the stage of almost contracting to the company' (Brian Wileman, CCSB).

Clearly, then, teams are important at the shop-floor level. Also, within particular projects teams can be important, with, for example, CCSB's Frontliners divided into teams for a number of business functions. Frontline is a CCSB programme of recruiting school-leavers to work for the company in a merchandising role while studying for an external degree from the University of London. Overall, CCSB makes good use of teamworking, although probably not to the same extent as some of the other companies.

The cultural dimension

One of the key aspects of a learning culture is to ensure that the company's employees are given responsibility for their own learning. This is a point that is repeatedly stressed by managers at CCSB. For example, the Personnel Director states that 'we have to say to people, "You have to take accountability for your own career." ' Equally, one of the senior managers at CCSB's largest bottling plant, Wakefield, emphasises the need to 'provide an open house in terms of people taking on board additional skills and responsibility for our own training, development and performance improvement' (*Winning Performance*, CCSB publication, 1994).

Another way in which CCSB has tried to create a learning culture is through the setting up of STAR TREK, a new management appraisal and development scheme. The LLLs, which were discussed earlier, are used in conjunction with STAR TREK. Eight performance criteria are identified by the STAR TREK acronym:

> **S**ound judgement;
> **T**ight money manager;
> **A**daptable;
> **R**esults-oriented;
> **T**hinks service;
> **R**adical thinker;
> **E**ffective leadership;
> **K**ey influencer.

If a development need is identified in any of the above areas specific LLL resources can be used to help rectify that weakness in an individual's performance. However, the LLLs are at present underused, perhaps suggesting that the learning culture at CCSB is not yet fully developed. One reason for this underuse is thought to be the nature of the material; it is considered to be slightly out of date and of the wrong type. In CCSB's manufacturing plants another factor is probably more important; employees work twelve-hour shifts and it is rather optimistic to expect people to work on self-improvement after working a shift of this length.

Another way in which CCSB has created a learning culture is by using directors as trainers.

> We have just launched a series of senior-management seminars that will be two-day affairs running across all the management disciplines. So we have walked away from the formal course approach that is a week here and a week there or going to business schools.
>
> (Keith Dennis, Personnel Director, CCSB)

The Personnel Director goes on to question the relevance of formal courses, and says that the new approach involves bringing in leading academics and getting them to tailor-make programmes which fit CCSB. Importantly, it will also involve specialists from within the organisation. For example, the Finance Director will spend time on the course talking about the key financial drivers for CCSB. This is then followed by external addresses from academics and consultants, with the goal of stimulating thinking and broadening people's agendas. One of the advantages of using directors as trainers on these courses is that it helps to stress the importance of learning and the company's commitment to it. Overall, we can see that CCSB is very keen to achieve a learning culture and has taken a number of significant steps towards achieving this goal.

CCSB has a very supportive culture that places an unusually high degree of emphasis on developing the ability of its employees. For example, by allowing employees to use the LLLs during working hours the company not only encourages self-improvement but also gives people a high degree of autonomy to decide how to spend their time. CCSB is satisfied that the vast majority of employees do not abuse this privilege. In terms of career development the company provides support programmes which help people analyse where they want to go, but it does not make outlandish promises with regard to career progression. The company strongly encourages employees to take responsibility for their own careers.

A key aspect of the culture at CCSB is the range of decisions that employees are allowed to make. In many organisations similar decisions would be the domain of middle or senior managers. A good example of this is the recruitment of new staff. Teams of people on the factory floor recruit their own members. The Personnel Department will put test mechanisms in place and administer the process, but the decision will rest with the team. At Wakefield all employees have full staff contracts; there are no hourly paid workers and employees do not clock in or out.

CCSB pays high salaries for its industry, typically £23,000 to £24,000 for a factory worker, together with generous benefits. The organisation has a flexible benefit programme, which it believes offers the widest range of benefits of any UK organisation. This allows people to choose between, for example, private health care and membership of a health club. All employees have the opportunity to have a car from the car list, up to a Jaguar if they are willing to pay for the difference between allowance and cost. The company has a profit-related-pay scheme which allows people to take up to £4,000 of their salary tax free. From time to time CCSB provides what it calls Outstanding Performance Dividends, amounting to an extra week's pay and given whenever the organisation has achieved exceptionally good performance. As we have seen, CCSB values highly the skills and abilities of its employees, and so it is only natural that it goes to great lengths to create a supportive culture to sustain their support and commitment.

In contrast to 3M, CCSB's approach to empowerment is far more systematic. In the Wakefield plant empowerment is seen as central to the success of the operation. One excellent example of this is the introduction of the sixth bottling line. The people designated to operate the line were given a significant voice in selecting equipment. Their input was a key influence in the choice of machinery and how it was installed, although clearly there were other considerations, such as cost. In the words of Brian Wileman, this 'gave the people who work on that line a much greater feeling of ownership and a feeling of accountability'. He also says that:

> they felt that it was their kit, they had had a lot of say in it and they were responsible. We've got over that now, and it's still climbing, but there's still a much better ownership of that particular kit, and they jealously say, 'It's ours.'

> (Brian Wileman, Plant Manager, CCSB)

Another way in which CCSB empowers its employees is through the company-wide BOP scheme. One of the senior Human Resource Managers (there are no job titles at Wakefield) described BOP as 'a method of opening up people input; a greater involvement of people input on a basis that we call "faster, fewer, better", by higher skills, multi-skilling, greater empowerment; thereby less numbers of people with a higher output, higher efficiencies' (Brian Wileman, CCSB).

BOP is really an umbrella term for a number of related programmes. One of these programmes emphasises multi-skilling and the more flexible use of labour. Another key part of BOP is illustrated by an example from Distribution. CCSB has been very keen to improve the skills of its drivers in order for them to carry out some of the functions of management prior to delayering, and as a way of encouraging them to subscribe to the continuous improvement of operations. Drivers have a wealth of knowledge about customers. They are the people within CCSB who visit customers more often than anyone else. In the words of the Human Resource Manager for Distribution: 'there's a huge amount of probably untapped knowledge and information. They are potentially able to influence customers very strongly because . . . there is quite a strong rapport that exists.' The move to upgrade skills has involved acceptance of an integrated package of terms, conditions and training which provides drivers with the incentives and ability to focus on the core objectives of the business. The Human Resource Manager for Distribution says that BOP is about 'trying to create an infrastructure to give the people the desire to succeed and the desire to find improvements'. This is reflected in the company's Wakefield factory, where 'they [the shop-floor workers] take ownership on the lines for the production, the quality, delivering the planned goods that their output is, the level required, to their customer – the warehouse' (Brian Wileman, CCSB).

This idea of the internal customer is prevalent throughout the company and ensures that quality is maintained at all points along the supply chain. We see from the above that CCSB has introduced a number of programmes with the goal of empowering its employees. CCSB's Managing Director states that 'we do not call ourselves empowered because empowered has connotations of you decide your own agenda and how you are going to do it', and he prefers to call the management style 'enabling'. The company's fluid culture means that new ideas can be taken on board relatively quickly and without excessive bureaucracy.

The practice of organisational learning: the case of Mayflower

The Mayflower Corporation describes its principal activities as 'the design, engineering and manufacture of car bodies, buses and commercial vehicle cabs, vehicle conversions and the production of synthetic webbing' (*The Mayflower Corporation plc, Annual Report and Accounts 1997*: 22). Mayflower is unique among the five case companies in that the company is still largely controlled by the man who founded it. This is reflected in the company's strong and visionary strategy, which is the most striking feature of its approach to organisational learning. The company's structure and culture have perhaps received less attention, and to an extent this is reflected in continuing variations in practice in different parts of the organisation.

The strategic dimension

Mayflower believes that 'the motor industry world-wide is moving into an era of fundamental change so radical that the shape of both original equipment manufacturers and suppliers alike will be totally reformed by the end of the century' (*The Mayflower Corporation plc, Annual Report and Accounts 1994*: 6). To ensure its success in this new environment Mayflower has a conscious strategy, involving four elements:

1   The integration of Motor Panels and Internal Automotive Design (IAD). The integration began in 1994 in North America and in 1995 in the UK.
2   Focus on core business. World-class products are sold to worldwide customers. This has meant the sale or closure of non-core activities.
3   Further development of core competencies. This is to ensure a leading role for Mayflower businesses. This has led to the establishment of the engineering centre at Coventry and a number of technical alliances.
4   Stretching beyond the boundaries. The concept of 'stretch' has been used to remove negative mind-sets and reward exceptional performance.

(adapted from *The Mayflower Corporation plc,
Annual Report and Accounts 1994*: 6–7)

It is evident that Mayflower has a clearly stated strategy for its future business direction. While learning is not an explicit element of this strategy, it is unlikely that the above elements could be achieved without a degree of learning having taken place. For example, the development of core competencies cannot take place without the acquisition of new knowledge. The establishment of technical alliances should similarly stimulate learning and the acquisition of new knowledge.

One organisational learning tool which Mayflower uses as part of its strategic development is the concept of 'stretch', which was introduced in 1994. Stretch is a concept which uses dreams and visions to set business objectives. By setting difficult goals employees are encouraged to think 'bigger' than they thought possible and to remove negative mind-sets that limit success. Stretch is a non-threatening tool that rewards progress beyond set goals. John Simpson, Mayflower's Chief Executive Office (CEO), describes stretch as 'a great success'. For this he relies on both the opinion of his fellow senior managers and the ideas and targets that have been generated as a result. He goes on to explain that it is a way of encouraging management to be more creative and that it is about 'trying to create a new set of targets that gives them more freedom than the budgets would to go out and aim at these higher and higher goals'. The Managing Director of IAD, Mike Bryant, similarly describes stretch as 'very good; I think it's to be encouraged'. He thinks that it 'provides a good discussion point and does allow us to see how far we could go with a trailing wind'. Powling reports that stretch is 'regularly used as a management tool encouraging a different way of looking at issues' (Powling, 1996: 60). The company believes that stretch has allowed executives to be more optimistic in their forecasting and strategic planning, and has removed some of the barriers to new ideas.

The clarity of Mayflower's vision of its future is arguably the most striking feature of its approach to organisational learning. The company's vision has been formed and shaped by its founder and current CEO, John Simpson. He says that 'the plan was, the vision was [when the company went public], that it would be a manufacturing, specialist engineering group'. At the time the group consisted of marketing companies, financial services companies, toy companies, all of which were losing money. These companies were sold and the group has since acquired Motor Panels, IAD, and Walter Alexander to give it the desired focus on engineering, and specifically on automotive engineering. The other main aspect of Mayflower's vision is that it sees itself as a global company. To a large extent this is necessitated by the demands of the original equipment manufacturers (OEMs). As we have seen, Mayflower believes that the motor industry worldwide is beginning a process of fundamental change that will radically alter the shape of both OEMs and suppliers. One aspect of this fundamental change will be the necessity for globalisation. All significant OEMs have moved their operations to a global basis, through either restructuring or merger. This process of globalisation will require suppliers to be able to operate on a worldwide basis, something that is a key part of Mayflower's strategy and vision. Mayflower hopes to achieve global status through both vertical integration, which will be the result of mainly organic growth, and horizontal integration, which will result, it is intended, mainly from growth through acquisition.

Mayflower's vision has been successfully shared throughout the company, and we can see that managers at IAD and at Motor Panels are convinced of the need for globalisation and for restructuring. The process has taken place in the UK with the formation of Mayflower Vehicle Systems, following the model applied in North America. The merger was welcomed by a number of key people in the two companies. IAD's Managing Director pointed to the requirements of OEMs to work with a small number of suppliers, while the Engineering Director at Motor Panels, John Fuller, emphasised the extent to which 'the skills of both companies overlap' and the fact that 'they [IAD] can do a similar job in terms of engineering'. Mayflower Automotive Division's HR Director, Mike Fell, was even more strongly in favour of the merger, saying: 'I have a vision of at least belonging to a greater whole.' Clearly, then, the vision has been successfully communicated to senior management in the subsidiary companies, but has it been communicated to the whole work-force? This is very difficult to determine. However, it is clear that the company has taken a number of steps to communicate its vision. For example, Motor Panels has launched a Communications Development Programme with the objectives of 'promoting a continuous dialogue across all employee levels and functions', and 'providing understanding of business deliverables and providing a vehicle for individual contribution' (*Communications Development, Mayflower Automotive Division*). Mayflower un-doubtedly has a strong vision, a strong picture of where it would like to be in the future, and it has made useful steps towards the sharing of this vision.

The nature of Mayflower's business means that scanning the environment and listening to customers are two key parts of its strategy and prerequisites for success, indeed survival. The company has to work closely with OEMs because it has relatively few customers, all of whom are extremely knowl-edgeable and demanding. Mayflower must satisfy the exact specifications laid down by the OEMs and tailor its performance to their demands. Mayflower's CEO describes the company's competitive advantage as its ability to 'do a complete service for you . . . they [Motor Panels] do the whole one-stop shop'. This is in response to complaints from OEMs experiencing problems when using different companies to carry out different stages of the design, engineering and manufacturing process. The approach taken by Motor Panels eliminates the problem of suppliers blaming one another for mistakes and delays. One problem with Mayflower's approach is that it lacks a systematic benchmarking programme, although many of its processes and strategies are compared informally with other companies, particularly Rover, Honda and a number of component suppliers.

The structural dimension

Mayflower's organisational structure is entirely different from either of the two previous cases. Mayflower has a small head office presiding over a number of relatively autonomous subsidiary companies. It is important to note here that there have been a number of changes in Mayflower's structure during the course of this research. The clearest example is the merger of Motor Panels and International Automotive Design (IAD). This happened first in North America, where Mayflower Vehicle Systems was formed during 1994. In 1995 a similar merger took place in the UK, with Motor Panels (Coventry) merging with IAD, while Motor Panels (Wigan) became a profit centre of the new company. These changes have allowed the company to become more streamlined and better co-ordinated. Most importantly, they have created a common sense of purpose.

As well as this high-level reorganisation of the company's structure, the individual operating companies have also made significant changes during the timespan of this research. An excellent example is the way in which Motor Panels has changed its structure from one based on functional departments to one based on project teams. This move to project-based (as opposed to functional) management is quite common and is driven by a coherent logic (see, for example, Hayes *et al.*, 1988; Bowen *et al.*, 1994). The new structure was copied by IAD and now forms a key part of the newly created Mayflower Vehicle Systems. The advantages are improvements in adaptability and a clearer picture of responsibilities within the organisation. It would appear that Mayflower has created structures that are highly appropriate for learning. However, it may take time for the benefits of these new structures to be fully realised.

Mayflower's ability to create and transfer new knowledge will be greatly influenced by the restructuring of Motor Panels and IAD that has recently taken place. Before the merger of these two companies, the Human Resource Director of Mayflower's Automotive Division said: 'we're not, at the moment, sharing the learning, that vast experience that the two companies have got.' The merger is reported to have helped in this respect, and the companies have already begun to work more closely together on projects. However, looking more widely across the group, Powling concludes that:

> there is a need to encourage more synergy between its existing portfolio of businesses in order to fully benefit and enhance their contribution. This should be developed as a competency led by Mayflower encouraging subsidiaries to share more for themselves and benefit from membership of a bigger team that engages in similar activities.
>
> (Powling, 1996: 62)

On a smaller scale, and in a similar fashion to 3M, Motor Panels has a database which details the skills of its employees. This is used mainly for selecting members of project teams, but also has the advantage of allowing people to identify colleagues with specific expertise and learn from them. Another benefit has been the ability to 'track the results of training and development programmes' (John Fuller, Engineering Director, Motor Panels).

Teamworking – and, in particular, project teams – are a central part of Mayflower's way of working. Almost all new work for customers takes the form of a specific project that must be completed to the customer's specification and requirements. In the somewhat understated words of IAD's Managing Director: 'projects deliver things . . . and the customer is very interested in projects'. At the beginning of 1994 (prior to its merger with IAD) Motor Panels' Engineering Department undertook a reorganisation which was specifically aimed at allowing project teams to operate more efficiently without the constraints imposed by functional departments. Patrick Crutchley, Project Engineer, Motor Panels, describes how each car is divided into sections (e.g. front end, underside, bodyside, roof and rear end). Each section, or zone, is then developed, to a great extent, separately. A project manager oversees the entire project, co-ordinating the four or five different zones. Each zone is developed by a team made up of an evolving group of staff. Initially, during the development of a concept and the styling, a typical team may be made up of five stylists, three designers and one production engineer. Later in the project, during the tooling, there may be one stylist, one designer, two production engineers and four toolers. This is likely to be followed by a handover period when responsibility for the project gradually passes from the engineering section to the production section. Motor Panels uses Gantt charts to help plan its projects. These go into great detail on each individual stage of the project and allow the company to plan its future resource needs. Team members are selected on the basis of their skills, the balance of skills across the team, their prior learning and their availability. We can see that the nature of Mayflower's business makes teamworking very important to the company and that this has been addressed by a number of measures aimed at making the project teams more effective.

One important element of Mayflower's organisational design is the emphasis it places on networking. The company's 1995 annual report extols the virtues of technical alliances. The company says that 'such alliances are expected to form an important part of future business relationships'. Another important form of networking takes place with customers and suppliers, who the Engineering Director at Motor Panels describes as 'an integral part of the team from day one'. He continues: 'the key suppliers are brought in, and the customer, MP [Motor Panels] and the suppliers work together to match the customers requirements to a set of deliverables at the right time, cost and quality compromise'.

The cultural dimension

In many ways Mayflower's culture and working practices are relatively tradi-tional on the shop floor, but this is gradually changing. New ideas have been brought in which encourage the development of employees and give them a more valuable role in the business. At Motor Panels a great deal of effort has been made to ensure that employees are comfortable with the new employee development programme that has been introduced. As the Human Resource Director of Mayflower's Automotive Division says, 'it'll be much more powerful if we can get these people feeling comfortable'. Motor Panels' Skills Matrix is another way in which the company provides a supportive atmo-sphere by explicitly recognising the skills of its employees. The company also recognises the danger of exposing some employees' skill deficiencies, and so skill-development levels will be displayed only at a local level in the factory, where 'it can be done with dignity' (Mike Fell, Human Resource Director, Mayflower Automotive Division). Mayflower sees empowerment as an important goal to aim for as part of its cultural development programme. One part of the ideal culture is described in an internal document as 'empow-ering factholders to make them the decision makers' (*Culture Development, Mayflower Automotive Division*). There have certainly been efforts at Motor Panels to treat people as though they have both the ability to learn and the ability to make decisions. The Human Resource Director of Mayflower

Automotive Division outlines one of the advantages of some of the changes introduced:

> at the operational level its implementation is so sensible – it's such a sign of relief that, 'Thank God, people are asking me. Great, I'm not asked to leave my brain at the gate and to just come in and be an automaton. I'm asked to be involved.'
>
> (Human Resource Director, Mayflower Automotive Division)

Similarly, one of the project engineers describes how the change from functional departments to project teams has led to responsibility 'passing from one member of the team to another as the project progresses'. Overall, we can see that, when the nature of the business is taken into consideration, Mayflower does try to provide a supportive culture for its employees and is reasonably successful. Empowerment certainly exists in staff areas and the company is gradually empowering its shop-floor workers.

Motor Panels has introduced a new employee development programme specifically aimed at increasing the organisation's willingness to change. Part of this programme is focused on cultural enrichment. This defines the culture that the company would like to achieve as one through which 'all employees willingly make their best contribution to achieve extraordinary customer satisfaction and maximise profit opportunity' (*Culture Development, Mayflower Automotive Division*). Despite this clear desire to create a learning culture, Mayflower Automotive Division's Human Resource Director admitted: 'We don't have a culture of learning yet. We don't take advantage of links with industries that we work with or educational establishments that we work with.' In summary, we can see that Mayflower has taken a number of steps in order to create a learning culture, something that it has identified as a *sine qua non* of excellent performance.

One further element Mayflower is trying to instil into its culture is a new quality programme. The company has chosen to link this closely to its training programme. It expects significant improvements in quality to come from the improved skills of its workforce. The company has achieved quality accreditations from General Motors, Ford, Chrysler, Jaguar, Navistar and Allied Signal. Motor Panels Inc. (the American subsidiary) was used as one of a small number of benchmark suppliers during the development of the North American automotive quality standard QS 9000. In 1997 the UK company Mayflower Vehicle Systems was awarded QS 9000 accreditation, one of only sixty-two companies in the UK to reach the standard required.

The practice of organisational learning: the case of Morgan Crucible

The Morgan Crucible Company plc is a manufacturer of specialised materials and technologically advanced components. Morgan regards its strengths as 'its people, materials technology, diversity of products and its worldwide sales, marketing and manufacturing networks' (*The Morgan Crucible Company plc 1996 Annual Report and Accounts*: 3).

Morgan Crucible's approach to organisational learning is interesting in that the company's structure almost inevitably means that practice is different from subsidiary to subsidiary. These differing practices are the result of the company's highly decentralised structure, which gives significant autonomy to individual operating companies. In many cases the Managing Directors of these companies are given powers that in many other companies would rest with head office.

The strategic dimension

Morgan Crucible's operating companies must each develop a strategy for presentation to head office, which will then be passed, modified or rejected. The Group Managing Director, Bruce Farmer, says that this means that 'each company has a bottom-up, top-down strategy which fits in with the divisional strategies, which fits in with the group strategies'. The main thrust of the group's strategy (named Strategy 2000) is to create global product groups which can compete successfully worldwide in selected advanced technology markets. The company has already created a number of global product groups, for example in crucible manufacturing, and intends to create more in the future. At the divisional level strategy is, in effect, a cut-down version of the group strategy and is characterised by a desire for growth. At the subsidiary-company level the strategies are likely to be quite different, although all will have been vetted by head office. This opportunity for the subsidiary companies to set their own strategies should allow them to develop along individual lines and to encourage learning if they think this is appropriate. However, learning is not an explicit part of Morgan Crucible's strategy at the group, divisional or subsidiary-company level.

Morgan Crucible has an excellent record of anticipating and responding to changes in its environment. A good example is the company's decision to globalise its operations, moving from only 35 per cent of its sales overseas in the early 1980s to 87 per cent of its sales overseas in 1995. This was in response to the recognition that there was little possibility of growth unless the company expanded overseas. It is interesting to note that of Morgan's customers in the early 1980s only 38 per cent exist today. In the words of the group's Managing Director: 'if we had just stopped in the UK and stopped in metal melting, we would not be talking today'. This is a good example of the company recognising the unattractiveness of its current environment and seeking to move beyond it. In terms of benchmarking, Morgan Crucible does not have a specific programme, but it will look at what is happening in other manufacturing industries to analyse the impact of specific issues. The Director of Group Personnel, Andy McIntosh, cites the introduction of European works councils as an example of an issue which induced the company to go out and look at other companies' responses.

One example of a Morgan Crucible company creating a whole new product as a result of its external awareness is the development of Foodlube by its subsidiary ROCOL. This is a lubricant which contains no mineral hydrocarbons and is therefore safe for use with food. In 1989 the government decided to ban the use of mineral hydrocarbons in food preparation because of research showing that they were unsafe. Scientists at ROCOL read reports of this in the newspaper and realised that this meant that there would be demand for a whole new range of mineral-hydrocarbon-free lubricants, something that had never been produced before. Although there was clearly still a tremendous amount of work to be done at this point, the idea for the new product was there as a result of the company scanning its environment and understanding the implications of changes in this environment.

Turning to look at Morgan Crucible's vision, the Director of Group Personnel states that the company 'has a very strong corporate strategy and vision which is then taken down into the various product groups and then subsequently down into the operating companies within those product groups'. The most important aspect of this vision seems to be the creation of a global group which is a leading supplier of high-technology materials. However, this vision does not seem to have been set down in writing; certainly it does not appear in any of the company's published material. At the subsidiary-company level the vision does not seem to have made a significant impact and was not considered important, probably because of the decentralised nature of the group.

At ROCOL quality is seen as part of the company's strategy and is described as 'an absolute maxim in everything that ROCOL does' (*Research, Innovation, Service, Commitment*, ROCOL internal publication). The company is clearly proud to have been accredited to ISO 9002 and BS5750, which the same publication describes as 'the most demanding quality standards available'. One example of the company's commitment to quality is its stated desire to increase the effective life-span of its lubricants by 400 per cent. At first sight this may seem good only as a way for the company to reduce its sales, but they believe that quality improvements of this type are necessary to success. It is difficult to know whether this commitment to quality is replicated at the other subsidiary companies, but the group seems to think that it is, and the company's newsletter is filled with stories of plants around the world achieving local and/or international quality standards.

The structural dimension

Morgan Crucible has a very decentralised organisational structure with a very small head office function – employing only sixty people compared to 12,000 in the whole group – guiding the operations of its subsidiary companies. The group has over 150 subsidiary companies, reflecting its belief that 'small is beautiful' (Bruce Farmer, Group Managing Director). The Director of Group Personnel explains that 'they [the managing directors of subsidiary companies] have a high degree of autonomy in running the business', and that 'we are a professional organisation with certain professional controls and disciplines, but there is a high degree of autonomy and ownership'. This is supported by evidence from the subsidiary companies themselves. The Managing Director of one subsidiary explains:

> the Morgan philosophy is one of centralised financial supervision but decentralised operating control, which means MDs are not only profit responsible and accountable but they take all their own decisions within their business. There are no decisions taken for them by Windsor [the location of the group's head office]; that is not the group philosophy.
>
> (Philip Wright, Managing Director, Morganite Thermal Ceramics)

Another senior manager at a different subsidiary expressed the same idea, but more simply: 'they [head office] leave us alone and yet at the same time fund us, which is a great situation' (Graham Bailey, General Manager, Lubrication, ROCOL). Clearly, the senior managers, both at head office and in the subsidiary companies, are satisfied with the company's structure, but we need to ask whether it encourages or hinders learning. We can assume that by giving autonomy to its subsidiaries the group is creating the opportunity for them to learn, rather than shackling them by imposing unnecessary bureaucracy. The danger of Morgan Crucible's approach is that the strict financial disciplines imposed on the subsidiary companies may inhibit their ability to learn.

Morgan Crucible's structure means that learning is largely left to the subsidiary companies. However, the company does run central training programmes, spending over £500,000 a year in addition to subsidiary-company activities. The Director of Group Personnel explains that 'we are providing learning opportunities and development opportunities for the subsidiary companies, which we organise and fund, but which are provided for the subsidiary'. The best example of this is the Morgan Management Training and Development Programme, which is organised by the group but attended by managers from the subsidiary companies.

Morgan Crucible seems to place less emphasis on teamworking as a formal process than the other case companies do, although this by no means indicates a lack of teamworking across the company. At ROCOL both the Product Development Manager, Bill Hopkins, and the General Manager of the Lubrication Division, Graham Bailey, stressed the importance of creating cross-functional teams which encourage different departments to work together. Similarly, the Product Development Manager of the Safety Products Division, Catherine Ripley, pointed out the need for commercial people to stay close to technical people and vice versa. One area where Morgan Crucible is very strong is its ability to build and maintain networks. The Group Managing Director says that 'there is a tremendous amount of networking that goes on'. The Managing Director of Morganite Thermal Ceramics, Philip Wright, explains that 'the Norton operation [the home of Morganite Thermal Ceramics] has links worldwide with other Morgan crucible-manufacturing operations. I now head a worldwide group of crucible companies.' He is the Chairman of the Crucible Executive, the body which manages the global product division, and which represents an excellent way for the individual company managers to build a global network. At ROCOL the Managing Director, Don Neil, emphasised the close links that have been formed between the company, the Ministry of Agriculture and the United States Department of Agriculture during the development and subsequent approval process for Foodlube. Overall, we can say that Morgan Crucible does not use teamworking to the same extent as some of the other case companies, but that it has certainly gone a long way down the road of creating global networks within its product groups.

At Morgan Crucible research and development is considered a divisional or subsidiary-company responsibility, and the company maintains three major research and development facilities to serve its four divisions. The Group Managing Director states that 'we do not believe in central R&D, so we don't have central R&D'. He goes on to explain that 'we have tried to set up a culture where we do not have salesmen. People go out and solve people's problems or do things better and come back with new ideas of what we could be doing.' Catherine Ripley, one of the Product Development Managers at ROCOL, stressed the importance of the continual development of existing products rather than new products or complete relaunches. This view was echoed by the Managing Director of Morgan Thermalite Ceramics, who pointed out that 'you have to approach improvement in a very focused and targeted manner'. Interestingly, he also pointed out the need to challenge the 'black art' that exists in crucible manufacturing. Previously, much of the knowledge needed to manufacture crucibles was held exclusively by the shop-floor workers, which meant that managers were reluctant to try to change anything because, in effect, they did not understand it. The company has tried to 'give people that have some knowledge of it [the black art] the opportunity to tell us about it, to challenge generally from the perspective of how or why'. Thus the company has tried to transfer the knowledge from its shop-floor workers to its managers. Another way to look at this would be as the conversion of knowledge from tacit to explicit (see Nonaka, 1991, 1994; or Chapter 2). In conclusion, we can say that Morgan Crucible lacks a co-ordinated policy of knowledge creation, but that it nevertheless manages to create new knowledge and successful new products because of the flexible nature of its structure.

The cultural dimension

At the subsidiary-company level there are probably as many different cultures as there are companies, each placing a different emphasis on learning. At ROCOL the culture is certainly one of encouraging ideas and the company is capable of taking advantage of seemingly simple ideas to generate new products. The company has managed to develop a range of successful new products that have kept it ahead of many of its competitors. One reason for this is the company's stated target of achieving at least 25 per cent of its sales from products that did not exist four years ago. In practice the company generates about 33 per cent of its sales from products introduced within the last four years. This target is very similar to 3M's new product objective, and it is likely that in this case ROCOL has learnt from 3M. At Morganite Thermal Ceramics there is much less emphasis on learning. In terms of new product development the company is reluctant to develop better, longer-lasting crucibles because this will inevitably reduce the number that it can sell. It therefore focuses its development efforts on two areas: those in which it is weak relative to its competitors; and those where it can make process improvements and thereby reduce production costs. For this reason learning is somewhat stifled at this particular subsidiary. Despite this, Philip Wright, Managing Director of Morganite Thermal Ceramics, emphasises that 'we are not in an environment which is heavily blame-orientated. If people make mistakes all I ask is that they should learn from them.' Overall, however, Morgan's efforts to encourage learning are fairly successful, although it does not have the same high profile as at 3M or CCSB.

Morgan Crucible's Director of Group Personnel claims: 'we recognise that we're only ever going to be as good as the people that we have within the organisation'. He goes on: 'over the last ten years we have made incredible step changes to our commitment to the development of our people'. He also cites the group's central training programme, which has the development of people skills at its core. The Group Managing Director is even more upbeat about the culture in the company: 'we have got an achieving organisation, we have got a caring organisation, we have got one in which most people enjoy what they are doing'. This sounds like a recipe for the ideal workplace, but we need to examine what the company does to create a supportive culture. One thing that Morgan Crucible has encouraged is employee share owner-ship, and in the UK 62 per cent of employees now own shares in the company. Evidence on the effectiveness of employee share ownership is very mixed, but Morgan Crucible believes that this will encourage employees to feel that they are part of the company and be more committed to it. In the subsidiary companies, where the effects of the group's commitment to people should be seen, the message is similar. At Morganite Thermal Ceramics, the Managing Director has introduced new bonus and profit-related pay schemes, which have made the workforce more committed and have aligned the goals of the employees to those of the company. The Managing Director spends one day each quarter talking to the entire workforce about the company's perfor-mance and its future prospects. Again, this is designed to win the commitment of the employees. At ROCOL the story remains the same, with people talking of the 'excitement and enthusiasm' generated by projects.

As we have already seen, Morgan Crucible's subsidiary companies have a high level of autonomy in managing their operations, suggesting that the managing directors of these companies are empowered. Have they in turn empowered their employees? The group's Managing Director points out that the number of levels in the organisation has been reduced to five, necessitating the devolution of responsibility to relatively low levels. He also points out that the company has tried to 'push accountability way down the line'. The Director of Group Personnel expresses similar sentiments, speaking of 'the pushing down of profit responsibility right down as far as you can, the opening up of communications, being more free with information to all levels of employees, opening up the whole organisation to all the employees within it, encouraging ownership of the business'. The Managing Director at Morganite Thermal Ceramics 'hates the word empowering because it is a buzzword we do not use here', but he nevertheless goes on to say that 'we are empowering them [the managers] to run their side of the business and supporting them to do it'. Having said this, it would be hard to conclude objectively that the company's workers are highly empowered. Perhaps this is unfair in comparison to the company's past record, but it is certainly correct in comparison with some of the other companies in the study. However, the company has managed to create quite a supportive culture as a result of its efforts to communicate with employees and involve them in the business.

The practice of organisational learning: the case of Siebe

Siebe plc is Britain's largest diversified engineering group (*Siebe plc Report and Accounts 1996*). Its main area of expertise is in the field of control equipment (*Engineering Excellence*, internal publication). Siebe's market capitalisation is over £5 billion, enough to make it one of the UK's top 100 companies. Siebe is in some ways similar to Morgan Crucible in that its organisational structure is nominally highly decentralised. However, the company differs in that, while still largely decentralised in an operational sense, it places more emphasis on central direction and on direction at the divisional level. This is most apparent in the tight financial controls placed on operating companies. The company's strategy is primarily focused on growth, something that it has been very successful in achieving in recent years.

The strategic dimension

Siebe has three publicly stated long-term goals:

> Global Engineering Leadership – to be recognised as one of the top three global competitors in each of its core engineering sectors.

Customer Value Leadership – to provide its customers with the best combination of product technology, quality, service and price, in other words, best available value.

Shareholder Value Leadership – to consistently deliver a long-term total return to shareholders ranking in the top ten per cent when compared to the UK engineering sector and its international peer group of competitors.

(*Siebe plc Report and Accounts 1995*: 5)

These are the company's formal goals and no mention is made of learning as a specific objective. More informally, growth – through both new product development and acquisition – is seen as central to the company's plans. We can say that the company probably has innovation as a goal but does not see learning as a focus. At an operating-company level the strategies are likely to be slightly different, although there are strict financial controls which help to align the individual companies' strategies to the overall strategy. At Siebe's CompAir subsidiary the Managing Director spoke of the need to 'get out of fire-fighting and into a more disciplined, quality-improvement programme'. This is reflected in the company's more down-to-earth day-to-day objectives or critical success factors: producing products and services that satisfy customers' needs; profitable business growth; looking for continuous waste reduction; fully effective employees; effective financial planning and control; and effective communication (*On the Road to World Class Performance*, CompAir internal publication). Again, these objectives do not include learning as a specific goal. While a target such as 'fully effective employees' might imply a leading role for training and learning, it is a secondary thought and more of a means than an end.

According to the Vice-President of Human Resources, Siebe's vision statement 'really focuses on the idea of growth, customer satisfaction and market focus, and it has two legs really to the mission or the strategy; it combines organic growth and acquisition'. This vision is then:

shared both by the local policy objectives and through the exchange that happens in a performance review system and is shared down through the structure by virtue of preparing for business reviews, preparing for budget reviews, and you'll find an assortment of communications throughout Siebe that take that even down to the person on the factory floor.

(Vice-President of Human Resources, Siebe)

This is a purposeful vision and the company certainly attempts to communicate it. The problem with Siebe's approach is that there is a risk that the company's subsidiaries may decide to establish incompatible local visions. This is certainly the case at CompAir, where the vision is 'to satisfy our customers totally by achieving *excellence* in everything we do' (*On the Road to World Class Performance*, CompAir internal publication). While this may not directly conflict with the vision set by Siebe, it will certainly create confusion if the employees are receiving two different messages. CompAir's internal publication *On the Road to World Class Performance* gives the company's mission: 'to satisfy our customers' needs for Compressed Air Products and Services profitably through continuous improvement and innovation', and a set of critical success factors which support the vision. In summary, we can see that Siebe has created a vision and has recognised the need to communicate this throughout the company. However, the success of this group-wide vision will remain limited while subsidiary companies are creating their own local visions.

Siebe has a number of activities that allow it to gain information on and from its environment. While the company has no general benchmarking strategy, the company does undertake benchmarking programmes in certain areas. A good example of this is the company's new management development programme, which is benchmarked against internationally established standards. The company uses standards that were established by Peter Fleming, a well-known psychologist in the fields of learning and development criteria, who surveyed over 18,000 people. Siebe's Group Development Director emphasised the importance of market research when making decisions on which products should be developed. He also mentioned the importance of filtering this information and treating its recommendations with care. A key danger is that market research will give a picture of customers' current requirements, not their requirements in two or three years' time when any product development programme has come to fruition. He considers that two of Siebe's weaknesses are 'inadequate market intelligence' and 'inadequate learning from other industries'. This suggests, in all likelihood correctly, that Siebe needs to go much further in its efforts to understand its environment, particularly in terms of being prepared for changes that are likely to affect the organisation.

Learning as a way of developing new products is a key goal for Siebe. The company states: '[our] growth strategies are solidly based upon our development of new products, incorporating the latest design and manufacturing technology' (*Siebe plc, Report and Accounts 1995*: 5). Siebe's Group

Development Director also, unsurprisingly, regards new product development as a strategic goal, although he goes on to explain that the company looks more to improving existing products than to developing entirely new technologies. In order to accelerate the speed with which new products are developed the company has implemented 'concurrent design' and 'design for manufacture' practices. This has led to a 40 per cent reduction in the average lead-time to design and commercialise new products. While the group has certainly been reasonably successful in developing new products, much of its growth in sales has been attributable to acquisition rather than the creation of new knowledge. The links between Siebe's many operating companies seem relatively weak and this is likely to hinder the transfer of knowledge between them.

The structural dimension

Siebe has a small head office based in Windsor and over 120 companies around the world. Siebe's Vice-President of Human Resources, Richard Bradford, describes the structure as 'very, very lean'. He emphasises the speed of reaction that this structure allows within Siebe: 'speed in terms of making judgements, speed in terms of responding to the issues, and speed in correcting problems that occur.' Financial control in Siebe is very tight and this means that ongoing data is available throughout the organisation very rapidly. The relative smallness of Siebe's operating companies allows it to remain relevant, quick and effective at the individual business level while maintaining financial control at the centre. The company believes that it has managed to achieve the – almost paradoxical – advantages of a very controlled organisation and, at the same time, of a very small, agile organisation.

Siebe's Vice-President of Human Resources says that one of the major changes in the company in the next few years will be that 'the company does more and gets more out of its people by virtue of a process of team-building'. The group's Development Director says that teamworking is the best way to develop new products. Unusually, however, he goes against the catalogue of praise for teamworking by pointing out that placing too much reliance on teams can stifle new ideas. At CompAir Hydrovane the Managing Director regards teamworking as a 'very, very important aspect of developing any cultural change'. In fact he goes on to describe the value of teamworking very simply: 'without teamworking you won't be successful'. We will look later at the way people volunteer for particular project teams rather than being selected, but this is only one aspect of how CompAir's project teams are organised. Each project team is given a sponsor, who will usually be a senior manager, and who is responsible for leading the project, agreeing the project's parameters and measurements, calling the meetings and focusing the team on the issues which are important to meet the objectives of the project. All this information is documented and displayed on the company's notice boards. The project also goes through various stages of authorisation, and checks are made for links to other projects. This is a very structured approach to teamworking which has both advantages and disadvantages. Within the company's training and development programme training often takes place on a departmental basis, training one team at a time. However, the company also recognises that there are benefits to be gained from training cross-departmental teams.

With regard to networking, Siebe has created a number of joint ventures around the world which allow it to take advantage of local expertise. The most notable of these are in Russia, where the Control Systems Division is working with Gazinvest, the investment arm of Russia's gas distribution company, and China, where the company has a majority position in the Shanghai–Foxboro Company joint venture. While the company makes use of joint ventures to enter unknown foreign markets, one possible weakness is the failure to create strong links between the different companies within the Siebe Group. Thus Siebe's scientists do not work together in the same way as those at 3M, and potential innovations may go to waste because they do not reach the part of the company most suitable for their development.

Siebe's management development programme is, according to the Vice-President of Human Resources, 'majoring on what we call the knowledge worker', but it does not seem to be anything other than a standard training programme. The topics are thinking strategically; focusing key resources while maintaining flexibility; managing priorities; defining performance expectation and quality; taking ownership, responsibility and accountability; influencing and interpersonal awareness; and continuously improving people, products and processes. These are all important topics, but hardly any different from those focused on by the majority of other management development programmes.

At Siebe total quality management (TQM) is essentially seen, quite rightly, as an operating-company responsibility. At CompAir the company has introduced a very thorough TQM programme, in turn engendering significant change in the culture. One of the most important aspects of the programme has been, in the words of the subsidiary company's Managing Director, to 'get away from this fixation that quality is all about product'. The need for training prior to the implementation of the change programme was also emphasised. The Managing Director explains that 'over a period of time you have a total quality management programme, you have business as usual, then you have the two merging together, and then, in time, total quality is part of day-to-day, business-as-usual activity'. This view of quality as an everyday, everybody activity fits perfectly with the ideals of a learning organisation; it has certainly been effective in changing the culture at CompAir and may have resulted in improved effectiveness.

The cultural dimension

At Siebe the leanness of the structure means that the company has to draw much of its learning from outside, and so a learning culture does not exist in the form envisaged by leading enthusiasts for organisational learning. The Vice-President of Human Resources argues that 'being a lean structure, you're going to have to be very selective on people. So from a pure learning point of view it's going to be hiring somebody with the talent coming in.' In CompAir, one of Siebe's most important operating companies, the focus is placed on the development of existing products as opposed to the creation of entirely new products and technologies. This has perhaps served to detract from the degree of learning within the culture, as people have become focused on continuous improvement rather than genuinely new research. In terms of incentives for innovation, the company has a much sought-after award, unsurprisingly called the Siebe Award. The award takes the form of an old deep-sea diving helmet, which was the firm's first product, set atop an inscribed trophy base. It is given out by division and group to those who successfully introduce new products.

As we have seen, Siebe already likes to refer to the participants in its management development programme as 'knowledge workers', suggesting a significant level of investment in managers. The company certainly supports its top managers financially by giving them bonuses for both personal performance and business performance: a stock option plan and a deferred compensation plan, which allows certain executives to gain tax advantages. However, the concern here is with the company's employees as a whole, not just the more senior managers. At CompAir one of the company's critical success factors is 'fully effective employees' and the question is thus: what does the company do to support its employees and make them fully effective? The first answer seems to be to recognise that the employees have a reserve of skills and resources, and also that they can be enhanced by further training.

There is a close relationship between having a supportive culture and having high levels of empowerment; unsurprisingly, some of the ways in which CompAir empowers its workers – for example by letting them choose which teams they would like to be a member of – also help to build a supportive culture.

At Siebe the Group Development Manager felt that empowerment was necessary for the success of any project. At CompAir Hydrovane the Managing Director explained the way in which the company now invites people to participate in project teams as opposed to assigning a particular person to a particular team. He says that this is intended to 'try to get the commitment from them to that scope and activity'. It is difficult to argue with the idea that people will be more committed to a task they have decided to do voluntarily. Siebe's Vice-President of Human Resources joins the almost unanimous criticism of empowerment, saying: 'I don't like the term empowerment but I do like the term ownership – and I think we'll get more ownership from employees.' It is difficult to say whether Siebe's employees are highly empowered or the culture is very supportive. However, the company has clearly made some important concessions towards offering greater responsibility to those taking the actions.

Case studies of organisational learning practice: a summary

The case studies above show the way in which each company approaches organisational learning in practice. There are many differences and similarities between the approaches adopted by each company. We have seen that each company has adopted different policies in terms of strategy, structure and culture. 3M has focused mainly on creating a culture in which learning and innovation are both highly valued and rewarded. It has also created a unique and highly complex structure, both formal and informal, which allows it to capitalise on the many technologies it has developed. CCSB is significantly different from the other case companies in that the creation of new products is not part of its *raison d'être*. Its focus has thus been on managerial and process innovations. The company's relatively young age and its high earnings have allowed it to implement progressive human resource policies which coincide with many of the principles of organisational learning. Mayflower is perhaps the most entrepreneurial of the five case companies, and this is reflected in the company's strong and visionary strategy. The company's structures and cultures differ considerably between subsidiary companies, although this matter is now receiving considerable attention. Morgan Crucible has a highly decentralised structure which gives a high degree of autonomy to individual operating companies. This means that there is not a uniform company approach to learning, rather that learning differs in its intensity and effectiveness from subsidiary company to subsidiary company. Siebe has a very clear strategy focused on globalisation and growth. It is similar to Morgan Crucible in having a devolved organisational form. Again, this means that learning practices differ within the group.

The above suggests that organisational learning is best viewed as a fairly loose construct. Insofar as the case companies are learning organisations, they are all learning organisations in different ways. They display strengths and weaknesses in different areas, and these strengths and weaknesses are often the results of events in each company's history or of contemporary external circumstances. This calls into question the usefulness of organisational learning as a distinct competitive tool. In Chapter 4 we will use these five case studies as the basis for the development of a theory of best practice in organisational learning, although this is made difficult by the marked differences in the companies' approaches.

4 Best practice in organisational learning

Introduction

It is difficult, but nevertheless essential, to attempt to determine best practice in the field of organisational learning. Only through the development of a model of best practice can reliable recommendations be made to business about the value of organisational learning. In this chapter we attempt to determine best practice through the analysis of the critical case studies developed in the previous chapter, supported by secondary sources and questionnaire results. The chapter is organised into two main parts. In the first, 'The characteristics of organisational learning', we develop a model showing the key characteristics of organisational learning practice and outline 'ideal' behaviour, i.e. behaviour most likely to lead to organisational learning and enhanced organisational effectiveness.

The second part, 'The five case companies and best practice in comparative perspective', places the five case companies in comparative perspective and assesses their respective attempts to achieve best practice. We will draw extensively on the case studies from the previous chapter, but these will be supplemented by self-assessments carried out by managers in each case company. This, in turn, is complemented by the author's more critical comparative assessment of the organisational learning practice of each case company. Comparative analysis of the key characteristics of organisational learning practice is followed by an integrative section comparing and contrasting the case companies' approaches to organisational learning practice as a whole.

The characteristics of organisational learning

The method established to determine best practice in the field of organisational learning is to compare and contrast the original case data presented here with those of previously published evaluative studies. We also utilise the results of the questionnaire survey, which add more general insights into organisational learning practice. We use these three sources to develop a model showing the key characteristics of organisational learning practice. These characteristics are then explained in detail and 'ideal' behaviour outlined.

In order to evaluate each company's approach to organisational learning it is first necessary to create a set of criteria against which the companies can be assessed. The existing literature utilised here includes, but is not confined to, the work of Marquardt and Reynolds (1994), Senge (1990a), Pearn *et al.* (1995), Watkins and Marsick (1993), Graham (1996) and Tobin (1993). Each of these authors, as might be expected, has his or her own personal ideas as to what constitutes a learning organisation. However, an attempt has been made to draw out common themes, from both the case studies and the literature. The evidence of the five original case studies remains the central foundation on which the view of organisational learning represented here is based.

The justification for the choice of approach – using a set of characteristics to describe best practice – is that it offers the best way of making sense of the complex behaviours involved in organisational learning. It is only by breaking down organisational learning into its constituent parts that we can come to terms with the concept as a whole. While we must, of course, remember that the characteristics are closely interrelated – and this is specifically acknowledged below – it is only by defining individual characteristics that we can discuss best practice in a meaningful way.

A detailed rationale for each of the nine learning characteristics will be developed during the course of this part of the chapter. By way of introduction, Table 4.1 lists the nine characteristics, together with a short description of each and an explanation of its contribution to organisational learning and effectiveness.

We can see from Table 4.1 that to achieve the status of a learning organisation is demanding for any organisation. The nine organisational learning characteristics identified are closely related. The three primary characteristics, as given in the previous chapter, may be thought of as establishing a context or framework within which the remaining six characteristics exist to a greater or lesser degree. We begin, therefore, by considering the strategic, structural and cultural dimensions of organisational learning.

Table 4.1 The characteristics of organisational learning

Characteristic	Description	Contribution to organisational learning and effectiveness
Learning strategy	Learning is a deliberate and conscious part of the strategy	Learning becomes a habit and an everyday occurrence
Flexible structure	A simple, streamlined structure that helps learning in the company	Reduces bureaucracy and restrictive job descriptions Encourages cross-functional co-operation
Blame-free culture	Learning is valued and encouraged, and the environment is blame-free	Learning becomes automatic and natural A blame-free culture encourages experimentation
Vision	The organisation has a clear vision of the future which is shared in all quarters	Establishes an overarching goal which encourages everyone in the organisation to pull in the same direction
External awareness	The organisation uses scenario planning, benchmarking and related techniques to scan its environment	Improved understanding of its environment allows an organisation to anticipate change and prepare its response
Knowledge creation and transfer	The creation of new knowledge is seen as central to the work of the organisation and people can easily learn and utilise knowledge from other parts of the organisation	The creation of new knowledge leads to new products and processes Transferring knowledge allows successful ideas to be widely disseminated
Quality	The organisation focuses on total quality management (TQM) and strives for continuous improvement	Improved quality reduces waste, improves the organisation's reputation and increases sales
Supportive atmosphere	Excellent results require happy, productive individuals, who feel a sense of ownership and empowerment	Commitment is a two-way street and an organisation that treats its workers with respect can expect respect in return
Teamworking	Small groups of people work closely together Networks are effectively teams operating outside the organisation	A key way not only of combining the existing knowledge of a group, but also the ability of its members to create new knowledge

Learning strategy

The first primary characteristic of a learning organisation is the possession of a learning strategy. We would expect a corporate strategy that embraces both learning and innovation as specific goals, and a learning strategy which is both deliberate and conscious. The ability to learn faster than competing organisations should be seen as a key source of sustainable competitive advantage. The organisation needs to make an explicit decision to place learning at the top of its list of priorities and put in place the necessary conditions for learning to occur. This means that all aspects of the company should be deliberately geared towards learning. As strategy must be endorsed, if not necessarily created, by top management, an inherent feature of a successful learning strategy is high-level commitment to learning. In an organisation with a learning strategy learning is no longer a discrete activity, but a part of each individual's and each team's full-time job. Managerial decisions are seen as contingent rather than definitive. In a successful learning organisation learning is a constant part of the strategic decision-making process. It becomes integrated with everyday work and runs in parallel to, and in support of, ordinary activities. As we have seen, the two characteristics that are most closely related to the idea of a learning strategy are vision and external awareness.

Flexible structure

The second of the three main characteristics of an ideal learning organisation is a flexible structure. A small, streamlined structure is recommended to help learning within the company. The organisation needs to create a climate of 'smallness' regardless of the size of the company. This can be done by encouraging teamworking, by the creation of small, autonomous profit centres, or by downsizing the company and creating a small, core workforce. A truly flexible structure should do away with traditional ideas such as rigid job descriptions, strict hierarchies and excessive bureaucracy. In the case of a large company, structures may need to vary between operating units to correspond with differing market conditions. A key aspect of a learning organisation is the importance it places on cross-functional working, and structure has an important role in facilitating and encouraging this. Cross-functional co-operation allows the organisation to gain an overall picture of the business, reduces the political content of management decisions and significantly improves the co-ordination of the organisation's operations.

The other characteristic closely related to a flexible structure is that of team-working. In particular, cross-functional teamwork and multi-functional project teams encourage both structural flexibility and the flow of knowledge and learning between different departments.

Blame-free culture

A learning organisation should provide a climate in which learning is valued and encouraged. Mistakes need to be seen, not as a black mark against an individual's record, but as an opportunity for improvement and a chance to learn. Organisations thus need to create a blame-free environment in which employees have the courage to experiment. Marquardt and Reynolds (1994) believe that four cultural aspects can enhance an organisation's ability to learn: incentives for innovation, learning from experience, the learning habit and corporate support. *Incentives for innovation* mean rewarding employee ideas and initiative, leading to more ideas and higher levels of initiative. *Learning from experience* means taking advantage of past mistakes and encouraging feedback to aid learning. *The learning habit* refers to a culture of continuous learning in every part of the business, while *corporate support* means a strong top-level commitment to learning. This often manifests itself as a high percentage of payroll costs or total revenue devoted to training and development. Graham suggests that in a learning organisation 'corporate values and principles are formally articulated and are a source of inspiration and unity. They provide a framework for behaviour and performance that helps to reduce bureaucracy' (Graham, 1996: 17). She goes on to list the values commonly expressed in learning organisations: respect for individual freedom, honesty, learning from mistakes, and appreciation of the personal and business significance of continuous learning. The characteristic which is most closely related to culture, and in the development of which culture is most important, is a supportive atmosphere. A blame-free culture and a supportive atmosphere are likely to be mutually reinforcing.

Vision

One of Senge's five 'disciplines' of a learning organisation is a shared vision. He asserts that you 'cannot have a learning organization without shared vision' (Senge, 1990a: 209). A shared vision is required to overcome the powerful forces supporting the maintenance of the status quo. Successful learning can occur only if it is undertaken in pursuit of a specific goal.

A shared vision provides a picture of the organisation's desired future and a goal which people can strive for. In their 1994 book *Competing for the Future*, Hamel and Prahalad argue that 'any company that cannot imagine the future won't be around to enjoy it' (Hamel and Prahalad, 1994: xi–xii). Without a vision this image of the future will be hard to generate and even harder to share. Many organisations have visions, but few have been successfully shared throughout the organisation. Creating a vision that is genuinely shared by all requires communication – consistent, repeated communication from the top of the organisation. If a shared vision does exist this can provide the drive and the excitement needed to move the organisation forward.

External awareness

A learning organisation recognises that its external environment is forever changing. As the rate and magnitude of this change increase, so external awareness becomes more and more important. A high level of external awareness usually manifests itself in three ways: the organisation scans its environment, the organisation affects its environment and the organisation chooses its environmental target. A key form of learning is to anticipate change and thus be ready to adapt if and when the change takes place. This makes environmental scanning, perhaps in the form of scenario planning, an important aspect of organisational learning. If the change does take place, then an organisation that has spent time planning different scenarios may already have experience of the new environment. A step on from scanning the environment is affecting the environment. If change is ongoing, then the organisation can, and should, try to influence that change to make it as favourable as possible. Choosing the environmental target means selecting the part of the environment with which the organisation will interact. Thus, when selecting benchmarking partners organisations will try to choose partners who are successful in the same business or a related business. In contrast, when entering a new market organisations will attempt to select one with weak competitors and high growth potential. Many organisations use SWOT (strengths, weaknesses, opportunities and threats) analysis or one of its more sophisticated derivatives to aid their strategic decision-making and help identify areas where they are strong and where good opportunities exist. This amounts to classic strategic positioning, but taken to a higher level of intensity in response to increasing rates of change and levels of complexity.

Knowledge creation and transfer

In a learning organisation the creation of new knowledge should be seen as central to the work of all parts of the business, not the exclusive province of a research and development department. The ability to take knowledge from other parts of the organisation and learn from what they are doing is also an important source of competitive advantage. Drucker, arguably the most distinguished management thinker and writer of the century, says that: 'knowledge is *the* primary resource for individuals and for the economy overall' (Drucker, 1992a: 95). If this is true the creation of new knowledge must be a key process for both organisational learning and organisational effectiveness. Equally, if knowledge is a valuable resource, then the need to share it, deliberately to communicate it to the entire workforce, becomes apparent. Going further, if knowledge is so important (and few would disagree with this assertion) there is much to be gained by sharing key information with customers, suppliers and distributors. This sharing of knowledge has many advantages, not least the improved access that the company will have to the knowledge of the customers, suppliers and distributors in such a reciprocal arrangement. Increasingly, the use of modern technology is an important way for companies to transfer knowledge and encourage learning. Sillince (1995) suggests that knowledge and understanding are the key to successful strategic change and that information technology, particularly a group-decision support system, can be an effective way of transferring such information. This may mean the use of telecommunications in training applications or even the use of artificial intelligence and so-called expert systems. The creation of an online database detailing employees' expertise or the widespread use of an electronic mail system should encourage and facilitate knowledge transfer (see Sillince, 1996, for an account of the issues surrounding the use of electronic communication systems in organisations). Importantly, all employees should be encouraged to become familiar with the way the business as a whole operates. They are given access to information regarding sales targets, financial indicators and business plans. This information, which is traditionally the preserve of managers and executives, gives employees the knowledge required to take more decisions for themselves.

Quality

Quality is now accepted as a *sine qua non* of business success and thus is an obvious part of a learning organisation. Senge says that 'good management techniques are enduring. Quality control, for instance, was treated as a fad here [in the West], but it's been part of the Japanese business philosophy for decades. That's why they laugh at us' (Senge, quoted in Griffith, 1995: 15). Quality has certainly been a foundation stone for Japanese success. Hayward (1996) suggests that the concept of quality as a crucial component of the production process had already taken a hesitant hold in Japan during the late 1940s and early 1950s. It took until the 1990s for most Western writers and managers to agree that the quality movement is more than just a fad. In a company that is focused on total quality management (TQM) and strives for continuous improvement there is a constant desire to do better. For this reason, such a company has much in common with a learning organisation. Indeed, in some respects, TQM may be seen as synonymous with organisational learning, or at least as a first step towards becoming a learning organisation. The typically incremental nature of TQM means that it is naturally akin to organisational learning. TQM requires everyone in the organisation to be continually learning to perform more effectively, something very close to the key ideas of organisational learning. Tobin emphasises the need for learning organisations to be committed to quality, describing quality as 'a measure of the skills, knowledge, and abilities of the people involved in the learning effort' (Tobin, 1993: 240). Interestingly, Lessem (1991) sees quality and learning as the two dominant factors in organisations, viewing learning as the process and quality as the end. He fuses the two concepts to form a more fundamental concept for those interested in organisational learning: total quality learning. Again, this serves to emphasise both the importance of quality and its close relationship with organisational learning.

Supportive atmosphere

Learning organisations understand that excellent organisational results are built on happy, productive, empowered individuals. Learning organisations should be aware of the delicate balance between the needs of the individual and the needs of the organisation. In other words, there has to be a balance between production, on the one hand, and productive capacity, on the other. This is best illustrated with reference to Aesop's fable of the goose and the golden egg. This is the story of a poor farmer who discovers that his goose has laid a golden egg. The farmer cannot believe his luck and becomes only more incredulous the next day when his goose lays another golden egg. Day after day his goose lays more golden eggs and soon the farmer is very wealthy. With his increasing wealth comes increasing greed, until one day the farmer decides to kill the goose and get all the eggs at once. But when he kills the goose and opens it up he finds no golden eggs, and now there is no way to get any more. The farmer has destroyed the goose that produced them. According to Covey (1992), this story shows that individual performance depends on two things: what is produced and the capacity to produce. As well as encouraging employees to produce, organisations need to encourage them to improve their capacity to produce.

Once people have the capacity to produce excellent results they need to be empowered to ensure that they fully utilise that capacity. 'Empowerment' is one of today's biggest management buzzwords, and as such is often shunned by practising managers. However, while they may be quick to criticise the term itself, few managers would disagree with the underlying ideas.

Traditional definitions of empowerment focus on the sharing of power with employees, thereby enhancing their confidence in their ability to perform their jobs and their belief that they can be influential contributors to the organisation. Responsibility is pushed as close as possible to the point where actions are taken and decisions made. As the role of managers has changed from one of controlling and planning to one of coaching and leading, so the need – and the opportunity – to delegate has increased. Empowerment is little more than delegation built into the culture, so that, rather than being an occasional occurrence, delegation happens automatically every day. Learning organisations realise that empowered workers can, in most circumstances, make better decisions than managers because they have access to the best information.

Teamworking

Teamworking is a central part of any learning organisation, for the simple reason that membership of a team is an excellent way for knowledge to be both shared and created within the organisation. Teams are key ways not only of combining the existing knowledge of a group of people, but also of combining their abilities to create new knowledge. Teamworking involves working in groups inside the organisation, while the associated idea of networking refers, in effect, to teamworking that takes place outside the organisation. The organisation can benefit from using teams because they can result in internal synergy, while networks can result in external synergy. Increasingly, the accepted wisdom is that no traditional corporate structure, however decluttered or delayered, can provide the speed and flexibility needed in today's highly competitive markets. Team-based structures, internal and external, are the most commonly prescribed solution to the need for speed and flexibility. Watkins and Marsick go so far as to claim that 'team learning is key to building a learning organisation' (Watkins and Marsick, 1993: 96). They go on to say that, 'when a team adopts something new, members reinforce one another's thinking and spread these ideas faster and further through their combined contacts elsewhere in the organization' (*ibid.*).

Katzenbach and Smith (1993) draw on their experience in a number of organisations, including 3M, in concluding that the team will be the principal building block of company performance in the future. Teamworking is now widespread in industry and there is little to suggest that this will change. My own survey of 160 organisations in the South-east of England showed that the majority of responding organisations had, in the opinion of their Human Resources Directors, quite high or very high levels of teamworking: 61 respondents (38.1 per cent) reported 'quite high' levels of teamworking, while 31 respondents (19.4 per cent) reported 'very high' levels.

One particular variety of team, the cross-functional team, can be important for its ability to bring diverse skills and knowledge together. Grant (1996) argues, citing Imai *et al.* (1985) and Clark and Fujimoto (1991), that cross-functional product development teams are not difficult to set up. He suggests, however, that the challenge is for the team to access the breadth and depth of functional knowledge pertinent to the product, and then integrate that knowledge.

Networks are less widespread than teams at present, but are likely to be used increasingly in the future, and this process will be accelerated by globalisation. Networks can bring the advantages of speed, flexibility and focus, which are so desirable in increasingly competitive marketplaces. In effect, a network can create a small company, with all its inherent advantages, inside a large one, which brings the attributes of global power and extensive learning. Hastings (1993) is one of the foremost advocates of organisational networking, and he particularly emphasises the importance of sharing knowledge.

Organisational learning: the characteristics combined

From the above it should be apparent that best practice in organisational learning requires a high level of performance across a number of characteristics. It requires an integrated policy which takes account of strategy, structure and culture. At a strategic level the key requirement is for learning to become a specific goal of the organisation. This must be combined with a clear vision of where the company wants to go and what it wants to be. This vision needs to be shared throughout the company and employees need to 'buy in' to the company's vision. This vision, and the company's strategy as a whole, should be outward-looking as most of the drivers for organisational change will come from the external environment.

Structurally, the key attribute of a learning organisation is flexibility. This can be achieved through the use of modern organisational methods such as matrix structures, self-managed teams, project teams and networks. Perhaps most important, however, is a lack of bureaucracy, which is often achieved through downsizing and decentralisation. Where bureaucracy does exist, a learning organisation needs informal channels through which the bureaucracy can be bypassed and quick decisions taken.

Turning to address the cultural dimension, we can see that culture is one of the key determinants, if not *the* key determinant, of whether the organisation can practise organisational learning effectively. Without a culture that encourages learning and that does not attribute blame to individuals who make mistakes, no organisation will be able to become a learning organisation. As Lundberg states:

> organizational culture both fuels and fosters learning in organizations, as well as learning by organizations. Managing for learning by members and by the organization is managing with and through culture.
>
> (Lundberg, 1996: 507)

The process of socialisation in organisations, through which individuals learn to conform to organisational norms and practices, is a major source of learning and the key direct influence of culture on the learning process. Indirectly, however, culture has an impact, to varying degrees, on all other aspects of organisational learning, and indeed all other aspects of organisational life.

Best practice in organisational learning: a restatement

The case studies presented in Chapter 3 demonstrate that different organisations understand organisational learning to mean different things. This makes it difficult to establish one model of best practice which is applicable to all organisations. In Chapter 6 we discuss the relevance of organisational learning to different organisations, but it is likely that even if organisational learning is relevant to a range of organisations it will look very different from place to place. While we have established that the different characteristics of organisational learning are interrelated, it is nevertheless clear that no organisation will excel in all areas. Inevitably, the actual implementation of organisational learning practices in any organisation will be a matter of improvisation. Indeed, an important research study led by Michael Beer of Harvard Business School (Beer *et al.*, 1990) advocates a deliberately improvisational approach to implementing strategic change, arguing that this is more effective than traditional corporate change programmes. The necessarily improvisational nature of the creation of a learning organisation means that those books and courses advocating a particular programme are likely to be fundamentally flawed. Notable examples of such deterministically prescriptive books include those by Thurbin (1994), Pearn *et al.* (1995) and Braham (1995). Advocates of the 'one right way' of building a learning organisation leave themselves dangerously open to the wide range of circumstances in which their ideas simply do not fit. The characteristics of organisational learning must be broadly defined and left open for interpretation by managers in their particular organisational context. For some managers, organisational learning may be seen more as an aspirational model of what can be achieved given ideal conditions than as a prescription for how to manage their business more successfully. This is not to say, however, that the characteristics identified here are not meaningful in a general sense. Their value is enhanced by the fact that they have been created from evidence gathered from five successful companies.

The five case companies and best practice in comparative perspective

We now turn to compare and contrast the five case-study companies and examine the extent to which they have grasped the opportunity that organisational learning represents. We compare the five case-study companies with each other and with the model of best practice that was established in the first section of this chapter. Naturally, we make extensive use of the case studies detailed in Chapter 3. This information is supplemented by self-assessments carried out by managers in each case company and by my own critical assessment of each company's overall performance. We also assess the companies' performances in terms of each of the characteristics of organisational learning. Finally, we compare and contrast the overall strategy, structure, culture and performance of each of the five case companies. We develop a typology that shows that the case companies fall into two groups: on the one hand, those companies that are highly integrated, centralised, highly co-ordinated, organised and dominant in their markets; on the other hand, those companies that are entrepreneurial, decentralised and unfocused. Crucially, the financial performance of the five case companies is analysed and used to assess the potential implications of the dichotomy for long-term organisational effectiveness and performance.

Company ratings

Table 4.2 summarises the in-depth analysis which follows and creates what is, in effect, an organisational learning rating for each company. Each company has been given two ratings. The first rating is derived from the case-study research presented in the previous chapter and is an attempt to create a relatively objective assessment based on systematic analysis of practice in each company. The second rating is the average of ratings given by two, three or four senior managers from each company. Each manager was presented with each of the nine descriptions listed above and asked to rate his or her organisation on the same scale as was used in the objective assessment. This was, in all cases, carried out with the assurance of anonymity to encourage respondents to be more open and honest.

Table 4.3 is effectively a simpler, reordered version of Table 4.2, which we will use to help to create the two groups of companies shown in the next section. It summarises Table 4.2 by giving just each company's total rating, rather than the rating for each characteristic of organisational learning. The companies are also reordered to begin with the company gaining the highest author rating and finish with the company with the lowest author rating. This differs from the usual practice of showing the companies in alphabetical order.

Looking first at managers' own assessments of their companies, it is clear that the standard deviation and the range of scores are quite low. The most highly rated company, CCSB, scores 32.33, while the lowest-rated company, Morgan Crucible, scores 31.00, a mere 1.33 points lower. The small range between the highest and lowest scores is likely to be the result of managers' unwillingness to give their companies very high or (especially) very low scores.

My own assessment of the five companies, based on the analysis in the first section of this chapter, shows that 3M and CCSB are the two companies that conform most closely to the ideal of the learning organisation, according to the

Table 4.2 Ratings of the five case companies

	3M		CCSB		Mayflower		Morgan Crucible		Siebe	
	Author rating	Company rating	Author rating	Company rating	Author rating	Company rating	Author rating	Company rating	Author rating	Company rating
Learning strategy	4	3.25	4	3.67	3	3.33	3	3.5	3	3.33
Flexible structure	3	2.75	4	3.67	3	4	4	4	3	4
Blame-free culture	4	4	4	3.33	3	3.33	3	3	2	3.33
Vision	5	4.5	5	4.33	4	3.67	2	3.5	3	3.67
External awareness	4	3.75	4	3.33	4	3	3	3.5	2	3
Knowledge creation and transfer	5	3	3	2.67	3	3.67	3	3	3	3.67
Quality	4	3.75	4	4	4	4.33	3	3.5	4	3.67
Supportive atmosphere	4	4.5	4	4	2	3	3	4	3	2.67
Team-working	3	2.75	3	3.33	3	3.33	2	3	3	4
Total	36	32.25	35	32.33	29	31.67	26	31	26	31.33
		n=4		n=3		n=3		n=2		n=3

Notes:
Each company is ranked on a scale of 1 to 5 where:
5 indicates that the company is ideal or close to ideal for learning;
1 indicates that the company is unsuitable for learning.
n = the number of managers questioned in each company.

Table 4.3 The five case companies ranked by total ratings

Company	Author rating	Company rating
3M	36	32.25
CCSB	35	32.33
Mayflower	29	31.67
Siebe	26	31.33
Morgan Crucible	26	31.00
Mean scores	30.40	31.72

established criteria. My scores follow reasonably closely the scores given by managers themselves, with the same two groups emerging, albeit with a much greater range between the highest- and lowest-scoring companies. Mayflower does worse than the leading two companies, while Morgan Crucible and Siebe are a little further behind again. Overall, however, all the companies do reasonably well, with each company achieving high standards in certain areas.

The five case companies: a dichotomy

What Table 4.3 shows, however, is that the case companies can be placed into two distinct groups. 3M and CCSB scored significantly higher, in terms of both their managers' scores and the author's own scores, than Mayflower, Morgan Crucible and Siebe. Of the two groups, the first, comprising 3M and CCSB, is characterised by the companies' centralised, organised, highly focused nature. Companies in the second group, comprising Mayflower, Morgan Crucible and Siebe, tend to be more entrepreneurial and decentralised, but less focused and co-ordinated. This dichotomy is displayed in Table 4.4, which lists the companies in each group and their identifying characteristics. Clearly, this characterisation is by no means perfect, and does not hold true for all organisations when looking at each point of differentiation. In particular, as we will see, Mayflower has, over the time-scale of this project, moved closer to Group One. Certainly, its financial performance is markedly superior to the other Group Two companies. However, the overall picture is of a strong set of differences, which justifies the creation of the two groups. The implications of the differences between the two groups will be discussed in the remainder of this chapter as we try to discover why the companies in Group One are ahead of those in Group Two when most of the characteristics of organisational learning are considered.

Point of comparison: level of centralisation

The first point of differentiation between the two groups of companies is the level of centralisation. In both 3M and CCSB operations are relatively centralised, with the head office inclined to keep a tight rein on operations. In marked contrast, Mayflower, Morgan Crucible and Siebe all have highly decentralised operations in which a great deal of responsibility for day-to-day operations is passed to divisional and/or subsidiary-company managers. In this section Chandler's (1994) analysis of the functions of the headquarters

Table 4.4 The two groups of case companies

	Group One	Group Two
Companies	3M	Mayflower
	CCSB	Morgan Crucible
		Siebe
Characteristics	Centralised	Decentralised
	Focused	Unfocused
	Co-ordinated	Entrepreneurial
	Dominant in their industries/markets	Usually a major player but often number two or three
	Products use related technologies	Sometimes unrelated technologies
	US-owned	UK-owned
	Record of excellent performance	Relatively ordinary performance

(HQ) in a multibusiness firm is used (see Table 4.5). This allows the different functions of the case companies' HQs, and thus each company's level of centralisation, to be differentiated.

Mayflower has a very small head office, which presides over a group of relatively autonomous subsidiary companies. John Simpson, Mayflower's CEO, sees the head office's role as being mainly monitoring, saying that 'nothing is controlled from here [the head office]; everything is controlled from the [subsidiary] company head office'. He also regards Mayflower's recent acquisitions, such as Walter Alexander and SCSM, as separate companies which will maintain their separate identity.

Morgan Crucible describes itself as 'operating a very decentralised management structure with subsidiary and associated companies, varying in size from 100–400 people, having a considerable degree of autonomy' (*Morgan: The Materials Technologists*, internal company publication). This is supported by the following quote:

> if you look at our Holding Company, we are a Holding Company and a head office which is very much subsidiary-company-oriented. We're an overhead here at the centre; it is the subsidiary companies that are doing the business for us out in the marketplace.
>
> (Andy McIntosh, Director of Group Personnel, Morgan Crucible)

Table 4.5 Planning and control systems for multibusiness firms

	Financial control	Strategic control	Strategic planning
Size of HQ	Small	Large	Large
Mechanisms of control			
• *budgets*	Strong	Moderate	Weak
• *strategic plans and reports*	None	Moderate	Strong
Responsibility for strategic definition	Business units	Divisions	Corporate HQ
Interbusiness-unit dependencies within divisions	Low	Moderate	High
Chandler's examples	ITT	DuPont up to 1980	IBM up to 1980
	Hanson Trust	GE in the 1980s	DuPont in the 1980s
Examples from case companies	Morgan Crucible	Siebe	Mayflower

Source: Adapted from Chandler (1994: 339).

This view is supported by subsidiary-company managers, such as Philip Wright, Managing Director of Morganite Thermal Ceramics: 'the Morgan philosophy is one of centralised financial supervision, but decentralised operating control, which means MDs [managing directors] are not only profit responsible and accountable, but they take all their own decisions within their business.' This view is also subscribed to by Don Neil, Managing Director of ROCOL Limited, a Morgan Crucible subsidiary. The prevailing view, then, is that Morgan Crucible is a highly decentralised company, and this is confirmed by *The Times*, which describes Morgan Crucible as an 'industrial holding company' (Barrow, 1995). In terms of Chandler's characterisation of the role of the HQ unit in the multibusiness firm, Morgan Crucible fits the profile of a financially controlled firm. It has a small HQ, strong budgetary controls and relatively low interbusiness-unit dependencies.

Siebe's structure is broadly similar to Morgan Crucible's. The company has a very small head office and numerous subsidiary companies organised into three divisions. Siebe's Vice-President of Human Resources describes the company as a combination of centralised and decentralised. He says:

> we're tightly controlled in certain areas and highly decentralised, highly autonomous in others, i.e. we have strong financial reviews . . . but on the other hand we're very loose in the sense that those people who are driving a given business get to make the fundamental decisions about the

business and the way it ought to go in comparison to their competitors.
(Richard Bradford, Vice-President, Human Resources, Siebe plc)

Given that the main responsibility of head office is the financial control of subsidiary companies, Siebe seems to fit the model of a relatively decentralised organisation, albeit with the usual controls from the centre.

These differences in organisational structure may be more a result of the different ways the companies have grown in the past than part of a deliberate plan. 3M and CCSB's growth has been largely organic, with any acquisitions quickly and effectively absorbed into the corporate structure. The Group Two companies have also achieved significant organic growth but, relative to Group One, growth by acquisition has been very important in this group. While the companies have often made efforts to absorb their acquisitions, this has often meant that they have taken the form of a new subsidiary company or a new division, rather than becoming a closely co-ordinated part of a systematic organisational structure. There is no clear consensus regarding whether centralisation or decentralisation is likely to lead to higher performance, but these differences in company structure between the two groups may have significant implications for the way the companies practise organisational learning. The two centralised companies may find it easy to make new practices work company-wide, but they will be less likely to benefit from some of the advantages of decentralisation, such as increased speed of decision-making and less bureaucracy. The lack of decentralisation in 3M and CCSB is partially compensated for by their relatively high levels of empowerment, which offer some of the same advantages.

Point of comparison: level of focus

The second differentiator between the two groups is the level of focus. 3M and CCSB are both highly focused on certain activities, and have a clear idea about how and why their businesses succeed or fail. While it would be difficult to describe 3M as focused on core activities – or, in Peters and Waterman's (1982) phrase, as 'sticking to the knitting' – the company's diverse range of businesses are all related and share related technologies. The company's recent decision to demerge its data-storage and imaging-systems businesses into a new company called Imation was part of a strategy to remain focused on core businesses. John Mueller described the situation as follows:

the bottom line is that we found ourselves looking at two strikingly different types of businesses that needed different criteria to judge the ultimate success of the business financially and/or from a competitive standpoint. Within that light, it really looked to be the case that both businesses would prosper better if they were distanced from one another.

(John Mueller, Chairman and Chief Executive, 3M UK)

3M, on this evidence, recognised its inability to manage such diverse businesses and chose to remedy the problem by creating a separate company. CCSB is focused on a very narrow range of products, all owned by its two parent companies and all in the soft-drinks market. At the other extreme, Morgan Crucible has a long line of products, such as slip-resistant flooring, marking paints, speed bumps and lubricants, which seem to be unrelated to its core business of speciality and high-technology materials. Siebe is another company which does not focus solely on its core activities. It has three divisions: Temperature and Appliance Controls, Control Systems and Diversified Products. The first two comprise the core of the group's business, but the third division operates in areas such as compressors, breathing apparatus, cables, and health and safety equipment, which do not have any obvious link with the group's main focus.

Mayflower is probably the most focused of the three Group Two companies, concentrating on automotive engineering. During the period of research work for this book it has made a conscious effort to become more focused on this core business area. However, the company has in the past been involved in a highly diverse range of industries, from paper products to toys. Peters and Waterman make the advantages of a high degree of focus apparent:

> our principal finding is clear and simple. Organizations that do branch out (whether by acquisition or internal diversification) but stick very close to their knitting outperform the others. The most successful of all are those diversified around a single skill – the coating and bonding technology at 3M, for example.
>
> (Peters and Waterman, 1982: 293)

Those companies that are highly focused are also well placed to adapt learning that takes place in one part of their business and apply it throughout the business. This is true of both managerial innovations, which will be more easily applied in similar settings, and technological innovations, which will be more easily utilised in similar businesses. Peters and Waterman's view is supported by more recent work such as Bain's *Successful Management*, in which he documents the way 'parent companies continue the trend towards simplifying their businesses and selling off unwanted parts' (Bain, 1995: 81). Bain goes on to describe the way in which 'acquisitions will continue on a more global basis as companies position themselves more strongly within desired areas' (*ibid.*). This, in fact, is exactly the strategy adopted by Mayflower in its attempt to become more focused: selling off non-core businesses, while at the same time acquiring a global presence in the business of its choice. The company's recent acquisitions include International Automotive Design (car design and engineering), Walter Alexander (bus body design and manufacture) and SCSM Holdings (a US supplier of metal pressings and body subassemblies). Couchman reports that, 'in the past, the success enjoyed by MVS [Mayflower Vehicle Systems] was not strategy driven' (Couchman, 1996: 2). However, the company's strategy has probably now advanced sufficiently to be considered as focused, but Morgan Crucible and Siebe remain committed to their diversified businesses.

Point of comparison: level of co-ordination

It is would be unfair to characterise 3M and CCSB as bureaucratic. 'Co-ordinated' or 'tightly knit value chain' are better descriptions. The intention, however, is to distinguish these two companies from the three companies in Group Two, which are clearly more entrepreneurial. 3M, in particular, has a highly complex matrix-type organisational structure which means that it is difficult for the company to respond quickly to changes in the marketplace. This was one of the main reasons for the company's decision to demerge its data-storage and imaging businesses – the fact that the company was too bureaucratic to meet the needs of fast-changing businesses such as information technology and imaging. CCSB is co-ordinated rather than entrepreneurial in the sense that it does not go out to search for new opportunities but is happy to stay in its current markets. For this reason the company tends to be tightly managed and focused on effective day-to-day administration, rather than on new developments and opportunities.

Mayflower, inspired by John Simpson, the company's founder, has displayed exceptional entrepreneurial ability. Simpson's original company, Olympic Packaging Group, which he founded at the age of 28, started off by buying and selling paper products. The company graduated to manufacturing paper products and acquired Mayflower Securities, a small group of companies in paper-tube manufacturing. Simpson then adopted a highly acquisitive strategy: 'to cut a long story short, [Mayflower] went on developing and buying and selling companies and making me a lot of money'. Eventually, however, Mayflower was left with a group of companies in marketing, financial services, toys and many other areas, all of which were losing money. This was far removed from Simpson's original goal of creating an international group of specialist engineering companies. To achieve this goal Simpson took his company public, sold off the companies he had acquired and set about building a new engineering group based around Motor Panels, his first acquisition in the engineering field. At the time of the Motor Panels acquisition, in 1991, Mayflower's market capitalisation was £6 million; by 1995 it had reached £197 million; and by 1998 it was £615 million, a remarkable rate of growth. This entrepreneurial story demonstrates the difference between Mayflower and the companies in Group One, which, while successful in their own right, achieve their success in an entirely different way.

Morgan Crucible and Siebe have both adopted similar entrepreneurial strategies. They have attempted to grow very rapidly through both organic growth and acquisition. While this strategy may have led to the lack of focus detailed earlier in this chapter, both companies have achieved their desired goals of rapid growth. This has necessitated a high degree of entrepreneurial activity, both in acquiring new companies and in expanding existing companies.

The high levels of co-ordination of the Group One companies may make it more difficult for them to implement some of the ideas of organisational learning. For example, the second characteristic of a learning organisation, a flexible structure, requires reduced bureaucracy and less-restrictive job descriptions. Such a flexible structure may be easier to achieve in the Group Two companies, but the research findings show that 3M and CCSB both have highly flexible structures, certainly more flexible than those of Mayflower, Morgan Crucible or Siebe. Thus it seems that 3M and CCSB have succeeded in spite of their relatively high levels of co-ordinated activity.

Point of comparison: level of market dominance

Market leadership or dominance is considered a key strategic goal by many corporations. The strategic advantages of such market leadership are significant. The problem when assessing market dominance is the difficulty of clearly delineating individual markets. However, there is little doubt that the Group One companies, 3M and CCSB, dominate their main markets. CCSB, in particular, is the clear leader in its main market, soft drinks. The company's flagship product, Coca-Cola, enjoys 36 per cent brand loyalty, which is twice that of its nearest competitor. Diet Coke enjoys an even higher rating in its market segment, with a loyalty share of 38 per cent – the highest of any soft drink. CCSB is the dominant soft drinks company in the UK, with sales far in excess of any of its rivals, PepsiCo included. Overall, CCSB has 41.1 per cent of the total UK soft-drinks market. According to *Beverage Digest*, the US trade publication, Cadbury Schweppes's brands have 8.5 per cent of the UK soft-drinks market, while Coca-Cola's brands have 32.6 per cent, of which Coke itself accounts for 18.6 per cent (quoted in Oram, 1996: 1).

3M operates in such a range of markets that it cannot be leader in them all, but it is clear that the company has a very strong position in many of its markets. For example, 3M (and now Imation) has over 40 per cent of the UK's branded computer-diskette market and over 55 per cent of the world's half-inch computer-tape market (Lance Quantrill, Marketing and Public Affairs Manager, Imation Europe). Other examples of markets where 3M or Imation is dominant include sanding products, reflective materials, medical imaging and industrial tapes. The advantages of a dominant market position for organisational learning lie in the success that such a position implies. Organisational learning ideas should be much easier to implement against a background of established success.

It would be unfair to characterise Mayflower, Morgan Crucible or Siebe as a company that is not a leader in its market. All three companies have sectors in which they are prominent players. However, while their strategies are to be a major force in their markets, they do not dominate large sections of their markets in the same way as 3M and CCSB do. Siebe and Morgan Crucible are both dominant in specialist sectors. Siebe, for example, manufactures more appliance controls than any other company in the world. Morgan Crucible is a world leader in technical and thermal ceramics, and has over 30 per cent of the developed world's crucible market. Indeed, Siebe's stated strategy is to dominate its specialist markets (August, 1996). However, both companies also compete in segments in which they are relatively weak. For example, Tecalmit, Siebe's garage equipment and fluid-systems business, has a major presence in the UK and Europe but is relatively weak in the rest of the world. At Morgan Crucible the company's presence in areas such as non-slip flooring, electro-optics and nuclear safety is not consistent with a strategy of dominating its core markets.

The question of Mayflower's position in its market is difficult to address in a definitive manner. The company can offer a complete service to OEMs from design, through engineering, to manufacturing. The company is not the dominant player in any of these areas (with the possible exception of pressing aluminium), but when the complete service is considered the company is unique in its ability to offer all three of the key elements mentioned above in-house. With this ability to offer in-house solutions becoming increasingly important, the company's market position is improving. Indeed, Couchman argues that MVS has enjoyed success 'due to its dominant position in the UK market. The only real choice open to customers is whether to use MVS or do the operation in-house' (Couchman, 1996: 2).

Overall, however, there is a key difference between 3M and CCSB, which dominate their main markets, and the other three companies, which dominate relatively few of their target market segments. Morgan Crucible and Siebe, in particular, compete in a number of segments in which they are relatively weak.

Point of comparison: use of related technologies

Another point of comparison between the two groups of companies is whether or not their products make use of related technologies. This factor is related to the level of focus on core activities, but differs in that a company can have a range of essentially different activities yet achieve significant synergies through the use and development of related technologies. In the case of both 3M and CCSB it is clear that the companies' various products are indeed based on closely related technologies. Figure 4.1 shows the way in which a large number of different products, in seemingly unrelated areas, have flowed from 3M's expertise in microreplication, a technology that began with the humble overhead projector and now extends to optical fibres, magneto-optics and liquid-crystal displays. Microreplication is the art of covering surfaces with millions of minuscule, and identical, structures. This seemingly humble technology resulted in over \$1 billion worth of 3M's sales in 1995, and this is expected to increase by up to ten times by 2001 (Stewart, 1996). 3M estimates that it has thirty-three distinct technology platforms, each of which can generate multiple products for multiple markets. Each of the company's over 60,000 products is based around some combination of these technology platforms. 3M is continually auditing its technologies, ensuring both that they are the right technologies for the future and that the company fully capitalises on the opportunities that the technologies offer.

As application of the microreplication technology illustrates, significant synergies are available to different businesses within 3M working with the

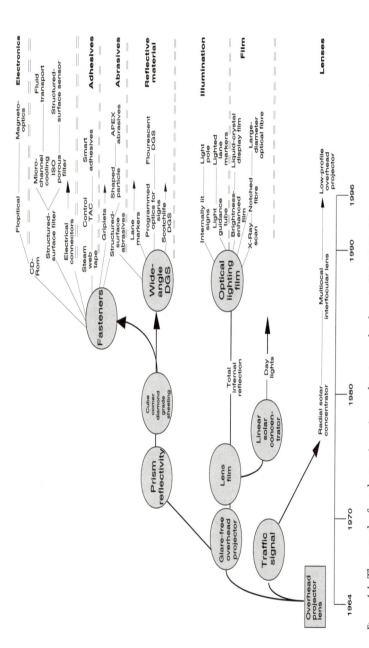

Figure 4.1 The growth of products using microreplication technology in 3M (1964–96)

Source: Adapted from Stewart (1996).

same technology. *The Economist* notes that 3M's intention, at the time of its demerger, was to 'specialise in about two dozen core technologies' (*Economist*, 1995: 109). The dissemination of new technologies around the company is actively encouraged and is a specific responsibility of the company's scientists. John Howells, 3M UK's Technical Director, offers the example of a new adhesive system developed by one of the company's senior scientists in the US. This new technology allows the company to stick things, such as Teflon and Polythene, that would be difficult to stick with standard adhesives, and so represents a significant potential breakthrough. Howells explains that:

> the technologies are owned by the corporation, but we encourage and expect our R&D people in all our businesses to capitalise and make use of them. So we would not see, for instance, one technology used by one business. We want as many businesses in all sorts of different markets and industries to use these as fast and as capably as possible. So ten or eleven businesses are already looking at this technology before it has even been launched.
>
> (John Howells, Technical Director, 3M UK)

This specific focus on technologies and their dissemination across the company demonstrates the way in which 3M's products are based on a number of related technologies, giving the company valuable synergies in product development and allowing it to derive the maximum benefit from each new technology that it develops.

CCSB does not use technology platforms in the same way as 3M but it is clear that its products are closely related by virtue of the company's focus on a single market – soft drinks. Of course, the soft-drinks market can be sub-divided into smaller niche markets, but the basic technology and expertise required to service those different markets remains the same. CCSB is responsible for adding water and other ingredients to product concentrate from the Coca-Cola Company, Cadbury Schweppes and other franchisers such as Appletise plc and Perrier UK. It bottles, sells and distributes the finished products. CCSB also undertakes below-the-line marketing activities. These activities may differ slightly from product to product, but they are certainly similar and do not require different technology or expertise.

Many of Morgan Crucible's and Siebe's products are based on related technologies. In Morgan Crucible's case many products are based on the company's expertise in working with speciality materials. Indeed, the company describes itself as 'engaged in the development, manufacture and marketing of technologically advanced materials, chemicals and components' (*Morgan: The Materials Technologists*, internal publication). While at first sight it seems that this means that Morgan Crucible's products do rely on related technologies, the way that the company's research and development activities are structured shows that the technologies are not closely related. In contrast to the efforts 3M makes to ensure that each division capitalises on the company's technologies, Morgan Crucible's research and development facilities are decentralised and each works for a different division. While there is some sharing of technology between the Technical Ceramics and Thermal Ceramics Divisions, there is little evidence of technologies being shared across the company. The company's global product groups encourage technological developments to be shared between countries but do little to encourage learning between different product areas.

Siebe's situation is somewhat similar to Morgan Crucible's in that the company has many products which rely on related technologies, but it also has some products which rely on technologies seemingly unrelated to its main products. Siebe's obvious strength is in control equipment, and many of the products in Temperature and Appliance Controls and Control Systems Divisions share similar basic technologies. However, some products, particularly some of those in the Diversified Products Division, seem to be more the result of an attractive acquisition opportunity than the opportunity to harness an existing technology to a new use. Siebe is described by August as 'the systems controls maker' (August, 1996), and again we must question the logic of the company's presence in a range of other businesses which do not make use of related technologies.

The argument here is that, following on from the section on the level of focus, companies whose products utilise related technologies will be better able to share learning throughout the company. Moreover, because different parts of the company use related technologies, any individual advance is likely to prove significantly more fruitful for the company as a whole. Following this logic, 3M in particular has a significant advantage over Mayflower, Morgan Crucible and Siebe in that any technological breakthroughs that it makes are likely to be beneficial to more than one part of the company. Additionally, the company can make breakthroughs by combining different but related technologies, something that the company has done with great success in the past.

Point of comparison: ownership

The penultimate differentiating factor between the two groups is ownership. While Mayflower, Morgan Crucible and Siebe all have significant overseas operations, they are all owned and based in the UK. 3M, by contrast, is an American company based in St Paul, Minnesota. At the time this research was carried out CCSB lay somewhere between 3M and the Group Two companies, being 51 per cent owned by Cadbury Schweppes of the UK and 49 per cent owned by the Coca-Cola Company of the USA. Cadbury Schweppes's decision to sell its share to Coca-Cola Enterprises means that the company is now wholly US-owned (see Oram, 1996, for full details of Cadbury Schweppes's decision). With organisational learning and many associated ideas having originated in the United States, it is possible to speculate that 3M's senior managers may have been exposed to such ideas before their counterparts in the UK companies.

As we will see in the section on the relevance of organisational learning in Chapter 6, research shows that US companies have a lead over their UK and European counterparts when considering the implementation of organisational learning ideas. US companies are often said to be characterised by more progressive management practices than UK companies. They are also considered to be more susceptible to the latest management ideas and fads, which they invariably adopt two or three years before their UK rivals. This is not necessarily the case here, however. The UK companies seem to be just as committed as 3M and CCSB to the idea of organisational learning, but they perhaps lag behind in implementing many of the necessary practises and techniques. This is likely to have more to do with their relative starting points than with their keenness to adopt such ideas.

Point of comparison: performance

Precise comparison of performance between the five case companies is difficult, but for each company general conclusions about performance can be drawn, with varying degrees of confidence. 3M is, by almost any measure, a high-performing company. Between 1985 and 1996 it scored in the top ten on *Fortune*'s list of Most Admired Companies ten times (Stewart, 1996). Exact comparisons with earlier years are difficult to make because of the demerger of the Imation businesses. However, in 1995 (the most recent year for which data are available) the company's return on capital employed was 23.4 per cent, more than double the average for the S&P 400. Interestingly, since the demerger 3M's market capitalisation has increased, from $22.406 billion on 31 December 1994 to $36.320 billion (for Imation and 3M combined) on 18 April 1997. 3M, we can conclude, is worthy of a place in the group of high-performing companies.

CCSB's performance is very difficult to evaluate because the company does not publish independent accounts. However, it has achieved a dominant position in the soft-drinks market, outselling its nearest competitor by three and a half cases to one. In 1995 the company achieved record volume, record market share and record profits. As mentioned above, since mid-1996 CCSB has been owned by Coca-Cola Enterprises, itself a subsidiary of the Coca-Cola Company, which was named by *Fortune* as America's Most Admired Company for 1996. So, while CCSB's performance is difficult to evaluate in terms of hard financial data, the justification for its place in our group of high-performing companies is apparent.

The performance of Mayflower, Morgan Crucible and Siebe is much easier to determine. We can utilise the stock market's ability to place a definitive figure on a company's worth. Table 4.6 shows the performance of each company relative to the *Financial Times* All Share Index.

Mayflower is clearly the highest performer of the three, having outperformed the market as a whole by 43.2 per cent from May 1992 to May 1997. In May 1997 Siebe's performance was 6.5 per cent above the market average, while Morgan Crucible was 7.5 per cent below. A fairly similar story is apparent for performance over the year to 11 May 1997, although Siebe has done well by this measure. Interestingly, when compared to just the engineering sector, Siebe and Morgan Crucible performed worse still, respectively 4.9 per cent and 17.4 per cent below average between May 1992 and May 1997. Mayflower, by contrast, outperformed the automotive engineering sector by 42.9 per cent over the same period.

Table 4.6 Performance relative to *Financial Times* All Share Index

	May 1996–May 1997 (%)	May 1992–May 1997 (%)
Mayflower	46.9	43.2
Morgan Crucible	1.4	−7.5
Siebe	22.0	6.5

Note: Share price information taken from the *Financial Times* and correct at 11 May 1997.

Overall, Table 4.6 provides powerful data to support the conclusion that Mayflower scores well on performance, while Morgan Crucible and Siebe are both, *relatively*, poor performers. It is important to note, however, that the absolute performance of Morgan Crucible and Siebe is by no means poor. Both companies have managed to achieve good levels of profitability while growing rapidly.

It is clear, then, that two distinct groups exist in terms of performance. 3M, CCSB and Mayflower are recognised as performing well above average, while Morgan Crucible and Siebe look ordinary by comparison. Thus the dichotomy shown in Table 4.4 breaks down for this point of comparison because of the excellent performance of Mayflower. This issue is considered further in the next subsection.

Overall implications of this dichotomy

The long-term implications of this dichotomy are difficult to determine. The first question we must ask is whether the differences between the companies will narrow, or whether they will persist or even widen. 3M's decision to demerge its data-storage and imaging-systems businesses to form the new company Imation is likely to lead to even greater levels of centralisation, focus, market dominance and use of related technologies in the new 3M company. Cadbury Schweppes's decision to sell its 51 per cent stake in CCSB may have similar, although probably less obvious and immediate, effects on CCSB. It is likely that these two companies will maintain their excellence, in terms of both organisational learning and overall business performance, for the foreseeable future. Mayflower has been making significant strides towards its stated goal of becoming a major global automotive engineering group. It has become increasingly focused, with all the major companies in the group making use of similar, closely related technologies. Additionally, Mayflower has already achieved highly impressive financial results. By contrast, despite their stated desire to be major players in their global markets, both Morgan Crucible and Siebe remain committed to their diverse businesses, a policy that has brought them some success to date but which also has inherent disadvantages. Their financial performance lags significantly behind that of Mayflower.

It is likely that all five companies will continue to adopt organisational learning ideas. This is certainly the stated intention of managers in the five companies. For 3M and CCSB, this is likely to take the form of consolidating existing policy and practises, together with incremental improvements where possible. Mayflower needs to maintain its existing policies and goals, but it has further to travel than 3M or CCSB to create a successful and sustainable learning organisation. There is a need for further integration of the company's operations to achieve synergies at both operational and strategic levels. Such integration would also result in enhanced opportunities for learning throughout the group.

Based on the above analysis, there is a need for Morgan Crucible to become more focused, concentrating on its strengths in speciality materials, rather than being merely an industrial holding company. This will also allow it to take a more company-wide approach to organisational learning. At present there is a deliberate policy of relatively little direction from the centre, but this means that diverse management practices develop, to the detriment of learning throughout the group. Again, we must note that Siebe's position is very similar to that of Morgan Crucible. The company must become more focused on its core strengths in appliance and temperature controls and control systems, an area which is very wide-ranging in itself and which has enormous potential. The Diversified Products Division is likely to take up a disproportionate amount of management time, considering that it offers little, if any, group-wide synergies. The company needs to reassess carefully the advantages and disadvantages of its commitment to each of the businesses in this division. A greater focus will allow the company to have a specific, company-wide learning policy and to introduce practices which encourage learning in each of its remaining businesses. Should Morgan Crucible and Siebe choose to undertake the restructuring implicit in these recommendations they will be able to close the gap with 3M and CCSB relatively quickly. It is interesting to speculate whether such changes in policy would help Morgan Crucible and Siebe to reduce the performance advantage enjoyed by 3M, CCSB and Mayflower.

What is clear from the above is that the case companies which are closest to the ideal of the learning organisation are also those which have the highest performance. 3M and CCSB are the nearest to being learning organisations and have achieved consistently high performance over a number of years. Of the three Group Two companies, Mayflower has made the most progress towards becoming a learning organisation and has also achieved by far the best results. Morgan Crucible and Siebe are furthest from the ideal of the learning organisation and have the lowest performance. As we will see in Chapter 6, there are a number of significant problems with attributing high performance to organisation learning. Thus we must be careful not to imply that organisational learning causes high performance. However, the inference from the above is clear: those companies which are closest to being learning organisations also have the highest performance.

The five case companies and best practice in comparative perspective: a restatement

In this section we have seen that all five case companies score well in comparison with the model of best practice that we established earlier in this chapter. This is true both in terms of the ratings that managers gave their own company and in terms of the ratings that each company has been awarded by the author. Managers were generally unwilling to give particularly high or low ratings to their companies, and this problem was accentuated by taking the average of a number of managers' scores. 3M and CCSB received higher scores from their managers than did Mayflower, Morgan Crucible and Siebe. This picture was also apparent in the author's scores for the five companies, with 3M and CCSB again receiving the highest overall scores. From the scores it became clear that two distinct groups of companies could be discerned: Group One, consisting of 3M and CCSB, and Group Two, consisting of Mayflower, Morgan Crucible and Siebe. We noted, however, the efforts made by Mayflower to replicate many of the characteristics displayed by the Group One companies, particularly in terms of focus and the use of related technologies. A number of distinguishing factors were then outlined and discussed. The Group One companies were centralised, focused, bureaucratic, dominant in their markets, produced products using related technologies and were US-owned. The Group Two companies, by contrast, were relatively decentralised, unfocused, entrepreneurial, sometimes not dominant in their markets, sometimes produced products using unrelated technologies and were UK-owned. The general implications of these differences for organisational learning in the five case companies are that 3M and CCSB have been able to come closer to the ideal model of best practice discussed in earlier in this chapter. Factors such as greater focus, market dominance, use of related technologies and earlier exposure to organisational learning ideas as a result of their US origins have enabled them to progress further towards becoming learning organisations than Morgan Crucible, Siebe and, to a lesser extent, Mayflower. By considering the performance of each case company, we were able to show that those companies which came closest to the ideal of the learning organisation were also the highest performers.

Conclusion

In the first part of this chapter we developed a model of best practice in organisational learning. This is based on the research related in the previous chapter and on a wider analysis of the secondary literature. Nine key characteristics of a successful learning organisation are given, each with an explanation of why it is important and what sort of behaviour is appropriate. We acknowledge the complex interrelationship between the nine characteristics and organisational effectiveness. Each characteristic is necessarily broadly defined and considerable scope is left for managers to adapt the characteristics to individual organisational situations. They form an aspirational model which managers can use as a window on what can be achieved given ideal conditions.

The second part of this chapter compares and contrasts the five case companies, in general and in terms of organisational learning. We show the dichotomy that exists among the five case companies. The five case companies can be divided into two groups, one comprising 3M and CCSB, and one comprising Mayflower, Morgan Crucible and Siebe. These two groups display significantly different characteristics in terms of strategy, structure and culture. This section outlines a number of points of comparison between the two groups which show the strength of the dichotomy. It also considers the impact of each of the differences on organisational learning in the case companies. We conclude that 3M and CCSB are both significantly more advanced in their approaches to organisational learning than Morgan Crucible or Siebe. Mayflower remains in the second group but has made significantly more progress than Morgan Crucible or Siebe. 3M, CCSB and Mayflower have achieved significantly higher performance than Morgan Crucible or Siebe. Interestingly, the high-performing companies are those that have progressed furthest in becoming learning organisations.

In the Chapters 5 and 6 we will examine in more depth the accuracy of this view of the five companies. This, admittedly somewhat schematic, analysis of each organisation represents a picture of current practice in organisational learning. By addressing various key themes in organisational behaviour, structure and strategy, we will look in much more detail at the ideal learning organisation, before turning our attention to the actions necessary to create such an organisation. We will also look in detail at how each company's success or failure in becoming a learning organisation is likely to affect its organisational effectiveness.

5 Organisational learning and leadership

Introduction

In this chapter we will explore the key management topic of leadership. Many companies are now making clear, at a senior level, their desire to become a learning organisation or, indeed, already claim to be a learning organisation. In these circumstances the need for an exploration of the processes behind this phenomenon is evident. The central issue which we will address here is the relationship between organisational learning and leadership. Most importantly, we will look at the latest leadership theories and assess their relevance for business and management in general, and organisational learning in particular.

We also ask whether the fact that organisational learning has become a strategic goal will assist in creating learning organisations. To this end, we examine the role of senior management in the creation of a learning organisation. We assess the role and importance of top-management commitment in creating a climate in which organisational learning can flourish. As with previous chapters, we will draw extensively on two main sources: the existing literature and research carried out within the five case companies. From the literature we use two key sources: first, work on leadership in general, such as that by Bennis and Nanus (1985), Conger (1988), Adair (1988) and Kotter (1990); and, second, work on leadership in learning organisations, such as that by Senge (1990b), Marquardt (1996) and Schein (1993).

In order to establish a meaningful empirical context, however, we present detailed case studies of leadership, strategy formulation and commitment to organisational learning in four of the case companies (unfortunately it was not possible to gain sufficient access to senior managers at Siebe to compile a comprehensive case study of the company's approach to leadership). The main research for these four case studies comprised interviews with the Chief Executives of the main companies: John Mueller, Chairman and Chief Executive, 3M UK plc; Derek Williams, Managing Director, CCSB; John Simpson, Deputy Chairman and Chief Executive, the Mayflower Corporation plc; and Bruce Farmer, Group Managing Director, the Morgan Crucible Company plc. Richard Northrop, Vice-President Europe, Imation plc, was also interviewed as the most senior manager in 3M's demerged imaging and data-storage businesses. Further interviews were carried out with the Managing Directors of three subsidiary companies and a number of other senior executives. In addition to these interviews, information is taken from interviews with various senior managers from a number of other companies. The case studies are used not merely to reflect concerns with the existing literature, but also to create a new perspective on the role of leaders in supporting and facilitating organisational learning. Before presenting the case studies, we look briefly at the twin issues of what constitutes leadership and why it is important.

What is leadership?

Leadership has been defined as 'a social process that involves determining the group's objectives, motivating behaviour in pursuit of these objectives, and influencing group maintenance and culture' (Lewis *et al.*, 1994: 425). Similarly, Burns defines leadership as 'inducing followers to act for certain goals that represent the values and motivations – the wants and needs, the aspirations and expectations – of both leaders and followers' (Burns, 1978). Put more simply, leadership is the ability to influence, motivate and direct others in order to attain desired objectives. Leadership is often defined and explored by differentiating it from management. Syrett and Hogg (1992) suggest that vision is the thing that most sets leaders apart from managers. They suggest that 'managers do things right, leaders do the right thing. Managers accept the *status quo*, leaders challenge it. Leaders create and artic-ulate vision, managers ensure it is put into practice' (*ibid.*: 5). Covey describes the difference between leadership and management slightly differ-ently: 'management is a bottom line focus: How can I best accomplish certain things? Leadership deals with the top line: What are the things I want to accomplish?' (Covey, 1992: 101). Similarly, he describes management as 'effi-ciency in climbing the ladder of success' (*ibid.*), whereas leadership is seen as 'determining whether the ladder is leaning against the right wall' (*ibid.*).

Bolling argues that what distinguishes a leader from an ordinary manager is 'the capacity to tackle immense problems: in other words, complex challenges without single clear-cut solutions' (Bolling, 1996: 65). From these definitions we can see that leaders are concerned with creating the organisation's strategy, while managers are entrusted with the job of putting the strategy into practice. Paradoxically for those seeking to differentiate between the two, leadership and management are increasingly seen as inextricably linked. There is little point in a leader formulating a grand strategy or far-reaching vision unless it is turned into real achievement – a process that inevitably requires managers.

The importance of leadership

Leadership is important in a number of ways and for a number of reasons. Adair describes leadership as 'an essential ingredient in effective and successful management' (Adair, 1984: ix). Lewis *et al.* suggest that 'being an effective leader has never been more important or more challenging' (Lewis *et al.*, 1994: 424). Peters is another authority who stresses the importance of leadership. In *A Passion for Excellence* (Peters and Austin, 1985) the 'three secrets of long-term excellence' are linked together by one other element: leadership. The third edition of *Bass and Stogdill's Handbook of Leadership* (1990) features a grand total of 7,500 bibliographic references, illustrating the enduring fascination of leadership for academic authors.

On an empirical level, Kotter and Heskett's (1992) in-depth quantitative study of the links between organisational culture and performance led them to conclude that the most important factor is a culture that is adaptive, i.e. one that seeks to anticipate and adapt to environmental change. Leadership is a particular consideration for Kotter and Heskett because they regard it as vital in the culture changes that are needed for organisations to become more adaptive. Whipp *et al.* (1989) reached a similar conclusion in their qualitative study of strategic change at Jaguar and Hill Samuel, in which they viewed a transformation of the organisation's culture (a task they assigned to the leaders in the organisation) as a prerequisite for radical strategic change.

Different authors attribute the importance of leadership, and its still increasing importance, to different factors, of which culture change is just one. Leonard-Barton (1995) sees leadership as important for technological reasons. She describes leadership as 'essential in order to build, nurture, and sustain core technological capabilities' (*ibid.*: 265). Syrett and Hogg (1992) attribute much of the importance of leadership to the increasing pace of change. They write: 'leadership has emerged as one of the most important business requirements at a time of permanent discontinuity' (*ibid.*: 5). Taking a slightly different approach, leadership is important for Bennis *et al.* (1994) because it arises from 'personal mastery' and because it results in 'group synergy'. Clearly there are a number of factors behind the importance of leadership, but it is safe to say that leadership is, for good reason, a topic of interest and importance to many managers and academics.

Leadership is important to those interested in organisational learning because learning organisations are likely to be created in a top-down manner. Thus the impetus for the creation of a learning organisation is likely to come from senior management. Even if the impetus comes from elsewhere, leaders within the organisation will have to be committed to organisational learning for it to have a chance of becoming reality. Senge has emphasised the importance of leaders in organisational learning, describing the building of learning organisations as 'the leader's new work' (Senge, 1990b: 7). Garratt (1990) takes a similar view, arguing that directors need to create a climate where people can learn through work and move their learning to where it is needed in the organisation. He regards a clear strategic role for the top team as vital to the creation of a learning organisation.

Leadership case studies

This section provides detailed case studies of how four of the case companies practise leadership. It also examines the way in which leadership in each company interacts with strategy formulation and with organisational learning. Unfortunately it was impossible to build a case study of leadership, strategy and organisational learning in Siebe because of the unavailability of the Chief Executive and other senior managers. However, comprehensive sets of interviews were undertaken at all levels of the other four companies.

Leadership, strategy and organisational learning in 3M

Leadership is probably given a less prominent role in 3M than in most other companies. Nonaka and Takeuchi argue that, 'at 3M, top management is not the focus of attention. The names of successive CEOs are relatively unknown, and what they say or do appears to be of little relevance to 3M employees' (Nonaka and Takeuchi, 1995: 135). Collins and Porras (1996) suggest that 3M has never possessed a visionary leader. Indeed, they use the company as the foundation for their belief that the importance of visionary, charismatic leaders has been greatly overstated. They argue that '3M represented something beyond visionary leadership . . . 3M could best be described as a visionary *company*' (*ibid.*: 12). 3M has had ten different CEOs since its inception, none of whom could be described as an archetypal, visionary leader. However, this is contradicted by John Mueller, 3M's Chairman and Chief Executive, who believes that 'the present Chairman has done a nice job in that he's come to two statements [which encapsulate 3M's vision] that I can certainly subscribe to, and I think over time will become inculcated within all our people'.

Middle and junior managers' view of leadership within 3M has been uniformly favourable, but, echoing Collins and Porras, they have tended to focus on the leadership from the company, rather than on the leadership given by an individual or a group of individuals. For example, Jeff Skinner, 3M UK's Management Development Manager, described 3M as 'a wonderful company to work for', while Mike Adams, a Research and Development Manager, described 3M as 'an excellent organisation to be a part of'.

3M's approach to organisational learning differs from that of most of the other case companies because it has a group which is specifically charged with ensuring that organisational learning takes place within the company. This group, Organisational Learning Services, is responsible for leading, on a practical level, all organisational learning initiatives in the company. Marquardt and Reynolds describe the work of 3M's Organisational Learning Services Group as 'providing learning guidance for its activities in 57 countries' (Marquardt and Reynolds, 1994: 279). One of the key early roles of the Organisational Learning Services Group was to create a core group of facilitators who could run workshops on learning for the rest of the workforce.

3M's strategy has been deliberately designed to be very broad. The leaders within the company have recognised that they cannot effectively control the exact direction of the company, only help it in the desired direction. The company has implicitly acknowledged the importance of what Mintzberg (1994) calls emergent strategies, and thus the intended strategy is somewhat less important as the organisation realises that it is unlikely to be realised in its originally conceived form. This contrasts markedly with many organisations, which create a definite strategy that they believe represents what *will* happen. When, because of unpredicted and unpredictable external changes, this strategy is unrealised the organisation is unprepared and does not know how to respond. Thus 3M's approach allows a high degree of flexibility in determining the final strategy and final outcome.

Stewart suggests that '3M has no strategy' and that this is 'a startling vice'

(Stewart, 1996). This, however, is an overly simplistic interpretation of 3M's leadership and strategic decision-making styles. 3M's strategic direction in terms of core businesses is certainly unclear, but this should more realistically be seen as the natural corollary of the diversity and innovativeness of the company. Stewart goes on to state that 'a well articulated strategy could have provided a vector for the innovative energy that steams out of every corner of 3M' (*ibid.*), but most commentators would argue that 3M's 'innovative energy' is exceptionally well provided for and harnessed for the benefit of the company. Stewart also suggests that a well-articulated strategy would have 'helped 3M work its way to a quicker and less drastic resolution of the long-simmering problems in its imaging and electronic storage businesses' (*ibid.*). However, the company seems to have solved whatever 'problems' there were with this business very effectively, with the demerger of the imaging and electronic-storage businesses leading to the creation of a smaller, more flexible company more suited to the demands of its markets. At the same time, the demerger has retained 3M shareholders' stake in the company, and the announcement of the demerger led to a large increase in the share price. Overall, 3M's strategy is less deliberate and less predetermined than that of many other organisations, but it is clearly incorrect to say that the company has 'no strategy' when, as we saw in Chapter 3, 3M has a clear vision, and a specific set of goals both in terms of innovation and financial performance. Certainly, in contrast to some of the other case companies, 3M's strategy is determined centrally, at head office, rather than in a multitude of subsidiary-company offices.

Thus in 3M we have a situation in which both leadership and strategy, perhaps for the same or similar reasons, do not have prominent roles. This might be expected to lead to difficulties with regard to organisational learning. However, in practice it is likely that the very lack of importance placed on leadership and strategy means that organisational learning has the chance to flourish without being impeded by 'newer, bigger, better' initiatives. In addition, the lack of immediate short-term strategies allows 3M to take a longer-term view and 'wait' for the benefits of organisational learning to accrue. The other reason for 3M's success in becoming a learning organisation, as was discussed above, is its creation of a single body, the Organisational Learning Services Group, to oversee all activities in this area.

Leadership, strategy and organisational learning in CCSB

Derek Williams, CCSB's Managing Director, describes the company's style as 'managing by accountability'. He also says that:

> the way we put it over [to the managers] is 'enabling'. We'll have a frame-
> work, we'll have a game plan, but we will not necessarily tell everybody
> right leg comes after left leg and run this way . . . We would give leader-
> ship. We do a lot of leadership.

(Derek Williams, Managing Director, CCSB)

The company has a number of core desires, but says that this list of desires
keeps growing. As managers are each given fixed budgets, they must give up a
current item of expenditure or find a new source of money if they want to do
something new. Paradoxically, while managers are given high levels of
accountability, both Derek Williams and Keith Dennis, the Personnel
Director, emphasise the lack of clarity in their leadership style. CCSB's
approach to leadership seems to conform to that recommended by Heifetz
and Laurie (1997). Heifetz and Laurie argue that leaders do not need to know
all the answers, but that they do need to ask the questions. They conclude by
stating that leadership requires a learning strategy. CCSB's leaders clearly
accept, in practice as well as in theory, that they do not have all the answers,
and this means that they allow their subordinates the opportunity to learn
and to supply the answers. Keith Dennis says: 'We do a lot of leadership. Not
a lot of clarity. We're not strong on clarity.' Derek Williams explains:

> I am very conscious that the clearer that I am being, the more imprecise I
> am being. If we say 'Do that, that's absolutely perfect', it might be right in
> Sainsbury's, but it would be totally wrong for Tesco, and it would not be
> clear, it would be confusion. It would be hopelessly wrong for KwikSave,
> and it would have no relevance whatsoever to a pub, and the guy that
> runs the vending division would think you were absolutely bloody
> bonkers.

(Derek Williams, Managing Director, CCSB)

He professes to be amazed by people who claim to have a strategy or a plan,
concluding that 'you've got to have a game plan, you've got to have deploy-
ment, you've got to have intentions, but you'd better avoid clarity'. In this
belief, Williams follows the view of Mintzberg, who suggests that 'too much
analysis gets in our way. The failure of strategic planning is the failure of
formalization' (Mintzberg, 1994: 321).

Most importantly, this view of leadership in CCSB is supported by a number of interviewees at lower levels of the organisation. This suggests that Williams's desire to create accountability and opportunity in the company is not mere rhetoric but has actually been put into practice. Hilary Moos, a CCSB Human Resource Manager, is one of those to support Williams's approach: 'He's tended to be fairly visionary in terms of where he likes to see CCSB going and how ideas are taken forward.' Beverley Stratton, another Human Resource Manager, expressed similar sentiments: 'I think without Derek [Williams] and Keith's [Dennis] support we would not have come as far as we have done – I think it is vitally important that you get that commitment from the top.' Hilary Moos went on to give an example of the Managing Director's supportive style of leadership: 'In terms of onward supporting of the scheme [Frontline], he is very supportive of it, wants to get to know the people involved in it, so there's a fairly strong sense of leadership from him.' Mike Hill, a Team Leader at CCSB's Northampton Distribution Centre and a more junior member of the organisation, also gave a positive view of the company's leadership and management style, comparing it favourably with other companies in which he had worked. Particularly good points were the level of autonomy given to individuals and the support that was given by senior managers. Interestingly, in contrast to 3M, the interviewees spoke of the leadership skill of the Managing Director, rather than of the excellence of the company as a whole.

CCSB's strategy is highly focused and the company is clearly targeted on achieving excellent results in its existing operations. It has clear aims and objectives, but these are quite limited in scope. For example, the company aims for record share, but record share in its existing markets. This is clearly a different, more limited, strategy than one in which the highest possible overall growth is targeted. The company's Lifetime Learning Links (LLLs) might not be directly comparable to the Organisational Learning Services Group in 3M, but they do provide a focus for many of the learning activities in the company. The company's leaders have clearly recognised some of the dangers of offering too much directive leadership, and so have developed a largely non-interventionist style which gives high levels of autonomy to middle and junior managers.

Leadership, strategy and organisational learning in Mayflower

Mayflower is unique among the case companies in that it is still run by the man who founded it. This means that the leadership style at Mayflower has been, and to an extent still is, a reflection of John Simpson's personal style. This, as would be expected, brings both benefits and problems. Andrew Powling, Business Planning Manager at Mayflower, describes the company's leadership style as 'enabling'. He also describes the way in which the management style has changed over the last few years and must continue to change:

> four years ago [in 1992] the business was about £30 million turnover [against £202 million in 1995]. So over a four-year period it has grown tremendously, and what we must make sure is that the management styles that are adopted must mature over that period of time as well. So, given that it is largely the same set of guys at the top, they were perhaps used to making decisions at a level which is now inappropriate.
>
> (Andrew Powling, Business Planning Manager, Mayflower)

Powling argues that the increased number of projects in the company means that the company needs to develop a style that enables the people it employs to run those projects to make decisions for themselves or put proposals forward. He believes that greater delegation is required than in the past, and that junior managers should put forward proposals rather than problems. Overall, however, he describes Mayflower's approach as 'enlightened'.

The stretch concept described earlier (see Chapter 3) is an important part of Mayflower's leadership strategy. Encouraging senior managers to set difficult targets for themselves creates a culture of taking responsibility for one's own performance at the top of the company. Mike Fell, Mayflower Automotive Division's Human Resource Director, has detailed the company's attempts to instil this type of culture throughout the company. He says: 'we empower fact-holders to make them decision-makers. In communicating with people and involving them, we need to understand that, at some stage, if we are truly going to involve them, we are going to have to delegate power.' However, he admits that the company still has a long way to go in achieving this.

Mayflower's structure differs significantly from those of 3M and CCSB in having a much higher degree of decentralisation. This naturally leads to differences between the companies' leadership styles. Powling believes that 'the majority of the companies [in the Mayflower Group] are managed in a relatively autonomous manner from Mayflower as far as reporting is concerned'. John Simpson echoes this even more strongly, saying: 'nothing is controlled from here [the group's head office]; everything is controlled from the company head office'. The company has a small team of executives who have overall control of the business, including John Simpson, David Donnelly,

Mayflower's Finance Director, John Fleming, who looks after acquisitions, and Terry Whitmore, who is responsible for the automotive group. John Fleming is responsible for the acquisition of new companies and runs these companies for a short period, typically six months, after their acquisition. Terry Whitmore is charged with exploiting opportunities for synergy between Mayflower's different subsidiaries, and as such he is the person designated to ensure that learning is shared across the group. This is achieved through benchmarking within the group, through the business planning process and through exchanges of personnel.

In summary, Mayflower's leadership style is in a state of transition as the company continues to grow very rapidly. The group has recognised that it needs to change from a directional style of leadership to a style that is empowering and enabling. This change is now under way, but it will take time, particularly in view of the high level of decentralisation, which makes it difficult to instigate a significant cultural change rapidly from the centre.

Leadership, strategy and organisational learning in Morgan Crucible

The leadership style at Morgan Crucible differs significantly from that in evidence at CCSB and 3M (and, to a lesser extent, from that at Mayflower). The reason for this is that the company has a very decentralised structure, with senior management at head office taking little or no role in day-to-day decision-making at subsidiary companies. This means that the leadership style naturally involves a very high degree of delegation by senior management, together with operational autonomy for middle and junior managers. As we saw in the previous chapter, following Chandler's (1994) method of analysis, Morgan Crucible is a company in which financial control is paramount. The Group Managing Director, Bruce Farmer, points out that 'we push account-ability way down the line and we only have sixty people in head office'. This should be set against the fact of a turnover of over £400 million in 1996. The company policy is to set simple goals across the whole group and then allow significant autonomy to divisional and company managers to set the strategy that will be used to achieve these goals. The goals the company sets include 15 per cent return on capital employed; 10 per cent PBT (profit before tax) growth per year; 25 per cent return on shareholders' funds employed; and a debt-to-equity ratio of between 35 and 70 per cent (depending on interest cover). Farmer summarises by saying that 'each company will be striving to achieve the operating profit, the growth, the return and the cash generation'.

While setting stringent targets, he is careful not to specify exactly how these targets should be achieved.

This style is, unsurprisingly, repeated in Morgan Crucible's subsidiaries. Philip Wright, Managing Director of Morganite Thermal Ceramics Limited, states: 'I am a firm believer in an organisation having a focus of very specific objectives that are well communicated upwards, downwards and across the organisation.' Thus he claims that 'the first thing I did here . . . was to publish some very specific objectives, and by publish I mean communicate'. He goes on to reiterate this point, but also to emphasise the importance of allowing employees to find their own way of achieving the targets:

> So the first priority in terms of my leadership style is to agree and then communicate clear objectives – not only financial objectives, but marketing objectives, manufacturing objectives, technical objectives, and to agree with the people that work directly for me how they will achieve those objectives and what their plans are, and then essentially you can let them get on with it.
>
> (Philip Wright, Managing Director, Morganite Thermal Ceramics Limited)

This view is supported by evidence from ROCOL Limited, another Morgan Crucible subsidiary. Don Neil, the Managing Director of ROCOL, also emphasises the importance of setting targets, although he has added further objectives to the financial goals set by Bruce Farmer. The extra objectives include producing at least 25 per cent of sales from products that did not exist four years ago and earning at least 40 per cent of revenue from exports. He has also initiated his own set of activities to encourage learning as little direction had been given from head office. The company does have a central management development programme, but other activities are largely the province of managers in subsidiary companies. Thus, for example, Morganite has initiated a successful profit-sharing scheme within the company, but without reference to the wider Morgan Crucible company.

Again, we must ask whether this leadership style, as espoused by senior managers, is reflected in the views of more junior employees. At the middle-management level interviewees were impressed by the level of flexibility and opportunity they were given. Steve Chapman, General Manager of the Technical Department at ROCOL, reported that managers in each department within the company could decide for themselves how their department should contribute to the goals of the company, subject of course to the need to co-ordinate with other departments.

One point that was made by Andy McIntosh, the Director of Group Personnel, was that the company was:

> being more free with information to all levels of employees, opening up the whole organisation to all the employees within it, encouraging ownership of the business, encouraging a much broader base of share ownership in the company, all the way through the various levels in the organisation.
>
> (Andy McIntosh, Director of Group Personel, Morgan Crucible)

Again, this view was supported by a range of employees at lower levels of the organisation. Catherine Ripley, Product Development Manager for Safety Products at ROCOL, said: 'we have a very close knit environment'. She then went on to detail how the different departments – sales, marketing, technical, commercial – work closely together in the new product development process. Thus staff at a relatively low level in the hierarchy were not only kept informed of the development of the product from day one, but actively involved at all stages of the process. This view was confirmed by William Hopkins, another ROCOL Product Development Manager, this time in the Lubrication Division. He believes that 'the important thing in doing a project like this is to get everybody behind it, and there was loads of excitement and enthusiasm behind the project'. He attributes this to the opportunity given to all the people working on the project to contribute to its success, arguing that they all felt genuinely concerned about the project's outcome.

Morgan Crucible's senior executives and divisional managers play a relatively small role in the management of the company's many subsidiaries. The running of each company is left largely in the hands of managers within that subsidiary. The role of the senior managers is seen to be setting targets – both for the group as a whole and for individual subsidiaries – and providing strategic direction. This direction, as we have seen in previous chapters, takes the form of expansion of its operations and product groups through acquisition, joint venture and organic growth (Cotton, 1996). Organisational learning within the company naturally reflects this style of leadership, with responsibility for learning initiatives largely being left in the hands of managers in individual subsidiaries. It is therefore unsurprising that different, and unrelated, sets of activities have grown up in the different divisions and subsidiaries.

Leadership case studies: some conclusions

The four case studies above show that although leadership styles in the four companies have many similarities there are also important differences. These differences have dramatic implications for the way in which organisational learning ideas have been implemented in the four companies. The relatively centralised leadership and strategic direction in 3M and CCSB, albeit with a high degree of autonomy for middle managers regarding day-to-day operational matters, has meant that senior management in both companies has been able to introduce co-ordinated learning activities throughout the organisation. The primary manifestations of this are 3M's Organisational Learning Services Group and CCSB's Lifetime Learning Links, both of which provide a focus for organisational learning activities in their respective companies. Interestingly, the strength of leadership in 3M derives not from the power or charisma of the Chief Executive or his executive team, but from the strength and tradition of the company itself. In CCSB the Managing Director has played an important role, but again much of the strength and success of the company is due to the strength of the company (in this case of its brands) and the traditions of both the Coca-Cola Company and Cadbury-Schweppes.

By contrast, leadership in Mayflower and Morgan Crucible is much more influenced by the individuals who have taken prominent roles in driving the two companies forward. However, because of the size to which the companies have grown it has now become impossible for these individuals to take responsibility for leading throughout the company. Thus, in each case, the CEO and his or her team restrict their role to allocating resources between subsidiaries, setting financial targets and co-ordinating the growth of the group, particularly in terms of new acquisitions. Operational decisions, and to some extent low-level strategic decisions, are the preserve of managers in individual subsidiaries. This decentralised approach to leadership and strategic decision-making has significant implications for the development of organisational learning in the two companies. Lack of a company-wide approach results from the decentralisation of leadership and decision-making; consequently, no single entity has the specific remit of encouraging the growth of organisational learning in the company.

Dissatisfaction with traditional ideas of leadership

Having considered leadership in four of the case companies, we now turn to consider the way in which new ideas of leadership have developed. We look first at the main driving force behind the development of these new ideas: the widespread dissatisfaction with traditional ideas of leadership. Senge describes traditional ideas of leadership as 'deeply rooted in an individualistic and nonsystemic worldview' (Senge, 1990a: 340). He outlines the problems with this view, saying: 'so long as such myths prevail, they reinforce a focus on short-term events and charismatic heroes rather than on systemic forces and collective learning' (*ibid.*). Senge is clearly deeply dissatisfied with traditional management techniques and theories, and it is not surprising that he advocates their replacement. We shall return later to the question of what, if anything, can replace these traditional ideas. First, however, it is necessary to examine whether other leading commentators take Senge's view and whether there is sufficient evidence to support it.

Marquardt agrees wholeheartedly with Senge, asserting that 'many leadership styles that were acceptable in the past will be unacceptable in the learning organisation of the future' (Marquardt, 1996: 106). He continues in a similar vein: 'hard-nosed managers who single-handedly and forcefully determined team direction, made key decisions, and pushed employees may prove destructive in today's organisation' (*ibid.*).

Schein offers a similar view, arguing that 'one of the most difficult problems of our age is that leaders, and perhaps academics as well, cannot readily admit that things are out of control and that we do not know what to do' (Schein, 1993: 85). He explains that there is:

> an unwillingness to violate cultural norms that leaders must always appear to be in control and to have solutions for all our problems. We are afraid that if we admit to our confusion, we will make our followers and students anxious and disillusioned.
>
> (Schein, 1993: 85)

Maira and Scott-Morgan offer a slightly different perspective: 'the very word *leadership*, and the way it resonates, embodies the problems many organizations are having: the word *leadership* connotes the behavior of the very few' (Maira and Scott-Morgan, 1996: 193). While agreeing with the authors above that leadership by command and control will not work any more, Maira and Scott-Morgan believe that leadership is coming to be the responsibility of many people, perhaps even all the people, in an organisation.

This dissatisfaction with the traditional leadership styles which is expressed in the literature is matched by opinion from the case companies. This is usually articulated more positively in the desire to move forward to a better leadership style, but is clearly rooted in dissatisfaction with traditional styles. For example, Mayflower Automotive Division's Human Resources

Director illustrates people's reaction to the implementation of a new employee-development programme: 'it's such a sigh of relief that, "Thank God, people are asking me. Great, I'm not asked to leave my brain at the gate and to just come in and be an automaton." ' If this is typical, then it is safe to assume that they were dissatisfied with previous arrangements.

New ideas of leadership and new organisational forms

The undoubted dissatisfaction that many people have felt with existing ideas of leadership has led to the rise of alternative ideas. The most well-established of these is transformational leadership theory, which originates in large measure from Bass's *Leadership and Performance Beyond Expectations*, published in 1985. The concept of self-managing teams is another alternative to the traditional ideas of leadership that we will consider, together with the development of corporate clusters and the new emphasis that many organisations are placing on delayering.

Transformational leadership

Transformational leadership is based on intrinsic motivation as a result of high levels of commitment, a shared vision or identification with corporate success. Thus it appeals to the high levels of Maslow's (1954) hierarchy of needs. More formally, transformational leadership has been defined as 'the process of influencing the attitudes and assumptions of organizational members and building commitment to the organization's mission and objectives' (Lewis *et al.*, 1994: 440). Transformational leaders are often described as charismatic – hence the alternative term 'charismatic leadership' – although Kets DeVries (1988) has endowed charismatic leaders with almost messianic qualities, describing charismatic leadership as a gift of grace possessed by prophets. Some commentators, for example Bateman and Zeithaml (1993), classify charismatic leadership as distinct from transformational leadership. They argue that, as well as being charismatic, transformational leaders possess two other critical abilities. First, they give their followers individualised attention. This can take the form of delegating challenging work, giving increased responsibility to followers, encouraging open communications and providing one-to-one mentoring to help develop their followers. Second, transformational leaders are intellectually stimulating. They make their followers aware of problems and potential solutions.

Bateman and Zeithaml describe transformational leaders as 'articulating the organization's opportunities, threats, strengths, and weaknesses', thereby 'stirring the imagination and generating insights' (*ibid.*: 429). These techniques allow problems to be identified, and the full commitment of followers is applied to finding and implementing high-quality solutions. Transformational leadership is perhaps best described as visionary leadership. The term 'visionary leadership' has the advantage of conveying the key role of both creating and sharing a vision in the transformation process. However, in this research the term 'transformational leadership' is used, for two reasons. First, it is the most widely used of the three terms and, second, it captures the essential meaning of all three terms, while 'charismatic leadership' and 'visionary leadership' capture only part of the whole idea.

Key to distinguishing transformational leadership from the more traditional transactional leadership is Bass's approach, which itself draws heavily on Burns's (1978) work. Bass views transactional and transformational leadership as separate dimensions, rather than as separate ends of a continuum. Thus, in his view, the ideal approach to leadership is a combination of both transformational and transactional leadership. There is thus no contradiction in describing an organisation as a successful exponent of transformational leadership while still acknowledging that it practises transactional leadership.

One leader who fits into the category of charismatic, visionary or transformational leaders is Derek Williams, Managing Director of CCSB. He joined the company when it was formed, in 1987. Prior to this he was Personnel Director, Manufacturing Director and then Managing Director of Schweppes GB. Williams has been responsible for consistently providing the business with vision and leadership. He adopted the visionary slogan 'No. 1 and Pulling Ahead' after reading it in a soft-drinks journal. As was noted above, he also receives praise from his staff for his leadership skills. Hilary Moos, a CCSB Human Resource Manager, speaking about one of his ideas, said:

> he's tended to be fairly visionary in terms of where he likes to see CCSB going and how ideas are taken forward, so if he has an idea it will tend to have a lot of weight thrown behind it, a lot of resource looked at it to see if it is feasible or not. Also, in terms of onward supporting of the scheme, he is very supportive of it, wants to get to know the people involved in it, so there's a fairly strong sense of leadership from him.
>
> (Hilary Moos, Human Resource Manager, CCSB)

Beverley Stratton, who succeeded Hilary Moos as Human Resource Manager for Frontline, expressed similar sentiments about Williams's role. She said: 'I think it is vitally important that you get that commitment from the top.'

Creating and communicating an inspirational vision is are key behaviours of charismatic or transformational leaders. An example of a company that has recently created a new vision is 3M. The company's UK Chairman and Chief Executive, John Mueller, suggests that 'it's only been in the last couple of years that I think 3M has really addressed the issue of a vision statement that is an umbrella for the whole company'. He attributes the length of time that it has taken to create a shared vision to the diversity of the company. He goes on to explain how the Chairman of 3M worldwide has acted as a transformational leader in creating the vision.

At Morgan Crucible there seems to have been a deliberate attempt to create transformational leaders. The company has tried to achieve this by giving individual business managers 'strategic responsibility for the development of a specific product on a global basis' (Andy McIntosh, Director of Group Personnel). This means that the individual manager is forced to create a vision not only of where his or her particular business is going, but also of the future of the product group as a whole. He or she has to communicate this not only to the staff in the individual business, but to the managers – and, through them, to the employees – of the other businesses. One example of such a transformational leader is Philip Wright, Managing Director of Morganite Thermal Ceramics and head of the worldwide product group of crucible companies. He is described as both as 'running a very important subsidiary company' and as 'a product champion' (Andy McIntosh, Group Personnel Director).

The literature on transformational leadership naturally focuses on the role of senior management, but it is apparent that managers at all levels of the organisation can apply transformational leadership. The thrust is to increase the motivation of subordinates by creating feelings of trust, loyalty and respect. The leader makes his or her subordinates more aware of their importance and their ability to contribute, and this is reflected in the higher levels of motivation and commitment that subordinates then display. This can be achieved through the empowerment of individuals, and by appealing to high-order motivations such as self-actualisation and creativity.

Self-managing teams

Teamworking has been one of the most fashionable management ideas of the 1990s. Bennis *et al.* remind us that 'it is not so long ago that workers were described as "hands" and the successful manager was of the "I command, you do as I say" stereotype' (Bennis *et al.*, 1994: 115). They go on to say that 'attitudes have changed and the new notion that has taken root and is likely to spread is that of the manager as the leader of a team' (*ibid.*: 115). Self-managing, or self-managed, teams are the latest twist on the idea of teamwork. Dumaine (1990) says that self-managing teams can also be called cross-functional teams, high performance teams, and even 'superteams'. He describes the workings of a self-managing team as:

> a superteam arranges schedules, sets profit targets, and – gulp – may even know everyone's salary. It has a say in hiring and firing team members as well as managers. It orders material and equipment. It strokes customers, improves quality, and, in some cases, devises strategy.
>
> (Dumaine, 1990: 40)

If this is how self-managing teams perform, then it is easy to see why Dumaine refers to them as superteams. Further alternatives to the term self-managing teams exist: Haines and McCoy (1995) describe such teams as 'self-directed work teams', Peters (1992) uses the term 'self-contained project team', while Marquardt (1996) prefers 'self-managed work teams'. Companies also have various names for self-managing teams; for example, General Electric's are called 'Work-out Teams'.

Manz and Sims (1995) offer an equally positive and optimistic view of self-managing teams, and go further than Dumaine by offering empirical evidence to support the benefits of utilising self-managing teams. They suggest that companies that have self-managing teams have a strong, positive impact on productivity, and they suggest that the improvement may be of the magnitude of 50 per cent.

Among the case companies, Mayflower is a major exponent of self-managing teams, which are referred to as project teams. These teams evolve with the life of the project, and so people leave the team and are replaced by those with skills relevant for the next part of the team's task.

CCSB likewise places great emphasis on self-managing teams. In Chapter 3 we looked at the strong emphasis that CCSB's flagship factory at Wakefield placed on self-managing teams. Employees described their journey from competent operators, through competent teams and achieving teams, to self-managing teams. This progression recognises both the importance of self-managing teams and the potential benefits – the company regarding teams as a long-term objective rather than as something that could be implemented overnight.

Microsoft is one of the companies to make extensive use of self-managing teams. Founder and CEO Bill Gates believes that self-managing teams are the only way to keep the company feeling small. He argues that all Microsoft employees need to feel that they can make a difference (Rebello and Schwartz, 1992). More generally, Peters concludes that 'there is, overall, significant progress to report in moving toward self-management' (Peters, 1992: 243).

Corporate clusters

Despite the obvious advantages of self-managing teams, there is by no means a consensus behind the idea. Quinn Mills (1991) develops a radical thesis which he claims goes much further than the idea of self-managing teams. Peters describes Quinn Mills's ideas as 'a sweeping alternative to hierarchy and even to the latest experiments in self-management' (Peters, 1992: 245). The prescription Quinn Mills offers is based around his idea of 'corporate clusters'. He defines a cluster as 'a group of people drawn from different disciplines who work together on a semipermanent basis' (Quinn Mills, 1991: 29). When answering the question 'Who is in charge in a cluster?' Quinn Mills lists two ways in which leadership takes place in a cluster. The first is within the cluster itself, with members meeting to 'review the quality of their work, to examine how well they work together, to make decisions, to decide direction, and to take disciplinary action against individuals and subgroups as necessary' (*ibid.*: 50). The second source of leadership is the individuals (the leaders) who, both on specific projects and in the cluster generally, provide supervision, direction and discipline. They are able to do this, not through their position in the hierarchy, but because they are granted the authority to do so by others in the group. Quinn Mills goes on to explain that:

> to act effectively, the cluster must have a method of resolving internal disputes and of making quick choices when necessary. Leadership in these areas goes to those who are accepted as the most competent – either best at the techniques involved or in handling people.
>
> (Quinn Mills, 1991: 51)

Examples of corporate clusters are relatively few and far between. Quinn

Mills uses British Petroleum, General Electric Canada, Du Pont and Xerox as examples of companies that have developed corporate clusters. However, each of these companies has used corporate clusters only in a small part of its operations. In British Petroleum's case this was the central engineering unit; General Electric Canada used a variation of corporate clusters for its centralised financial services; Du Pont has them in its information services unit; while Xerox uses them more widely, but by no means throughout the business. More generally, Quinn Mills describes corporate clusters as widespread in consulting, accountancy and law firms. It is perhaps in these types of professional organisations that corporate clusters are most appropriate and will prove most effective.

Given his description of the workings of corporate clusters, it is easy to see why Quinn Mills describes them as 'a dramatic change from traditional management' (Quinn Mills, 1991: 7). However, the differences between corporate clusters and self-managing teams are less clear cut. Quinn Mills admits that self-managed teams that work without significant hierarchical control become much like a cluster organisation, but he attempts to differentiate corporate clusters by describing the cluster concept as 'broader'. He writes: 'a cluster is more diverse in composition, being ordinarily made up of persons of different specialities and disciplines. Most important, clusters emerge from a different spirit and philosophy' (*ibid.*: 40).

Whether or not clusters and self-managing teams are conceptually – and in reality – different, it is clear that they both represent important new organisational forms, with strong links to many of the ideas behind the learning organisation. Equally, both concepts have profound consequences for the role of leadership in organisations. Leadership is no longer solely the responsibility of managers, and the hierarchy is no longer the key determinant of who is expected to provide the leadership in a given situation.

Delayering

The delayering of management and the concomitant flattening of organisational structures are having a profound impact on the nature of leadership in organisations. Reducing the numbers of middle managers has meant that authoritarian leadership styles and the close supervision of employees have had to give way to more progressive methods. As organisations delayer, leaders will increasingly be required to deal with a wider span of responsibilities and more direct reports. Thus they will need both to exercise greater delegation and to instil greater trust in their subordinates.

Delayering has taken place, to a greater or lesser extent, in all the case companies, as well as in many other large companies. Richard Bradford, Vice-President of Human Resources at Siebe, says: 'I think everybody is moving to leanness.' Morgan Crucible's Group Managing Director describes his company's delayering as follows: 'we have reduced the number of levels of management to five, from me down to the lavatory cleaner'. This reduction in the number of management levels is naturally reflected in the company's decentralised structure and the pushing of accountability down to subsidiary companies. Likewise, it means that a different leadership style is required of managers, with, for example, greater levels of delegation and the empowering of employees.

Importance of leadership in organisational learning

On the cover of *The Fifth Discipline* Senge (1990a) uses a quotation from *Fortune* which demonstrates the close connection between leadership and organisational learning. *Fortune* says: 'Forget your old, tired ideas about leadership. The most successful corporation of the 1990s will be something called a learning organization.' The important thing to note here is that *Fortune* sees the learning organisation not as replacing tired, old ideas about management, or about organisation, or about managing people, but as replacing tired, old ideas about leadership.

The learning organisation as a strategic goal

Many organisations are now making the creation of a learning organisation a key part of their long-term strategy. Unless learning is a conscious part of the strategy it is difficult to see how the organisation can make a realistic claim to be a learning organisation. Marquardt and Reynolds argue that 'for many people the most critical element for becoming a learning organization is a deliberate and conscious learning strategy' (Marquardt and Reynolds, 1994: 66). They view learning as the key to productive competitiveness and the *sine qua non* of learning organisations.

Camillus (1997) reviews the two classic models of strategic management in the face of change: the predictive paradigm and the learning paradigm. The predictive paradigm rests on the presumption that a combination of analysis, experience and insight can lead to reliable predictions. The learning paradigm, by contrast, emphasises flexibility, experimentation, response and learning. This learning paradigm of strategic management thus has much in common with the basic concept of organisational learning. However, Camillus argues that the current business world is characterised by lumpy discontinuous change – which is inimical to these two models. He asks how organisations can manage external shifts in change drivers, such as that from electronics to information, and internal discontinuities, such as the growth in professionalism and knowledge bases. He proposes a new proactive managerial mind-set in which both organisational structure and strategy are seen as fluid, something he refers to as the transformational paradigm. While he suggests that this proposed mind-set represents a new paradigm, it is remarkably similar to that advocated by many writers on organisational learning. However, the opening of the debate about whether learning should be a deliberate strategic goal is important to the development of organisational learning.

As part of the questionnaire survey conducted for this book, respondents were asked to say whether they believed their company to have a conscious learning strategy. Of the 159 respondents who completed this question, 59 said that their company did not have a conscious learning strategy, while 100 said that their company did have a conscious learning strategy (see Table 5.1).

These answers suggest that one of the most important prerequisites for the creation of a learning organisation is in place in the majority of large and medium-sized companies. A number of managers questioned in the case companies also described their organisation as possessing a conscious learning strategy or, indeed, as being a learning organisation. 3M's Human Resource Director said that '3M would describe itself as a learning organisation', while the Management Development Manager said that 'the primary focus of the company is for people to learn'. 3M's Chairman and Chief Executive acknowledges the importance of learning, but without making any claims for the company's success: 'there is a sincere recognition that we have to foster an environment that is conducive to learning and change'.

At Morgan Crucible the Director of Group Personnel said that 'we would classify ourselves as a learning organisation'. He also described the company's 'very strong corporate strategy and vision' as encompassing learning.

CCSB's Personnel Director described his company as a learning organisation, but only 'in part'. Interestingly, as we saw in the case study above, the

Table 5.1 Conscious learning strategy

No	Yes
59 (36.9%)	100 (62.5%)

Note: One respondent did not answer this question

Managing Director claims that the company has no clear strategy and says: 'I am amazed when people say, "We have a strategy, we have a plan, let's stick to it."' He argues that too much clarity creates 'heaps and heaps of confusion', and that 'clarity does not exist. No such thing.' He even states, paradoxically: 'I am very conscious that the clearer I am, the more imprecise I am being.' In this context, it is not surprising that there is no clearly articulated conscious learning strategy. Despite this, it is clear from the company's behaviour that the underlying strategy is one in which learning plays a key role.

At Procter and Gamble the Managing Director described learning and innovation as key parts of the company's strategy, while at Mayflower the strategy includes 'recognising and harnessing the potential learning' (Mike Fell, Human Resource Director, Mayflower Automotive Division).

As part of this research a number of managers in each of the case companies were asked to rate their organisation on a number of characteristics, using a scale of 1 to 5. One of the characteristics was the company's strategy and the ideal description was: 'learning is a deliberate and conscious part of the strategy', with the objective that 'learning becomes a habit and an everyday occurrence'. The results of this part of the research can be seen in detail in Chapter 4 but, in summary, it was quite clear that managers in the five companies regarded learning as a deliberate and conscious part of their strategy.

Clearly, if these companies are representative of the corporate world – and the survey results suggest they are – then learning is a part of the strategy of a majority of large and medium-sized organisations. This does not answer the question of the effectiveness of such a strategy, but the widespread existence of learning as a part of the conscious strategy of organisations is, on its own, indicative of an important source of potential competitive advantage.

From top-management commitment to the commitment/acceptance of the whole workforce

As we saw in Chapter 2, there are a number of antecedents which, when communicated via the relevant filters, can combine to create top-management commitment to the creation of a learning organisation. In this section we look at how the process moves on from top-management commitment to the commitment or at least the acceptance of the whole workforce, and then to the actual creation of a learning organisation. As Figure 5.1 shows, there are a number of stages that must be gone through before the organisation can make a realistic claim to have become a learning organisation.

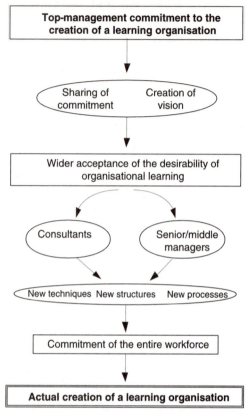

Figure 5.1 The creation of a learning organisation: from top-management
commitment to the commitment of the whole workforce

The first and probably the most important roles of top management in the creation of a learning organisation are the sharing of commitment and the creation of a vision. These two 'tasks', which can be encapsulated in the idea of a shared vision, if accomplished successfully should lead to wider acceptance of the idea of the learning organisation. In our survey of the Human Resource Directors of 160 UK-based companies, 61.8 per cent of respondents said that their company had a vision that was shared by most or all of the employees (see Table 5.2 and Figure 5.2).

Prior to this question respondents had been asked to describe their company's vision. A space was left for each respondent to write his or her own answer. This elicited a wide range of responses, from the inclusion of a laminated card spelling out the company's vision to the one-word answer

Table 5.2 Shared vision

No employees	A few employees	About half of the employees	Most employees	All employees
4 (2.5%)	23 (14.4%)	30 (18.8%)	74 (46.2%)	25 (15.6%)

Note: Four respondents did not answer this question

'confused'. The majority of company visions expressed the desire to be customer-focused and to be the market leader in their chosen field. None of the companies gave creating a learning organisation as their vision, although many of the answers suggested that something very close to a learning organisation would be required to achieve the vision.

Marquardt argues, correctly, that top managers 'should not only articulate the vision, but be active early participants in its actualization' (Marquardt, 1996: 96). He argues that senior mangers should be strong advocates or champions of learning, and that their modelling of a learning organisation is 'the most powerful way to disseminate the vision and inspire others within the company to join the bandwagon'.

If the organisation has successfully shared its wish to become a learning organisation, then consultants and/or senior and middle managers who have accepted the desirability of the learning organisation concept can then be assigned the task of creating the necessary techniques, structures and processes to help build the learning organisation. Once these techniques, structures and processes are in place, this, together with further attempts to share the vision, should create a climate in which the whole of the workforce is committed to the creation of a learning organisation. Failing this, if the organisation can at least achieve the acceptance of the whole workforce, then it should still be possible, albeit more difficult, to create a learning organisation.

The general importance of senior-management commitment to new projects or changes was acknowledged on a number of occasions by middle

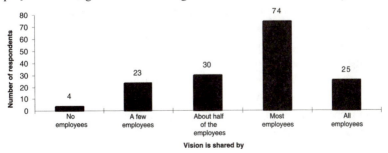

Figure 5.2 Shared vision

managers in the case companies. A good example of the importance of senior-management commitment to a new idea is Derek Williams's support for Frontline. Hilary Moos, the Human Resources Manager in charge of the programme, was asked about the importance of the original idea having come from the Managing Director. She described his role as 'very important' and explained that an idea from the Managing Director will 'tend to have a lot of weight thrown behind it, a lot of resource used to look at it to see if it is feasible or not'. She went on to outline the Managing Director's support for the scheme, saying: 'in terms of onward supporting of the scheme, he is very supportive of it, wants to get to know the people involved in it, so there's a fairly strong sense of leadership from him'.

New leadership roles in learning organisations

It should be clear from previous chapters that structure and infrastructure in learning organisations differ from structure and infrastructure in traditional companies. If structure and infrastructure are different, then it follows naturally that patterns of decision-making will be different and therefore that leadership roles will be different in learning organisations. An interesting perspective on leadership roles in general is offered by Farkas and Wetlaufer (1996). They argue that effective Chief Executives adopt one of five distinct leadership approaches. They call the first of these the *strategic approach*, and argue that Chief Executives who adopt this approach believe that their most important job is to create, test and design the company's long-term strategy. The second approach is the *human assets approach*. Chief Executives in this group believe that their main job is to impart certain values, behaviours and attitudes. The *expertise approach* is adopted by Chief Executives who believe that they must select and disseminate an area of expertise that will be a source of competitive advantage, while the *box approach* is adopted by Chief Executives who believe that they can add the most value by creating, communicating and monitoring an explicit set of financial and/or cultural controls. Chief Executives who adopt the *change approach* believe that their most important role is to create an environment of continual reinvention.

Turning to look specifically at leadership roles in learning organisations, it is likely that a leader who wishes to create a learning organisation will need to adopt a change approach. This will allow him or her to cultivate an environment of constant questioning and risk-taking, and frequent reinvention of business practices and products. However, elements of the other approaches, particularly the expertise and human assets approaches, are likely to be required as well. Various authors have considered the new roles that will be required of leaders in learning organisations. The work of two of the most prominent authors is discussed below, together with illustrations from the case companies.

Senge's leadership roles

Senge (1990a) gives three leadership roles that are critical for the building of learning organisations. They are the leader as designer, the leader as steward, and the leader as teacher. Each is considered in detail below.

Senge believes that the *designing role of the leader* has been neglected by many managers and commentators. He argues that 'it is fruitless to be the leader in an organisation that is poorly designed' (Senge, 1990a: 34). The cause of the neglect of design as an important leadership role is probably its background, behind-the-scenes nature. Organisation design, however, should not be seen as merely moving boxes and lines on the organisational chart. The overriding, overarching ideas of the organisation should be seen as a key part of the organisation's design. The creation of these ideas – the vision, purpose and the values of the organisation – is key to the creation of a learning organisation. One of the leader's key roles is thus designing or creating an environment in which learning can flourish.

Contradicting the view that design is neglected as a leadership role, a number of senior managers in the case companies have emphasised their role in designing their organisation. 3M's Chairman and Chief Executive emphasised the importance of organisation design by detailing his role in the company's Leadership and Organisational Development Committee:

> I'm now leading an effort for Europe, by way of a pan-European committee called Leadership and Organisational Development, which in many ways is beginning to focus on how we must continue to evolve as an organisation, to make certain that we are competitive and sustainable in the long run. At the heart of that is a sincere recognition that we have to foster and provide an environment that is conducive to learning and to changing, not just in the management ranks but throughout the organisation.
>
> (John Mueller, Chairman and Chief Executive, 3M UK)

He returned to this theme in a later interview when talking about the possibility of using Imation as a benchmarking partner, citing the importance of 'the Organisational Development Committee for Europe'.

Similarly, at CCSB the Director of Personnel described the way in which the personnel department's agenda 'has tended to change over the years and we've probably got more involved now in the organisation design and the performance of the organisation'. When asked how he influences the organisation design, he cited the twice yearly review with the Managing Director. The questions that are asked then include:

> What should we be changing? Why should we be changing it? What leverage can we get out of that sort of change? Or what are the external pressures that make it appropriate for us to change and therefore get better value out of people and the roles they perform?
>
> (Keith Dennis, Personnel Director, CCSB)

3M and CCSB are both clearly concerned with organisation design. Both are highly professional and successful companies, which have grown, largely organically, in the way that they have chosen for themselves. Siebe, Mayflower and Morgan Crucible have seemingly made organisation design less of a priority. This may be due to the fact that acquisition has been a relatively important source of growth, leading each company to grow by 'bolting on' additional subsidiaries, rather than creating new but highly integrated divisions or product groups.

The second of Senge's three leadership roles in learning organisations is the *leader as steward*. This refers to the leader as steward, guardian and advocate of what he calls the *purpose story*. This is an overarching explanation of why the leader acts in the way that he or she does, of how and why the organisation needs to go forward, and, most importantly, of how and why that progress is part of something larger.

It is difficult to find examples of purpose stories in the case companies because, by its very nature, each leader's purpose story will be different. In 3M, leaders' stories typically focus on the innovative nature of the company and their desire to create new products. At CCSB the Managing Director talks consistently about the need to be out of control and to avoid clarity. He talks about the need to find 'a way to deliver those attributes that we value and prize highly, i.e. to be out of control, to go in a different direction, to change our minds, to increase the pace, to be an enabling organisation'.

At Mayflower the Chief Executive's purpose story has extra relevance because of his role as founder of the company. He speaks consistently about his desire to 'build an international group of specialist manufacturing companies, which was my original vision and objective'.

The final leadership role that Senge defines as important in learning organisations is that of the *leader as teacher*. He argues that the ability to define reality is a crucial source of influence: 'much of the leverage leaders can actually exert lies in helping people achieve more accurate, more insightful, and more *empowering* views of reality' (Senge, 1990a: 353). Leaders, in Senge's view, must help people achieve a view of reality that is a medium for creating rather than a source of limitation. This, then, is the task of the leader as teacher. Leaders must be able not only to understand instinctively the reasons for change and the strategic direction of the company, but also to communicate, to teach, to conceptualise these insights so that they become widely understood.

CCSB is particularly keen to give all its employees an understanding of the business. This extends to the company's delivery men, who are expected, because they are often the most frequent visitor to a customer, to become involved in customer service and satisfaction.

Marquardt's leadership roles

Marquardt (1996) suggests six new leadership roles required of managers in a learning organisation. The six roles are: instructor, coach and mentor; knowledge manager; co-learner and model for learning; architect and designer; co-ordinator; and advocate and champion for learning processes and projects. Each is discussed briefly below, before we turn to look at their relationship with the three new leadership roles defined by Senge (1990a).

Marquardt sees the roles of *instructor, coach and mentor* as three distinct aspects of the leader's job. This is an acknowledgement of the fact that different learning situations, and different learners, require different styles of help from the 'teacher'. Karash (1996) also notes the importance of these roles, although he describes them as coaching and facilitating. CCSB has acknowledged the importance of these roles with its STAR TREK Programme, which helps employees to identify their development needs. The employee then agrees with his or her manager a plan detailing how these needs will be addressed. This process could require significant input from the manager, or the employee may be able to address the development need alone after being given access to the necessary resources.

Information will increasingly be the most important commodity in the organisation and one crucial role for leaders in learning organisations will be to act as *knowledge managers*. Marquardt argues that there is a need for a leader who can 'motivate and assist colleagues in the collection, storage, and distribution of knowledge within and outside the unit' (Marquardt, 1996: 107). The importance of this role is explicitly acknowledged by 3M, whose senior scientists have the task of disseminating knowledge as widely as possible in the company. Graham notes that 3M has 'two formally organised networks [which] keep scientists in constant contact and encourage cross-unit technology transfer' (Graham, 1996: 43). These are the company's Technical Councils and Technical Forums.

In the role of *co-learner and model for learning*, leaders will be expected to perform as devoted learners who demonstrate a love of learning. The leader realises that it is insufficient merely to tell employees what to learn. Successful exponents of this leadership role will encourage, motivate and help workers to improve their learning skills. This role is highly valued in CCSB, where managers make use of the company's LLLs to help guide their employees' learning. By visiting the Learning Centres with their staff, managers can help to identify appropriate learning resources.

The importance of the leader's role as *architect and designer* was demonstrated in Chapter 3, in which we saw the importance of the new techniques, structures and processes that are used to build a learning organisation. The leader has an important role in designing these new techniques, structures and processes, but even more critical is the leader's role in integrating these into a system that will be successful in the organisation's competitive environment. Another aspect of this role is that of organisation design, with the leader responsible for redefining the organisation and inventing new methods of selecting, training and rewarding people. The new policies, strategies and principles that are required must be put in place by the leader in order for everyone to *belong* to the new organisation.

Marquardt likens the role of *co-ordinator* to that of the conductor of an orchestra, who enables all the musicians to play their instruments to the best of their ability. In the same way, the leader of a learning organisation co-ordinates people's work in order to allow them to perform at their best. Another analogy is that of the coach or manager of a football team, whose job is to transform the set of individual players into a cohesive unit. This analogy of the organisation as a football team is popular at CCSB, where the Managing Director state: 'we are very strong on football analogies'. Unsurprisingly, he sees himself as the manager, responsible for co-ordinating the work of his players.

The role of *advocate and champion for learning* seems to be an extension of the co-learner role. Marquardt argues that 'robust organisational learning requires more than one advocate or champion if it is to succeed' (Marquardt, 1996: 108). As Figure 5.1 suggests, top-management commitment is a vital precondition for the successful creation of a learning organisation. Although it may be possible for anyone to be an advocate of learning processes and projects, senior management is often the best and most likely source of this advocacy. Clearly, the more advocates a project can collect, the faster and more successfully learning will take place.

The relationship between Senge's model and Marquardt's model

As Figure 5.3 demonstrates, there is a strong relationship between the two models of leadership. The strength of Senge's model is its ability to combine the different aspects of leadership required in a learning organisation into three key roles. The disadvantage of this is that the roles he has suggested are, necessarily, fairly vague and may be difficult for a practising manager to interpret and apply. Conversely, Marquardt's approach provides a more detailed set of roles that leaders in learning organisations need to fill.

The leader as colleague, peer and friend

Something that is apparent in the interviews with senior managers, but which is not emphasised by Senge (1990a) or Marquardt (1996), is the need for managers to be able to motivate their staff. The single most important attribute of a leader in any organisation is his or her ability to relate to people and to inspire them to achieve exceptional performance. There is an increasing recognition that the only way to achieve this is by treating people with respect, trusting them and expecting them to do the same in return. This should help to create the shared vision and commitment that is required to create a learning organisation. This need to treat people with respect and to trust them was a recurring theme in the interviews conducted for this research, and it also has a strong instinctive appeal.

At 3M the necessity of treating people with dignity and respect is a long-standing part of the company's culture and philosophy. However, 3M not only preaches this philosophy, but also applies it in practice. There is no better example of this than the way in which the company has handled the job losses resulting from the closure of its audio-video business (see Denton and De Cock, 1997).

At Mayflower a similar – although perhaps less well-articulated – approach is followed. Mayflower Automotive Division's Human Resource

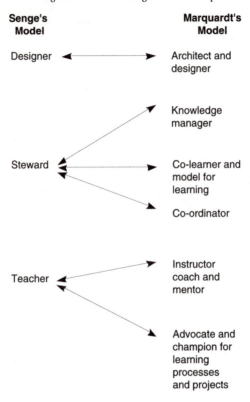

Senge's Model

Marquardt's Model

Designer ← → Architect and designer

Knowledge manager

Steward → Co-learner and model for learning

Co-ordinator

Teacher → Instructor coach and mentor

Advocate and champion for learning processes and projects

Figure 5.3 Leadership roles: the relationship between Senge's model and Marquardt's model

Director encapsulates their approach in the saying 'people have purpose, dignity and recognition'.

Leadership roles in learning organisation: are they relevant?

Although we have seen that there are a number of leadership roles which may be necessary for the successful creation and maintenance of a learning organisation, it is unclear whether these roles are necessarily unique to learning organisations. Only a few of the proposed roles required of leaders in learning organisations deal directly with learning; the others may be equally appropriate within any organisation. For example, the role of the leader as the designer of the organisation must be equally important whether or not the leader chooses a design that is appropriate to promote organisational learning. He or she could – and perhaps is more likely to – choose from a range of alternative designs, each of which would be an important factor in the organisation's success. However, the roles required for the creation of a learning organisation are sufficiently distinct for their elucidation to be valuable.

New leadership skills in learning organisations

It is clear that if leaders are to fulfil the new leadership roles expected of them in a learning organisation, then new leadership skills will be needed to equip them for these roles. There are two key skills which leaders will require if they are to build and sustain learning organisations: building shared vision and commitment, and creating a team-based organisation.

The most obvious skill that leaders in learning organisations will need is the ability to share their commitment to the organisation's success and the steps needed to realise that success. Marquardt (1996) suggests that leaders should attempt to blend extrinsic and intrinsic visions, communicate their own vision and ask for support, encourage personal visions from which emerge shared visions, and keep visioning as an ongoing process. In short, these are the skills that are required to achieve step two of Figure 5.1, namely the sharing of commitment and the creation of a vision.

We have seen the importance of self-managing teams, corporate clusters and related concepts. The successful leader of a learning organisation must develop the skills to plan, manage and co-ordinate such teams, while at the same time letting go of the day-to-day control of the teams' activities. Leaders will often have to deal with multiple teams, each working on distinct activities, at separate levels and to different time-scales. Leader must have the ability to become a trusted partner of each of the teams with which they are working.

Conclusion

Leadership theory has undergone many developments since the Second World War. Leadership styles that were acceptable and even successful in the past will be unacceptable and unsuccessful in the learning organisations of today and tomorrow. The case studies of leadership demonstrate that there is no place for the 'great man' theory of leadership in today's organisations. Senge (1990a: 340) also explicitly rejects the view of leaders as heroes. One individual, however great, can no longer act as an omnipotent, omniscient force, understanding and controlling all elements of the organisation. While individuals, for example Derek Williams and John Simpson, have played an important role in the development of case companies, they have not dominated their organisations or determined strategy in isolation from colleagues.

It is apparent from practice in the case companies that strategy can no longer be determined in the form of a long-term plan decided by senior management which is then rigidly adhered to. The increasingly rapid pace of change has made long-range planning almost obsolete – hence books such as *The Rise and Fall of Strategic Planning* (Mintzberg, 1994). Indeed Williams's statements that he is amazed by companies that have a strategy and that 'you'd better avoid clarity' encapsulate the central thesis of Mintzberg's book. What is clear from these statements, and from the lack of precision in 3M's strategy, is the importance of recognising that intended strategies are increasingly unlikely to be realised in their entirety. Thus leading organisations are seeking to make their strategies more flexible, to allow for environmental uncertainty and to allow effective emergent strategies to develop. The external drivers which have necessitated the switch to more flexible strategic decision-making processes are similar to those which have acted as antecedents to organisational learning itself. Factors such as the increasing pace of change, the increasingly global nature of the business environment and the increasing demands placed on all businesses by their customers contribute to the need for strategies to be flexible and adaptable. Such flexible strategies are best determined by a group of people with as much understanding as possible of the changes taking place in the market. As Mintzberg argues, 'effective strategists are not people who abstract themselves from the daily detail but quite the opposite: they are the ones who *immerse* themselves in it, while being able to abstract the *strategic messages* from it' (Mintzberg, 1994: 256).

Another key message of this chapter is that companies need to create structures which can promote leadership at all levels of the organisation. There is still a role for traditional transactional leadership practices, but these must be complemented by more people-centred leadership styles. Thus we have seen the rise of self-managing teams, corporate clusters, transformational leadership and delayering. Most notably, leaders must be able to undertake the variety of new roles that will be required of them in a learning organisation. These new roles include such diverse activities as organisation design, acting as a coach or mentor and managing knowledge. Most critically, leaders must learn to trust people and, by treating them with dignity and respect, can expect this trust to be reciprocated.

Success in these new roles will allow leaders to create two crucial elements of a learning organisation: a committed workforce and a shared vision. These, together with a team-based structure, will allow the leader to reap the rewards of creating a learning organisation. The vital leadership function is thus the creation of the environment in which organisational learning can flourish.

The case companies have all endeavoured to create progressive, people-centred styles of leadership. However, they have gone about this task in markedly different ways and with different results. With particular reference to organisational learning, the creation of a single entity to oversee learning in 3M and in CCSB has enabled these companies to advance rapidly towards becoming learning organisations. Mayflower and Morgan Crucible have chosen to decentralise management control and adopt a leadership style which emphasises subsidiary-company autonomy. This has led to relatively fractured and uncoordinated learning in these cases, but also to some interesting examples of successful local leadership.

Perhaps the most important lesson is that leadership roles are changing, and must continue to change in order for organisations to be successful in the future. For an organisation wishing to become a learning organisation, this change in leadership style is even more imperative. Thus contemporary leaders must fulfil new roles in order to create a shared vision and a team-based organisation, the two foundations on which effective learning organisations are built.

6   The usefulness and relevance of organisational learning

Introduction

In this penultimate chapter we critically evaluate both the usefulness and the relevance of organisational learning. The usefulness of organisational learning refers to the concept's ability to create meaningful benefits for those companies that determine to become learning organisations. The relevance of organisational learning depends on its applicability in everyday organisational settings. Put more simply, we ask and answer two questions: 'How useful is organisational learning?' and 'Who is it useful for?' The potential for organisational learning to contribute to organisational effectiveness is assessed in detail.

Scholarly discussions of organisational learning have often bordered on the utopian, far removed from the everyday decisions facing managers. Senge describes a learning organisation as an organisation in which 'people continually expand their capacity to create the results they truly desire, where new and expansive patterns of thinking are nurtured, where collective aspiration is set free, and where people are continually learning how to learn together' (Senge, 1990a: 3). It is hard to argue with this as a vision but critics have, to varying degrees, identified the great difficulties to be faced in achieving anything like the organisation described above. Senge himself admits that he underestimated the intensely negative reaction many managers would have to his methods, even when his theories enjoyed immense general popularity (Griffith, 1995). Pedler and Aspinwall describe the idea of the learning organisation as 'an attractive, if elusive, vision' (Pedler and Aspinwall, 1996: 1). Garvin takes a more overtly negative line, arguing that 'the topic in large part remains murky, confused, and difficult to penetrate' (Garvin, 1993: 78). In these circumstances the need for an assessment of the concept of organisational learning should be apparent. Thus we attempt to dispel the murkiness, explain the confusion and clarify the topic of organisational learning.

In order to assess the usefulness of organisational learning we need to look first to businesses which have applied the concept. This will allow us to examine whether becoming a learning organisation has, in practice, resulted in tangible benefits. If these businesses believe that adopting organisational learning has brought significant benefits this is an important first step towards determining whether organisational learning is indeed a valuable strategic goal. Placing reliance only on anecdotal evidence from learning organisations would be dangerous, however, and could result in a hagiographic account of organisational learning. It is important to remember that the views of those working in learning organisations represent only one perspective and are likely to be significantly more positive than the general view. Managers in learning organisations may be guilty of post-hoc rationalisation, justifying their position by citing benefits that, in reality, are difficult to attribute to organisational learning. For this reason, we pay due regard to the significant body of academic work critical of organisational learning. Notable examples include March (1991), Edmondson (1996), and Weick and Westley (1996). This approach allows a more balanced view of the topic to be presented.

The relevance of organisational learning, as we have said, depends critically on the applicability of the idea in a range of organisational settings. If organisational learning is effective only in theory, then clearly its relevance to managers and companies is severely limited. Likewise, if organisational learning is useful only in certain tightly defined settings its relevance will again be constrained. On the other hand, if organisational learning is applicable across a wide range of institutional settings, in different situations, companies, industries and countries, then it will be reasonable to assume that the concept has a high degree of relevance. In order to assess the relevance of organisational learning we will look first at the results of the questionnaire survey conducted for this research. By looking at 160 different businesses (listed in Appendix 2) of different sizes, across a range of industries, and from both the service and the manufacturing sectors, we can gain a valuable insight into the perceived applicability of organisational learning within a variety of contexts. This is, once again, combined with information from the five case studies, which give a more in-depth view of the prevailing situation. The results of this primary research are set against those reported elsewhere to create a comprehensive picture of organisational learning and its relevance. Valuable alternative sources include Shrivastava (1983), Sullivan and Nonaka

(1986), Wick and Leon (1993), and Ashton (1988). We begin, however, by returning to the question of usefulness and looking first at the question of how this can be assessed.

The usefulness of organisational learning

Miner and Mezias argue that 'although "learning" carries a positive connotation in many cultures, research on organizational learning clearly shows that it may or may not produce good outcomes' (Miner and Mezias, 1996: 93). Our evaluation of the usefulness of organisational learning comprises five main sections. First, we will establish a model of organisational learning that stresses the importance of action in determining usefulness. We then look at each of the four stages of this model in turn: individual learning, organisational learning, changes in behaviour and superior performance.

Determining usefulness: demonstrating the importance of action

Daft and Weick (1984) believe that action is represented by the internalisation of managers' (and presumably employees') experiences into the activities of organisations. While learning involves the acquisition of new information, this is not, on its own, enough to imply usefulness. The information certainly cannot be considered useful unless a change in behaviour results. Inkpen argues that 'for new information to impact organizations strategically, the information must be translated into behaviour or action' (Inkpen, 1995: 50). He believes, with direct relevance to our assessment of usefulness, that 'the link between organizational information and action and its influence on performance provides the basis for evaluating the effectiveness and "intelligence" of the organizational learning process' (*ibid.*). The chain of events necessary to imply usefulness to the concept of organisational learning is thus as shown in Figure 6.1.

The four-stage model in Figure 6.1 begins with two closely related and overlapping cognitive stages. Individuals are exposed to new ideas, add to their knowledge and start to think in different ways. This is then aggregated at an organisational level, with improvements in the organisation's stock of knowledge, and the organisation as a whole begins to think in a different way. This second step, the translation of individual experience to organisational memory, is key to our understanding of organisational learning, especially given the context of a battery of organisational constraints. The third step is

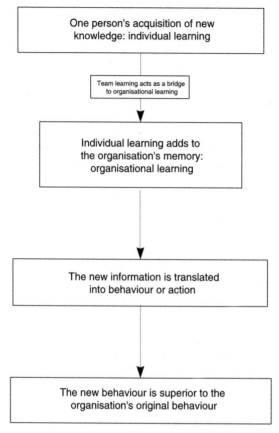

Figure 6.1 The usefulness of organisational learning: a schema

behavioural, since as individuals now think differently and organisations now have new knowledge patterns they both begin to act differently. The final stage is performance improvement, with the changes in behaviour at stage three leading to tangible improvements in collective results.

In order to conclude that organisational learning is useful, we must be able to show, first of all, that both individual learning and organisational learning can, and do, take place in organisations. This learning must then be applied by the organisation in the form of new behaviour or action. Finally, this new behaviour needs to be shown to be superior to the organisation's original behaviour. We will examine each of the steps in this process individually, but not in isolation from the preceding and succeeding steps. There is likely to be a degree of feedback from one step to another, which may have an important influence on the process as a whole. For example, the question of whether or not learning is applied in the form of new behaviour will have a major impact on the likelihood of further learning taking place. At each stage we examine in detail the problems that may prevent a smooth progression to the next stage.

Individual learning

Individual learning is the starting point from which most theories of learning, in general, and organisational learning, in particular, begin. For example, Marquardt asserts that 'individual learning is needed for organizational learning since individuals form the units of groups and organizations' (Marquardt, 1996: 32). Similarly, Senge believes that 'organizations learn only through individuals who learn. Individual learning does not guarantee organizational learning, but without it no organizational learning occurs' (Senge, 1990a: 236). March speaks of the 'mutual learning of an organization and the individuals in it' (March, 1991: 73). According to Argyris and Schön, 'individual learning is a necessary but insufficient condition for organizational learning' (Argyris and Schön, 1978: 20). Edmondson assigns an even more important role to individuals, arguing that 'the focus on learning gives rise to a cognitive approach, in which individuals' beliefs and insights are viewed as critical influences on organizational effectiveness' (Edmondson, 1996: 571).

From the above we can see that the leading writers on organisational learning are in agreement that individual learning is the critical first step on the path to organisational learning. There are, however, some problems associated with the study of individual learning, and it is to these difficulties that we turn next.

Individual learning in an organisational context

One of the problems with individual learning is that it is rarely encouraged – and is sometimes even implicitly discouraged – by certain organisational members. Often learning is encouraged, but only within very narrow parameters, with individuals encouraged to learn only if their learning offers a demonstrable improvement in their immediate job performance. Jones and Hendry argue that individual learning has:

> usually been considered purely in the context of production processes – that is, learning tends to be limited to training needs arising out of an

organization's need to have employees do a job properly within the narrow economic and political systems that govern how organizations are controlled.

(Jones and Hendry, 1994: 157)

Mumford notes that 'the individual learner can be helped or hindered by the organisation in which he or she works; the environment may not be absolutely fundamental, but it can be a powerful influence' (Mumford, 1994: 77).

Without wishing to be drawn too deeply into the complex debate concerning whether organisations as entities can do anything in their own right, there is undoubtedly a multi-level interaction between individuals and the organisation which needs exploring. March and Olsen (1975) describe learning as a cycle in which individuals' actions lead to organisational actions. These lead to environmental responses which affect both organisational and individual beliefs. Figure 6.2 shows Hedberg's (1981) graphical interpretation of March and Olsen's model. This model suggests that it is individuals who learn and act on their learning; organisations are regarded merely as a stage on which learning and action takes place.

The alternative model is exemplified by Cyert and March (1963), who give the impression that an organisation is an entity that can act and learn. In their analysis, organisations can exist in different states, and at any time an organisation will prefer certain states to other, less favourable, states. Uncontrollable external shocks affect the organisation, which responds according to its internal decision rules. The combination of external shocks and internal responses leads to an alteration in the state of the organisation. Thus a particular state is determined by the previous state, external shocks and internal decisions. Any decision that has resulted in a preferred state

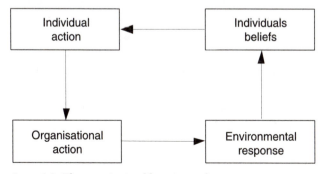

Figure 6.2   The organisational learning cycle

Source: Adapted from Hedberg (1981: 3), by permission of Oxford University Press.

becomes more likely to be used in the future, and this, in Cyert and March's abstract analysis, is the way in which organisations learn. The role of individuals is limited to their role in determining and applying the internal decision rules.

The literature remains unclear on the question of how individuals learn in an organisational context, but at the rational, intuitive level it is impossible to overlook their role. Few managers would be willing to subscribe to Cyert and March's view of organisations as entities that can learn 'on their own'.

Confusion between organisational learning and individual learning

It is apparent that many managers, and some writers, are unclear, usually with good reason, about what is meant by organisational learning. Often this lack of clarity manifests itself as confusion about the difference between organisational learning and individual learning. Fiol and Lyles believe that 'though individual learning is important to organizations, organizational learning is not simply the sum of each member's learning' (Fiol and Lyles, 1985: 804). Most commentators agree that although individuals are the agents of organisational learning the process involves more than merely the cumulative learning of those individuals. Hedberg goes further in arguing that: 'as individuals develop their personalities, personal habits, and beliefs over time, organizations develop world views and ideologies. Members come and go, and leadership changes, but organizations' memories preserve certain behaviors, mental maps, norms, and values over time' (Hedberg, 1981: 6). More concisely, he believes that organisations 'retain the sediments of past learning after the original learners have left' (*ibid.*). This suggests an important cultural element in organisational learning, a theme we will return to later in this chapter. Nelson and Winter, in their seminal book on industrial organisation and evolutionary theory, support this view by arguing that 'to view organizational memory as reducible to individual memories is to over-look or undervalue the linking of those individual memories by shared experiences in the past' (Nelson and Winter, 1982: 105).

From this perspective, the usefulness of organisational learning results not just from individual learning but, more importantly, from the development of organisational memory. From this perspective, learning is seen as a way of adding to the organisation's memory.

Team learning

As we have seen throughout this book, teams are very important in organisations in general and in learning organisations in particular. Watkins and Marsick (1993) see teams as the link between individual learning and organisational learning. They describe teams, groups and networks as the 'medium for moving new knowledge throughout the learning organization' (*ibid.*: 14). They also believe that 'the organization can take advantage of the teams' combined thinking to build new systemic capacity' (*ibid.*: 15). In this view, which is common throughout the literature, teams are a crucial bridge between individual and organisational learning. Team learning is one of Senge's (1990a) five 'competent technologies' which provide the vital dimensions in building learning organisations. Tushman and Nadler describe teams, committees, or task forces as 'arrangements [that] exert an important influence on organizational learning and innovation' (Tushman and Nadler, 1996: 145).

While the importance of team learning is widely accepted, some authors highlight the high level of complexity and the degree of difficulty associated with team learning (and with teamworking in general). Roth points out that 'team learning and associated organizational changes take place within a larger organizational context' (Roth, 1996: 231). He believes that, 'at various points in time, the differences between how a team learns to operate more effectively, and how the larger system continues to operate, create conflict' (*ibid.*). Critchley and Casey (1996) express similar sentiments, arguing that in many areas of management activity teams are unnecessary, and are more likely to promote puzzlement and scepticism than learning.

Despite these dissenting voices, most academics and managers would agree that teamworking is an essential part of almost any successful organisation. More importantly for our work here, team learning has the potential to provide a bridge between individual learning and organisational learning.

Training and learning

In this section we distinguish between what Leymann (1989) calls 'unorganized learning' and training, which is organised learning. Individual learning can result from training, but a successful learning organisation requires not only a comprehensive training programme, but also a way of encouraging, and benefiting from, unorganised learning. Jones and Hendry believe that, 'however much training and self-development takes place in organizations, people still learn using a second agenda' (Jones and Hendry, 1994: 157). This may involve informal processes, gossip, new skills, indeed all varieties of learning. They believe that Leymann's 'unorganized learning' is 'an important and integral aspect of individual and organizational development' (*ibid.*). This suggests that an emphasis on formal training and development may come only at the expense of other aspects of learning, a view which is supported by Argyris (1993). Jones and Hendry believe that 'much of what inhibits learning derives from how we have hitherto perceived people developing in organizations' (Jones and Hendry, 1994: 157). In practice, however, some organisations seem to focus on formal, prescriptive training and development programmes when trying to improve learning. This can be the case even when the organisation has explicitly stated its desire to become a learning organisation. Of the case companies, Morgan Crucible and Siebe have made training and development programmes the focus of their organisational learning efforts. Morgan Crucible's training and development programme consists of a comprehensive series of modules designed to 'enhance personal and professional performance' (*Morgan Management Training and Development*, internal publication). Siebe has a very lean structure, which means that the ability to recruit highly talented individuals is often placed above the ability to develop them. The Vice-President of Human Resources believes that, 'from a pure learning point of view, [the company's strategy] is going to be hiring somebody with the talent coming in that can grow'. Empirical evidence contradicts this view of organisational learning as a driver for increased training. The prevailing view is that changes in training and development occur, not as a result of attempts to achieve organisational learning, but more as a result of external pressures. The Employers' Manpower and Skills Development Survey found that the strongest motivator for changes in training and development was the desire to improve quality standards to meet increased competition (Dench, 1993). Common sense and the author's experience suggest that customer requirements are often another important reason for introducing more training. This driver may be the result of individual customers demanding better service, or it may be the result of an organisation's insistence that a supplier has quality standards, such as BS5750 or ISO 9000, in place.

Browne and Duguid (1991) argue that conventional learning theory, implicit in most training and development programmes, tends to endorse the value of abstract knowledge at the expense of actual practice. Thus learning is separated from working. They use workplace studies to show that espoused practice does not take account of the actual conditions of work. They recommend a 'communities of practice' approach to learning, in which workplace learning is viewed as a way of forming (or joining) communities and changing personal identities.

Overall, the evidence on the relationship between training and learning seems rather confused. It is likely that, while they may be seen as substitutes by some managers, the two concepts are relatively unrelated in practice. This is suggested by Leymann's (1989) division of learning into the organised and the unorganised. Thus training and development can be seen, not as a substitute for learning, but as an additional way of improving the skills and abilities both of individuals and of the organisation. An alternative view, exemplified by Jones and Hendry (1994), is to see training as a barrier, or a hindrance, to learning.

From individual learning to organisational learning

We have seen the importance of individual learning as the starting point for learning in the organisation, and have also seen that team learning can act as a bridge between individual learning and organisational learning. We now turn to the questions of the meaning of organisational learning and how it takes place. Definitions and explanations of organisational learning are given elsewhere in this book and their repetition here would serve little purpose. Thus we move first to examine the way in which individual learning and team learning can add to the organisation's memory and lead to organisational learning. This is followed by a detailed examination of some of the problems and criticisms surrounding organisational learning.

Child (1997) argues that organisational learning focuses on the individuals and teams within organisations which learn, but that the concept has difficulty in explaining how, and under what conditions, that learning is transformed into an organisational property. Even more critically, Czeglédy argues that 'organisations do not learn, people do; all frames of reference must follow from this social fact' (Czeglédy, 1996: 238). He argues that it is better to talk of learning in organisations rather than learning organisations. Further, he believes that there needs to be a shift from organisational learning as a bureaucratic, institutional monopoly to organisational learning as an individual activity informed by a range of social and cultural factors.

However, De Geus (1997) offers an interesting analogy from the natural world to illustrate how organisations – as distinct from individuals – can learn. He believes that, provided three conditions are met, an entire species can improve its ability to exploit the opportunities in its environment. The first condition is that the members of the species must have and use the ability to move around, and they must flock or move in herds, rather than sit in isolated territories. To meet the second condition, some individuals must be able to invent new skills or behaviours. The third condition is that the species must have an established process for transmitting a skill from the individual to the entire community, not genetically, but through direct communication. The presence of these three conditions will accelerate learning in the species as a whole, increasing its ability to adapt quickly to fundamental changes in the environment.

The closeness of the analogy between the way species and organisations can learn is clear. The first condition, showing that birds that flock learn faster than those that do not flock, suggests that organisations which encourage flocking behaviour will also encourage organisational learning. De Geus describes management development programmes as an excellent opportunity for flocking, particularly if the training is collaborative. Looking at the second condition, most organisations with several hundred employees should have at least a handful of people curious enough to look for new skills or behaviours. The third condition, the established procedure for transmitting a skill from an individual to the entire organisation, is what De Geus believes is lacking in many organisations. Again, he suggests management development programmes and skunk works (see Peters and Waterman, 1982: 211–12) as ways of disseminating knowledge across the organisation. Having looked at this interesting version of how organisational learning can, and does, take place, it is necessary to examine some of the more sceptical views on the subject.

Organisational learning: an oxymoron?

One of the most powerful criticisms of organisational learning derives from what some commentators believe to be the inherent contradiction between organisation, on the one hand, and learning, on the other. Two of the most articulate proponents of this view are Weick and Westley (1996), who argue that the phrase 'organisational learning' qualifies as an oxymoron. They believe that 'to learn is to disorganize and increase variety. To organize is to forget and reduce variety' (*ibid.*: 440). They argue that this tension between learning and organising is often overlooked by theorists, leading to uncertainty as to whether learning is something new and distinct or merely organisational change by another name. Figure 6.3 shows the author's own view of some of the sources of the tension that Weick and Westley describe. There is always likely to be conflict between the words in the left-hand column, which describe 'organisation', and those in the right-hand column, which describe 'learning'.

The view that organisational learning is devalued by the need to 'choose'

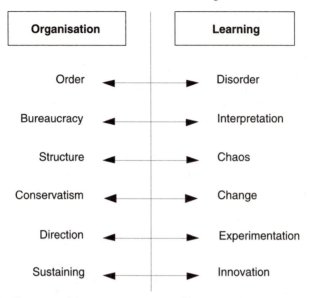

Organisation		**Learning**
Order	← — →	Disorder
Bureaucracy	← — →	Interpretation
Structure	← — →	Chaos
Conservatism	← — →	Change
Direction	← — →	Experimentation
Sustaining	← — →	Innovation

Figure 6.3 The tension between organisation and learning

between learning and organising falls into what Collins and Porras describe as 'the tyranny of the OR' (Collins and Porras, 1996: 43). Alternatively, the same concept can be described as a failure to 'embrace the genius of the AND' (*ibid.*: 44). Collins and Porras argue that successful, visionary companies 'do not oppress themselves with what we call the "Tyranny of the OR" – the rational view that cannot easily accept paradox, that cannot live with two seemingly contradictory forces or ideas at the same time' (Collins and Porras, 1996: 43).

According to Collins and Porras's view, successful organisations distinguish themselves through their ability to manage a series of paradoxes and contradictions. These include the ability to have a purpose beyond profit *yet* pragmatically pursue profit; to have a relatively fixed core ideology *yet* achieve vigorous change and movement; and to have a clear vision and sense of direction *yet* be capable of opportunistic groping and experimentation. In their view, the ability of these companies to manage the contradiction goes beyond mere balance – the company seeks to do well in the long *and* the short run; it seeks to be idealistic *and* highly profitable. Applying this concept to a learning organisation, the company must seek to organise *and* to learn, to innovate *and* to hold on to its core values, and to disorganise for learning *while still* organising for efficiency. This need to learn and organise contrasts markedly with Weick and Westley's view of organising and learning as 'essentially antithetical processes' (Weick and Westley, 1996: 440). Child takes a similar line to Collins and Porras by arguing that 'the tension associated with the paradoxes of organisational life promotes change and has the potential for stimulating organisational evolution' (Child, 1997: 65) In this view, the tensions described by Collins and Porras are actually beneficial to the organisation.

Peters (1992) is another to recognise the problems and possibilities of trying to combine order and disorder. He explicitly acknowledges the need to create a degree of 'chaos' in order to facilitate learning and change. Peters uses the example of Imagination, a creative services company currently helping to manage the Millennium Celebrations, which advocates 'tension and total flexibility'. To most people Imagination's business methods would seem wildly chaotic and unsuited to anything other than the creative businesses in which the company works. Peters, however, believes that all companies can learn from Imagination's lack of structure and hierarchy, and he sees the firm as a model for the future evolution of organisation design.

This theme, of combining order and disorder, is apparent in Peter's earlier work with Robert Waterman (Peters and Waterman, 1982). One of the eight characteristics of excellent companies they identify is the possession of 'simultaneous loose–tight properties'. They describe loose–tight organisations as 'on the one hand rigidly controlled, yet at the same time allowing (indeed insisting on) autonomy, entrepreneurship, and innovation from the rank and file' (*ibid.*: 318). Such an organisation would clearly confound the oxymoron of Weick and Westley's (1996) analysis, by being both organised and able to learn. One of the examples they use is 3M, which they describe as 'marked by barely organized chaos surrounding its product champions' (Peters and Waterman, 1982: 15). At the same time, they quote an analyst who believes that 'the brainwashed members of an extremist political sect are no more conformist in their central beliefs [than 3M managers]' (*ibid.*: 16). Thus, unlike Weick and Westley, Peters and Waterman see chaos as a necessary complement, perhaps even as an antidote, to organisation. There can be little doubt of the difficulty of achieving such a balance, but the advantages of achieving both a high level of order and a high level of learning are evident. As a compromise, we can view learning not as contradicting organisation, but as a way of reorganising, of moving from one state to another.

Organisation and learning: a synthesis

The question of whether organising and learning can co-exist effectively is at the heart of the controversy surrounding the usefulness of the organisational learning concept. A company that can achieve both will have a significant competitive advantage over a company that has to choose one or the other. In their conclusion, Weick and Westley argue that 'learning is an ongoing and implicit feature of the organizing process. By this we mean that as organizing unfolds, it does so in ways that intermittently create a set of conditions where learning is possible' (Weick and Westley, 1996: 456). They believe that organisation must be reduced, and doubt and curiosity cultivated. These changes juxtapose order and disorder, allowing 'sufficient order to sustain a learning entity and sufficient disorder to mobilize forgotten material and new alternatives' (*ibid.*: 456). This juxtaposition is said to represent 'a transient window of opportunity' (*ibid.*).

Weick and Westley thus accept the necessity of combining learning and organisation, but implicitly suggest that organisations must engage in what is effectively a 'trade-off' between the two. Thus, in their view, order and disorder cannot co-exist – the two concepts are seen as mutually exclusive. This contradicts the views of Peters and Waterman (1982), and Collins and Porras (1996), who argue that organisations can 'have their cake and eat it' by effectively combining order and disorder, organisation and learning.

A possible way of combining learning and organisation may be to consider the various spheres of activity within the organisation. Thus it may be possible to have order as a vertical process, but disorder as a horizontal process. 3M is a company that is highly organised in a structural sense and yet encourages learning in a cultural sense. This leads to high levels of complexity but, equally, underpins the company's exceedingly successful record on innovation. Morgan Crucible is highly organised at a holding-company level but less organised at a subsidiary-company level. This encourages learning in the subsidiary companies, but allows financial and organisational control to be imposed from Head Office.

The meaning of learning and organisation

Sandelands and Drazin (1989) point out that learning is an achievement verb. This means that learning refers to both an outcome and a process, giving it a circular, tautological sense. This double meaning serves to conceal rather than reveal the dynamics of the learning process and the exact nature of the outcome.

Organisation is an equally, if not more, difficult concept to define exactly. Sandelands and Srivatsan (1993) argue that organisations cannot be perceived, which has the unavoidable consequence of making it difficult to theorise about them. Weick and Westley believe that 'organizational scientists have too often resorted therefore to theories based on metaphors, as opposed to experience, hence abandoning the healthy tension between experience and conceptualization which drives the natural sciences' (Weick and Westley, 1996: 441).

If it is difficult to conceptualise organisations while using experience as a reference point, then, clearly, developing a useful theory of organisational learning will also be difficult. If the exact meaning of learning is unclear, either because of the double meaning of the word 'learning' or because of the confusion between individual learning and organisational learning, then this can only compound the problem. Weick and Westley believe that 'such side-stepping of issues [i.e. reliable explanations of organisation and learning] leaves us again with the depressing lack of a truly social science of organization or of learning' (Weick and Westley, 1996: 442).

Converting learning into action: achieving new behaviours

If organisational learning can be shown to have taken place, then the next step in demonstrating its usefulness is to show that learning has led to a change in organisational behaviour. If this is the case it becomes possible to contest the widely held view that the concept of organisational learning is no more than management rhetoric. If it can be shown that organisational learning does take place and leads to changes in the organisation's actions, then there can be no doubt that the concept has true meaning. Below we discuss three potential inhibitors of action. The presence of particular political power relationships, control structures and cultural precedents means that learning may fail to result in new behaviour. Politics, control and culture may lead to the maintenance of inappropriate behaviour and thus limit the development of new behaviours. Thus they can limit the organisation's ability to 'unlearn', to discard obsolete and misleading knowledge. Hedberg (1981) and Johannessen and Hauan (1994) are powerful advocates of the need for organisations to unlearn. Political, control and cultural factors are closely interrelated in many complex ways, and so there is a natural overlap between their effects on organisational learning.

Converting learning into action: the importance of politics

One criticism often levelled against the concept of the learning organisation is that it ignores the crucial role of organisational politics. In this view, the learning organisation is seen as a worthy idea that is doomed to fail at the hands of cynical organisational members. Organisational politics has been defined as 'the process whereby differentiated but interdependent individuals or interest groups exercise whatever power they can amass to influence the goals, criteria, or processes used in organisational decision-making to advance their own interests' (Miles, 1980). Senge (1990a: 273) defines a political environment somewhat more simply as one in which the 'who' is more important than the 'what'. He also admits that 'office politics and conservative thought patterns are far more ingrained in corporations' (Senge, quoted in Griffith, 1995: 15) than he expected when he originally put forward his ideas.

Jones and Hendry believe that organisations 'tend to engage only in acceptable learning – that is, learning which supports the organisation's structure and how people should act within it' (Jones and Hendry, 1994: 158). They argue that much useful learning may be negated by the influence of power and politics. Coopey (1996) maintains that power and politics are omnipresent, and that proponents of the learning organisation ignore the reality of political activity, power and influence, which are all likely to impede learning. In his thoughtful article, Coopey places the learning organisation in a framework of assumptions about power and political activity that is conspicuous by its absence in much of the literature. He argues that the characteristics of a learning organisation have an interesting effect on the distribution of power within an organisation. He believes that changes in structure and increments in collective knowledge will tend to favour those formally appointed as managers, especially at the most senior levels. Their enhanced access to the points at which power is exercised, both internally and externally, may help to build up and safeguard their power. Other members of the organisation who feel that their power and position is threatened may act defensively, restricting the possibility of learning resulting in new behaviour. Thus we have a situation where not only can the exercise of power and politics in an organisation limit organisational learning, but organisational learning itself can increase the importance of power and politics. This implies serious negative consequences for the long-term usefulness of organisational learning. This view is supported by Kanter's (1989b) finding that in new forms of organisation designed to deal with external turbulence political action increases considerably and political skills are at a premium. However, we must remember that power and politics will be important factors in any change programme and are by no means limited to organisational learning. Evidence from the case companies regarding the importance of politics is relatively limited. Many of the managers who mentioned politics did so in order to play down its importance. Richard Bradford, Vice-President of Human Resources at Siebe, tacitly acknowledges the role that politics can play in an organisation, but believes that Siebe has avoided this. He says:

> my experience is the leanness of the structure takes away from the polit-
> icalness of [the competition between managers for promotion]. People
> simply don't have the time or the inclination, they're trying to perform
> their task to achieve results, and if you're focused on the results you're
> not focused on the politicalness of the organisation.
>
> (Richard Bradford, Vice-President of Human Resources, Siebe)

By contrast, Mike Fell, Human Resource Director at Mayflower's Automotive Division, highlighted the defensive reactions of many people when confronted with the prospect of change. He outlined the question most often asked when a change is introduced – 'What's happening to my job?' – and then emphasised, in typically imaginative language, the need to show that 'their job is quite clearly Top of the Pops'. In Graham's (1996: 2) survey of organisational learning, 46 per cent of respondents cited company politics as a major obstacle to knowledge creation and information-sharing in their organisation. Noticeably, politics were seen as more important in large companies: 55 per cent of corporations with revenues of more than $10 billion cited political factors as barriers to the flow of knowledge, compared with only 34 per cent of firms with revenues of below $100 million.

In truth, the importance of politics is likely to vary from situation to situation, and from company to company. However, there can be little doubt that it is a significant consideration for companies seeking to become learning organisations. The ability to reduce, or at least manage, the impact of political considerations may be a major factor in helping to convert learning into action.

Converting learning into action: the importance of control

Argyris and Schön argue that 'to focus on learning without taking into account the legitimate need for control is to embark on a romantic and usually fruitless exercise' (Argyris and Schön, 1983: 3–4). Once again, echoing Weick and Westley (1996), this suggests that the learning organisation is essentially antithetical to good business practice. Clearly there will be an inevitable tension between learning, involving as it does the relinquishing of power, and control, which involves the exercise of power.

Pedler *et al.* (1991) take a relatively egalitarian view of control, although it is implicitly assumed that it will be managers who exercise control. By contrast, Garratt (1987) is more elitist, regarding direction-giving as the directors' 'brain function'. He believes that the role of the directors is to 'monitor what is happening in day-to-day operations, check what is happening in the wider environment, and then take decisions on how best to deploy the limited resources they control to achieve their objectives in the given conditions' (*ibid.*: 33). In Garratt's view effective directors are those who act on George Bernard Shaw's maxim: 'Get what you like or you get to like what you get.'

Coopey (1996) presents the question of control in an interesting way by discussing the drawing of a 'control boundary' between management and other employees. He argues that the continuing pressures on organisations operating in turbulent environments to become ever more productive means that the more optimistic predictions for shifting this boundary to give more responsibility to non-managers will not be realised. This is likely to have negative effects for both individual and collective learning if learning depends on control and responsibility. Likewise, if control lies elsewhere employees will have less opportunity (and less incentive) to apply what they learn. Hence, we hypothesise, based on Coopey's conclusions, that the maintenance of relatively centralised control, despite the rhetoric regarding empowerment, has inhibited learning in many organisations. This is disputed by managers in the case companies, however. They argue, seemingly in unison, that control has shifted towards (if not to) employees. At CCSB's Wakefield plant one of the most striking features is the level of autonomy and accountability given to the line workers. Empowerment is seen as central to the process and employees have secured a high level of control over their own work. One example of this is the policy of allowing staff to recruit others reporting immediately to them. Teams likewise recruit their own members. Control of recruiting decisions has thus passed down from the Human Resources Department to the shop floor. Siebe's Group Development Director, Harry Craig, believes that for any project to be successful control must be passed to the project group concerned. At 3M, Ken Jackson, Director of Human Resources, talks of the 'freeing up of job roles', while John Mueller, 3M's Chairman and Chief Executive, speaks of the 'value placed on initiatives of the individual'. Mayflower Automotive Division's Human Resource Director, Mike Fell, also emphasises the importance of delegating power, while Bruce Farmer, Managing Director of Morgan Crucible, speaks of 'pushing accountability way down the line'. The five case companies have the same experience of and views on the issue of control – concluding that more control must be passed to employees. The results from the case companies seem to be corroborated by the available empirical data. A survey of readers of *Personnel Management* by Saggers (1994) found that companies are devolving responsibility for training and development to line managers. It reported that 65 per cent of employers had increased the involvement of line managers in training over the previous two years, compared with 5 per cent who had reduced it. Similarly, a Training Trends survey among members of the Industrial Society (1996) found that 41 per cent of respondents thought that the trend toward the devolution of training budgets was unlikely to be reversed in the subsequent two to three years. It is difficult to characterise the statements of the interviewees listed above as mere management rhetoric because, in the majority of cases, they are supported both by internal examples and, more generally, by empirical data. On this basis we can conclude that control has, to some extent, become less centralised. This should help in converting organisational learning to new behaviour.

Converting learning into action: the importance of culture

Edgar Schein's work on corporate culture, together with his later work on organisational learning, highlights the importance of culture in encouraging effective learning. Schein says that an organisation's culture is: 'what it has learned as a social unit over the course of its history' (Schein, 1985: 12). He defines culture as composed of 'artefacts', such as dress codes and office layouts, 'values', which he says are often enshrined in stories, and 'underlying assumptions', which concern both behaviour within the organisation and the interaction of the organisation with its environment. Senge (1990a) calls these underlying assumptions 'mental models'. They are fundamental world-views, reflected in structures and processes, that reinforce the values of the organisation. Schein's major work, *Organizational Culture and Leadership* (1985), is predicated on the belief that managing cultural change is the key to successful leadership. Lundberg argues that:

> the more fully managers understand the effects, both intended and unintended, of the way they manage, the more likely they are to enhance learning in, and by, their organizations. Since cultures in organizations explain so much about their behaviour, it follows that an appreciation, and an informed understanding, of organizational cultures is not only useful but perhaps is a prerequisite for organization management now as well as in the future.
>
> (Lundberg, 1996: 491)

Clearly, in Schein's and Lundberg's opinion, an organization that can effectively manage its culture has gone a long way towards effective management.

The nature of culture and the way it is created and shared amongst a group of people mean that learning is inherent in culture. Many definitions of organisational learning show the importance of culture through their choice of phrases which mimic definitions of culture. Argote and McGrath believe that 'organizational learning focuses on how organizations acquire knowledge as they gain experience, how this knowledge is embedded in organizations, and what the effect of such changes is on later performance' (Argote and McGrath, 1993: 53). From this it is clear that culture is central to Argote and McGrath's view of organisational learning. Normann goes further by explicitly linking culture to organisational learning:

> I would interpret the increasing interest in the concept of culture as really an increasing interest in organizational learning – in understanding and making conscious and effective as much as possible all the learning that has taken place in an organization.
>
> (Normann, 1985: 231)

He argues that merely 'to be aware of culture is to increase the likelihood of learning' (Normann, 1985: 231). In a more general vein, Weick and Westley conclude that: 'conceptualizing organizations as cultures makes it easier to talk about learning' (Weick and Westley, 1996: 442).

We have seen that the concept of corporate culture offers a useful way of looking at organisational learning, and that managing culture is important in facilitating both change and learning. The twin questions of how culture effects the transition from learning to action and which type of culture is most conducive to organisational learning are considered below.

Lundberg believes that 'organizational culture both fuels and fosters learning in organizations, as well as learning by organizations' (Lundberg, 1996: 507). Ulrich *et al.* (1993) have also argued that to enhance learning a fundamental change in culture is required. However, Dibella *et al.* (1996) argue that this is not the case, citing their research at Fiat. They believe that 'organizations may enhance their learning by improving what they already do well. Improving what one already does is a less threatening way of developing learning capabilities' (*ibid.*: 377). Despite this dissenting voice, it is clear that the 'wrong' culture can inhibit organisational learning.

Many of the learning disabilities listed by Senge (1990a: 17–26) have their roots in an organisation's culture. One of the most striking examples of this is what Senge describes as 'The Enemy is Out There'. He believes that we all have 'a propensity to find someone or something outside ourselves to blame when things go wrong' (Senge, 1990a: 19). He continues by arguing that some organizations elevate this propensity to a commandment – 'thou shalt always find an external agent to blame'. One example of this phenomenon is the way in which departments within a company blame one another for difficulties. Marketing blames low sales on the poor manufacturing quality. Manufacturing blames quality problems on poor design by engineering. In turn, engineering blames design faults on interference from marketing. At a wider level, the failure of many Western companies has been blamed on Japanese competition. Often two sides in a dispute will each blame the other, with, for example, unions criticising management for poor pay and conditions, and management criticising unions for adopting restrictive practices and taking strike action. McGill *et al.* also recognise this problem in arguing that 'two common inclinations among managers are to blame others when things go wrong and to resign themselves to living with less-than-desirable situations' (McGill *et al.*, 1992: 15). Always seeking to blame someone else is an example of a cultural difficulty that impedes learning. The culture of blame means that those people capable of solving the problem do not do so because they believe it is someone else's fault. If the blame lies elsewhere, then so, the logic follows, must the solution. A blame-free culture in which allocating blame is unacceptable is thus a positive way of encouraging learning. Without the need to allocate blame, departments can work together to solve sales/design/quality problems, and management and unions can work together to solve their collective difficulties.

Another of the learning disabilities listed by Senge is 'The Fixation on Events'. He believes that:

> conversations in organizations are dominated by concern with events: last month's sales, the new budget cuts, last quarter's earnings, who just got promoted or fired, the new product our competitors just announced, the delay that was just announced in our new product, and so on.
>
> (Senge, 1990a: 21)

This tendency to focus on short-term events is reinforced by the media. After all, yesterday's news is no news. The problem with this fixation on short-term events is, Senge believes, that:

the primary threats to our survival, both of our organizations and of our societies, come not from sudden events but from slow, gradual processes; the arms race, environmental decay, the erosion of a society's public education system, increasingly obsolete physical capital, and decline in design or product quality (at least relative to competitors' quality) are all slow, gradual processes.

(Senge, 1990a: 22)

The way in which short-term events dominate people's thinking is a result of organisational (and societal) cultures that value short-term results. Values (a key part of culture) are often enshrined in the stories told in organisations, and if many of the stories are about short-term events this will inevitably perpetuate the idea that short-term results are valued and long-term results, the bigger picture, can safely be left for someone else to worry about.

Argyris (1990) offers a culturalist explanation for the failure of many management teams to learn from mistakes. This leads to a *Groundhog Day* situation in which the same mistakes are repeated again and again. Argyris believes that most managers find teamworking inherently threatening, especially when it examines problem areas. He believes that many organisational cultures reinforce this by rewarding people who advocate their views effectively, rather than those who enquire into complex issues. Many senior managers prefer someone who presents them with the solution to a minor problem to someone who points out a major problem with the company's current policies. Managers learn not to raise difficult issues so as to avoid looking uncertain or ignorant. Argyris describes this as 'skilled incompetence' – teams of people who are highly skilled at both avoiding learning and avoiding applying anything that they do learn. Mike Fell, Human Resource Director at Mayflower's Automotive Division, recognises the importance, and the difficulty, of avoiding this problem. He suggests that 'you've got to swallow a bit of pride occasionally. The benefit for the whole business could be massive. You could stop three other MDs making the same mistake by saying: "I didn't realise this. I've been in this industry thirty years and I did this last week. Christ, I feel embarrassed telling you, but please guys, it's a watch out." ' He acknowledges the difficulty of encouraging managers to do this, saying: 'that takes a bit of brave pills, that does'.

It is clear from Senge's (1990a) and Argyris's (1990) examples of learning disabilities that culture can inhibit learning and can prevent organisations from applying what they learn. Culture can prevent learning being converted into action because culture often leads organisations to adopt a highly conservative approach in preservation of the status quo.

Organisational learning: a source of superior behaviour?

If organisational learning has resulted in a change in behaviour the obvious question that must be asked (following Figure 6.1) is whether or not this new behaviour is superior to the organisation's original behaviour. If this can be shown to be the case it is difficult to avoid the conclusion that organisational learning is beneficial in changing organisational behaviour and improving performance. There are, however, a number of problems that must be overcome in order to conclude that any changes as a result of organisational learning are superior forms of behaviour. First, there is the inherent problem of measuring the results of any change programme: it is difficult to know what the behaviour would have been if the programme had not taken place. Second, there is the problem of causality: it is difficult to know whether the change in behaviour is the result of organisational learning. Third, even if benefits have been successfully attributed to organisational learning there is the problem of measuring their extent.

Identifying the benefits of organisational learning: the impossibility of knowing the non-occurring alternative

One of the key difficulties of determining the benefits of organisational learning is the fact that it is impossible to know what the results would have been had organisational learning not occurred. I call this problem the impossibility of knowing the non-occurring alternative. More formally, it is 'the application of counterfactual reasoning' – a well-known problem in history and the social sciences. It was most notably applied to questioning the impact of railways on economic development (see Fogel, 1964). Even if organisational learning has resulted in a change in behaviour, and even if this change in behaviour is better than the organisation's starting point, we are still unable to say that organisational learning is the best available strategy. This is because there is no way of knowing whether another strategy – one which the company could have adopted but chose not to – would have been more successful.

Many works which ascribe significant benefits to becoming learning organisations overlook this problem. This is most true when looking at case studies of individual companies. For example, Marquardt (1996) attributes

'Rover's incredible turnaround' largely to its decision to become a learning organisation. He writes:

> Rover has grown and benefited immensely over the past five years as an emerging learning organization. There has been a continuous flow of improvements initiated and generated through learning by empowered employees. Learning has indeed resulted in a better bottom line, happier employees, and a superior globalwide reputation.
>
> (Marquardt, 1996: 208)

Indeed, the chapter that this quotation comes from is entitled 'Rover – one organization's journey to success as a learning organization' (Marquardt, 1996: 193–208). To be fair to Marquardt, he is perhaps only reporting the views of Rover people: 'top management and employees are unanimous and quick to attribute the new prosperity to Rover's successful journey toward becoming a learning organization' (*ibid.*: 194). We could speculate as to other possible causes of Rover's success in the years 1990–5 – the benefits of privatisation, capital injection from British Aerospace, the results of its partnership with Honda – or we could question the extent to which it has genuinely been successful – plant closures, redundancies, four consecutive years of trading at a loss between 1990 and 1993, its eventual sale to BMW – but perhaps it is better just to question the wisdom of attributing so much to Rover's attempts to become a learning organisation. Equally, we cannot know how successful Rover would have been without its focus on learning. Indeed, other authors have presented a more ambiguous view of Rover's success (see, for example, Pilkington, 1996a).

Marquardt is not the only writer to fall into the trap of almost unquestioningly attributing successes to organisational learning. Tobin (1993) makes a similar misjudgement when assessing Digital's performance. He claims that 'Digital was successful in selling networks in the mid-1980s because it created a unique learning environment for all members of its networks-related businesses' (*ibid.*: 172). This raises more questions than it answers: what are the reasons for Digital's relatively lacklustre performance in the 1990s? How much of its success was due to learning? And, most notably for our analysis here, how well would it have performed without the emphasis on learning?

In the case companies a number of managers were also keen to talk of the benefits of organisational learning, and typically saw it as a valuable source of competitive advantage. Andy McIntosh, Director of Group Personnel at Morgan Crucible, says: 'I think any organisation that sets out to be a learning organisation is one which inevitably has a competitive advantage.' Similarly, at CCSB Keith Dennis, the Personnel Director, believes that 'learning and copying are both great forms of competitive advantage as long as you adapt them'.

In truth, the extent to which benefits can be ascribed to organisational learning depends, to a great extent, on the breadth of the definition of organisational learning. If organisational learning is widely construed – as an umbrella term for a disparate group of management practices, including quality programmes, training and development programmes, and organisational strategy development – it is likely that many benefits can be attributed to this basket of activities. If, however, organisational learning is seen as a distinct practice removed from existing management programmes and practices, then it is likely to be far more difficult to attribute any benefits to organisational learning.

Identifying the benefits of organisational learning: the difficulty of determining causality

Probably the most significant problem in determining the usefulness of organisational learning concerns the question of causality. The question we must ask is whether organisational learning causes an otherwise ordinary company to become successful, or whether successful companies choose to become learning organisations. Alec Reed, Founder and Executive Chairman of Reed Executive, offers a good illustration of the difficulty of determining causality. He argues that grand marble entrance halls are more likely to be found in successful companies. However, he points out that it is unlikely that the companies' successes were caused by the impressive nature of their entrance halls. Rather, the causality is reversed: it is likely that the success of these companies enabled them to lavish resources on their entrance halls which less successful companies would be unable to afford. Thus a grand entrance hall is a sign of success, but by no means a cause of success. The same argument could be made for grand dining rooms, expensive notepaper, lavish expense accounts, large bonuses or landscaped grounds as causes of superior performance.

Thus to show that organisational learning is useful it is not enough simply to show that companies that practise organisational learning are more successful than those that do not. This does not imply that all companies should adopt organisational learning as their route to success. If we are to conclude that organisational learning is a useful concept we must establish that organisational learning is the cause, or at least one cause, of superior performance.

One possibility is that organisational learning and success are mutually reinforcing. A virtuous circle is formed in which increasing investment in organisational learning leads to greater success, this leads to higher profits (assuming success is equated with profitability) and, in turn, to more money available for investment in organisational learning. This is similar to the situation which seems to prevail at 3M. The company has a large number of successful technologies, which it uses to create successful products. These products generate significant financial returns, which are invested in the company's efforts to create new technologies. These new technologies (or a combination of existing technologies) are used to create more successful products, which, in turn, increase returns. Similarly, it may be that companies that adopt the rhetoric of organisational learning, regardless of whether they practise it, are more likely to have adopted a series of other, beneficial policies, particularly those in related fields such as human resource management (HRM).

Identifying the benefits of organisational learning: measuring the results

Garvin (1993) is one of the few writers to address the need for a measurement of an organisation's rate and level of learning. He uses the old maxim, well known by managers, that 'if you can't measure it, you can't manage it'. The traditional solution to measuring learning is the use of learning curves and, later, experience curves. *Learning curves* show the way in which a company's costs decrease as it increases cumulative volume, while *experience curves* show that costs and prices in a whole industry fall as total production increases. The logical competitive strategy derived from these curves is simple. Companies must rapidly increase their production, ahead of their competitors, to enjoy the benefits of lower costs, lower prices and increased market share. These measures are clearly inadequate, for a number of reasons, when we are trying to assess the results of organisational learning. First, they take only a single measure of output (cost or price) and ignore other significant variables such as quality, design or time to market. Second, they imply that production volume is the ultimate cause of learning. This ignores the possibility of drivers for learning such as new technology, competing products and government regulation. Third, such measures tell us little about the sources of learning or why change takes place.

Another measure, the *half-life curve*, addresses some of the problems with learning and experience curves. A half-life curve, as it is used by managers rather than scientists, measures the time it takes to achieve a 50 per cent improvement in a specific measure of performance. It was originally developed by Analog Devices, a leading semi-conductor company. The half-life curve has the advantage that it can be used to assess a range of performance measures, such as quality rates, on-time deliveries, time to market and productivity. The reasoning behind the half-life curve is that companies with short half-lives are taking less time to improve and so must be learning faster than their competitors. Garvin believes that half-life curves or other performance measures are vital for determining whether changes in behaviour have produced results: 'without them, companies would lack a rationale for investing in learning and the assurance that learning was serving the organisation's ends' (Garvin, 1993: 91). The difficulty with the use of half-life curves, however, is that they do not help to establish causality.

Tobin is another to emphasise the importance of being able to measure the benefits of organisational learning. He believes that becoming a learning organisation, which he describes as a 'bet-your-job' or even a 'bet-your-company' investment, requires investments that 'cannot be made casually or without having clear, measurable goals' (Tobin, 1993: 227).

A major difficulty when trying to measure the benefits of learning is the non-quantifiable nature of many of the potential benefits. Some benefits, such as a reduction in time to market, are likely to be difficult to measure in purely financial terms, although they will be measurable. Other benefits, such as increased loyalty to the organisation from employees, will be almost impossible to measure meaningfully, although proxies such as labour turnover may be of some use. Tobin recognises this difficulty, arguing that it is 'not very wise to try to justify each separate program element on the basis of ROI [return on investment]' (Tobin, 1993: 241).

A wider problem with the measurement of organisational success in general is the lack of agreement on a single, definitive measure of even purely financial success. There are many possible financial indicators with which to assess company performance, each with its advocates and opponents, and its associated advantages and disadvantages. Each measure, however, offers only a limited view of an organisation's performance. In an attempt to alleviate this problem various writers have suggested the use of multiple measures, financial and non-financial, to assess organisational performance. Kaplan and Norton (1992), for example, suggest the use of a 'balanced scorecard' which provides a comprehensive set of financial and non-financial measures that encompass both internal and external perspectives. This allows all aspects of the organisation's performance to be linked and assessed. Taking a similar approach, Maisel (1992) offers a detailed 'balanced scorecard', taking in financial measures (profitability, growth, shareholder value), customer measures (time, quality, service, price), business process measures (time, quality, productivity, cost) and human resource measures (innovation, education and training people, and intellectual assets). This approach is likely to be much more useful when assessing, not only overall company performance, but the results of an organisational learning initiative. It is interesting to note that 3M and CCSB are both beginning to follow the approach of using a range of measures. 3M has published targets for sales generated from new products, earnings per share, return on capital employed and return on equity, while CCSB focuses on sales volume, profitability and market share.

Another major problem with measuring the results of organisational learning is the fact that many of the likely benefits will be realised only in the long term. This is a point that is ignored by both Garvin (1993) and Tobin (1993). Potential benefits such as increased employee loyalty and reduced staff turnover, an enhanced sense of *esprit de corps* and increased creativity are not only difficult to measure in financial terms, but likely to become apparent only gradually and to yield benefits into the long term.

A further related problem is knowing whether any benefits, measurable or otherwise, will be maintained in the long term. The difficulty of maintaining success has been highlighted by the problems faced by Peters and Waterman's (1982) so-called excellent companies. By 1987 the fortunes of some of the case companies had plummeted to such an extent that Peters began *Thriving on Chaos* (1987) with the line 'there are no excellent companies'. Five years after the publication of *In Search of Excellence* (Peters and Waterman, 1982) only 14 of the 43 excellent companies could still be classified as excellent using Peters and Waterman's original criteria. Atari, Avon, DuPont, IBM, People's Express and Wang Computers were among the most notable failures. This demonstrates the difficulty of maintaining success even in the medium term. The nature of many of the benefits of organisational learning means that they may be more sustainable in the long run. Potential benefits such as increased employee loyalty and enhanced creativity are likely to be difficult for competitors to emulate and so will be sustained sources of competitive advantage. However, there is as yet no way of knowing whether or not these advantages, such as they are, will be sustained in the long run.

The usefulness of organisational learning: a summary

The key message in this section has been that in order to be useful organisational learning must result in a change to behaviour that is superior to the organisation's original behaviour. The process begins with individual learning, which can, in turn, lead to organisational learning. This learning can then be applied and result in new behaviours. However, a number of factors (politics, control and culture) exist which can make the transformation of learning into action problematic. Once a change in behaviour has occurred, there are a number of problems that must be overcome before it is possible to conclude that the behaviour is superior. First, there is the impossibility of knowing the non-occurring alternative, which means that the drawing of conclusions about the usefulness of organisational learning relative to alternative techniques is fraught with danger. Second, there is the difficulty of determining causality. It is difficult to ascribe any changes in organisational performance to a single cause. In most cases the relationship between cause and effect is highly complex, and characterised by a high degree of mutuality and feedback. Third, there is the range of problems associated with measuring the effects of organisational learning. Many benefits are difficult to quantify, while other benefits may become visible only over a protracted period.

Overall, the usefulness of organisational learning can be considered in terms of two closely related, but nevertheless distinct, aspects. First, there is the question of its usefulness to academics as an explanation of organisational behaviour. Second, there is the question of its usefulness to managers as a guiding principle in the management of their businesses. Which of these – in some ways competing – tests of usefulness organisational learning passes depends on the way it is defined. If organisational learning is tightly defined – as in 'organisations are seen as learning by encoding inferences from history into routines that guide behaviour' (Levitt and March, 1988: 320) – it may well be useful as an explanation of certain, limited, types of organisational behaviour. Its usefulness to managers as a guiding principle, however, will be virtually nil if it is defined in this way.

If organisational learning is far more loosely defined, perhaps as an umbrella term for a disparate group of management practices – such as empowerment, teamworking, total quality management, vision definition and cross-functional working – its usefulness as a guiding principle for managers will be significantly greater. Equally, however, if organisational learning is so broadly defined its usefulness as an explanation of organisational behaviours will be severely limited.

The relevance of organisational learning

In the second part of this chapter we turn to look at the relevance of organisational learning. Many writers implicitly suggest that organisational learning is equally applicable to all organisations. Experience shows, however, that the search for one management solution that will work for all businesses in all situations is likely to prove fruitless. In his critique of *In Search of Excellence* (Peters and Waterman, 1982), Thomas points out that the authors 'generalized from the experience of particular types of firms in particular contexts to all firms in all contexts' (Thomas, 1993: 180). Even if we can say that organisational learning is a useful concept for businesses and/or for academics this does not mean that it will be equally useful for different groups. It may be that organisational learning is particularly relevant to certain groups but of little relevance to other groups. In this section we will assess the relevance of organisational learning to a range of different groups in a range of different situations.

Organisational learning in different situations

There are certain situations in which learning is likely to be particularly important for an organisation. For example, if an organisation launches an improvement to an existing product in an existing market the immediate need for learning may be relatively limited. On the other hand, if the organisation enters an entirely new market with an entirely new product it will have to assimilate a whole range of new information and behaviours. Thus the specific situation that the organisation faces may help to determine the relevance of organisational learning.

One situation that offers great scope for learning is the launch of an alliance or a joint-venture operation. Inkpen argues that 'one of the driving forces behind the increased use of strategic alliances is the realisation that self-sufficiency is becoming increasingly difficult in an international business environment that demands both strategic focus and flexibility' (Inkpen, 1995: 1). One of the areas in which self-sufficiency is difficult is learning, especially when an organisation needs specialised knowledge of an overseas market. Hamel (1991) argues that an important factor in the trend towards international joint ventures and strategic alliances is the use of the collaboration as a platform for organisational learning, giving firms access to the skills and capabilities of their partners.

A divergent view is offered by Pilkington, who doubts the value of Rover's learning from its joint venture with Honda. He argues that 'Rover did not learn enough from the Honda collaboration to forestall its sale by BAe' (Pilkington, 1996b:108). He concludes by arguing that in matters of capability exchange and organisational learning it is internal institutional settings, rather than external issues such as market entry and commercial risk-bearing, that need to be understood. More generally, however, Inkpen concurs with Hamel, arguing that joint ventures: 'can provide firms with access to the embedded knowledge of other organisations' (Inkpen, 1995: 1). He believes that the differences in skills and knowledge between partners can act as the fuel for learning. It is the identification and internalisation of these differences that leads to learning. Huber (1991) refers to the internalising of skills and knowledge from partner organisations as 'grafting', noting that this is a process which allows organisations to increase their store of knowledge by internalising knowledge not previously available within the organisation. Kanter is another to emphasise the importance of learning in joint ventures and alliances. She argues that a good relationship between the partners depends on the creation of 'a dense web of interpersonal connections that enhance learning' (Kanter, 1994: 97). Joint ventures and strategic alliances are thus an excellent environment for the application of organisational learning, and an area in which the concept is highly relevant as an explanation of organisational behaviour.

Similarly, when the organisation is part of a network of other organisations, which is often the case in Asian cultures, its opportunities for learning will be relatively high. Again, in these circumstances organisations should be relatively likely to apply the ideas of organisational learning, and the concept of organisational learning should be a relatively good way of explaining organisational behaviour.

Organisational learning in large and small organisations

Goffee and Scase (1995) argue convincingly that small organisations undergo significant changes as they grow. They build on Mintzberg's (1983) model of organisational structures and processes to show that each of the five parts of an organisation described by Mintzberg's model changes as the organisation grows bigger. One of the most significant changes occurs in the way in which the organisation creates information and takes decisions based on the information it possesses. This suggests that organisational learning is unlikely to be equally relevant for organisations of different sizes.

Tobin notes that 'small businesses that are attempting to become learning organizations have both advantages and disadvantages with respect to their larger counterparts' (Tobin, 1993: xxvii). He believes that one of the advantages possessed by smaller companies is the lack of a massive bureaucracy, which may continue to hinder the change efforts of larger companies. This should allow smaller companies to alter organisational design and business processes quickly, easily and effectively in comparison to larger companies.

Tobin sees the major disadvantage faced by smaller companies as the fact that they will typically lack a training and development function. He characterises small companies as 'so strapped for time, personnel, and funds that employee training and development has taken a backseat to more pressing needs' (Tobin, 1993: xxvii). He argues, however, that all small organisations will need to create a training and development function as they grow, and that this is best done with organisational learning in mind.

Graham's (1996) survey of organisational learning for the *Economist* Intelligence Unit found that large companies experienced greater barriers to learning, such as organisational politics. However, they were also making greater efforts to encourage organisational learning. Larger companies have a greater incidence of corporate programmes pursuing formal organisational learning applications. Additionally, their use of organisational learning tools and theories was increasing at a faster rate than in small companies.

The fact that small organisations face both advantages and disadvantages relative to their larger competitors when attempting to apply organisational learning makes it difficult to assess whether organisational learning is more relevant to one or the other. A tentative conclusion can be drawn that organisational learning is clearly applicable to large organisations. After all, most examples of successful learning organisations are drawn from the ranks of large organisations. Admittedly, this may be due to the fact that relatively little research has been carried out in small and medium-sized enterprises (SMEs). However, there is little or no reason to suppose that organisational learning should not be equally applicable to small organisations, with their attendant advantages of reduced bureaucracy and greater speed.

Organisational learning in different industries

Intuitively, organisational learning seems most likely to appeal in those industries where employees are clearly the main assets of the business. Obvious examples include professional organisations such as accountancy firms, management consultancies and advertising agencies. However, companies in these industries have not been especially prominent among learning organisations. Books that include case studies of successful learning organisations certainly include companies from a wide range of industries.

In my own survey of organisational learning practice all the participating organisations were classified by industrial sector using the 1992 Standard

Industrial Classification. Table 6.1 shows the distribution of the 160 participating organisations, which were aggregated into four sectors.

The results of this grouping of participating organisations by industrial sector was then cross-tabulated with the answers to the other questions in order to determine whether the extent of organisational learning varied between different industrial sectors. No statistically significant results were produced, which suggests that there is little difference in organisational learning practice between different industrial sectors. The one exception to this was in terms of the quality of products and the effectiveness of the quality programmes. When the answers to questions on these topics were cross-tabulated with industrial sector a weak, but significant, association was identified. This suggested that manufacturing organisations believed their product quality to be higher and were more concerned with the effectiveness of their quality programmes compared with organisations in the service sector. Insofar as organisational learning can be used to improve product quality and the effectiveness of quality programmes it may be more relevant in the manufacturing sector than in the service sector. Overall, however, there seems to be relatively little to indicate that organisational learning is not equally applicable and relevant to organisations in all sectors and industries.

Organisational learning in the public sector

One interesting question regarding the relevance of organisational learning concerns its applicability to public-sector organisations. A number of articles have examined the application of organisational learning ideas to organisations in the public sector, particularly in business schools, but also in the National Health Service (NHS). My own research has looked at the role of learning within a Training and Enterprise Council (TEC).

Kilmann explains the way in which the business school at the University of Pittsburgh formed an incoming class of 250 full-time MBA students into 'microcosms of the kind of organizational world that many businesses would be experiencing in the 21st century (and, indeed, is already being experienced by some global network organizations)' (Kilmann, 1996: 210). These

Table 6.1 Industrial sector of participating organisations

Manufacturing	Financial and business services	Wholesale, retail and communications	Other services
72 (45.0%)	45 (28.1%)	33 (20.6%)	10 (6.2%)

microcosms were termed MBA Learning Organisations or Management Learning Organisations. The students were given a four-day workshop on organisational learning techniques, and were then expected to select and design their own learning organisations of twelve to fourteen members. Kilmann believes that the use of this approach provided MBA students with the relevant experiences and necessary skills to function effectively in global learning organisations, and taught them how to build such organisations in the first place.

Ashton, however, takes a markedly divergent view. He asks: 'are business schools good examples of learning organisations?' and answers his own question by concluding that 'the obvious response is negative' (Ashton, 1988: 12). He believes that business schools have a very strong set of 'traditional' values and that there are significant blockages to changing these values. He suggests five new values which 'might be espoused as part of a more effective model for organisational learning in business schools' (*ibid.*: 13). These alternative values are that education means helping people to help themselves; manager performance depends on the focus of education; quality is important – and is defined by the 'customer'; change is part of our culture; and personal authority is based on competence in the learning process. Ashton thus suggests that business schools are poor learning organisations at present, but he clearly believes that the concept of organisational learning is relevant to them and that with application they might reform themselves.

Turning to look at a different type of public-sector organisation, Preston *et al.* (1996) have carried out an extensive study of culture, communication and learning in the NHS. They believe that within an NHS hospital a very traditional hierarchy of roles and professions exists, and that this hierarchy is understood by people at all levels. Their analysis suggests that hospitals are at present poor learning organisations, with the behaviour of organisational members constrained by their roles within the hierarchy and the traditional nature of the organisation's culture. They believe that more realistic and sensitive approaches are needed than have often been taken to date. These new approaches may allow hospitals to realise their potential as learning organisations.

While arguably not a public-sector organisation in the traditional sense, Surrey TEC provides an interesting example of a quasi-public-sector organisation. Ian Barclay, Marketing Consultant at Surrey TEC, offered a number of examples of Surrey TEC's approach to learning. The TEC makes considerable efforts to gain information from its customers to learn what they want and whether the TEC is supplying it effectively. They also learn from other

sources, for example from Coventry and Warwickshire TEC, Surrey's partners in a scheme to establish information sources used by local businesses.
Surrey TEC's development strategy (see Figure 6.4) demonstrates the importance it places on consultation, evaluation, measuring results, and constantly
refining the products and services it offers. Surrey TEC is clearly operating in
an environment that allows it a great deal of scope to learn. It has undoubtedly taken advantage of many of these opportunities and made a conscious
effort to put learning at the centre of its strategy and its operations.

From the above, we can see that a number of public-sector organisations
operate as effective learning organisations, while others are prevented from
doing so, often by their traditional management practices or their traditions
in general. Our conclusion, however, is that public-sector organisations can
function effectively as learning organisations, and that the concept of organisational learning already goes a long way to explaining organisational
behaviour in some public-sector organisations.

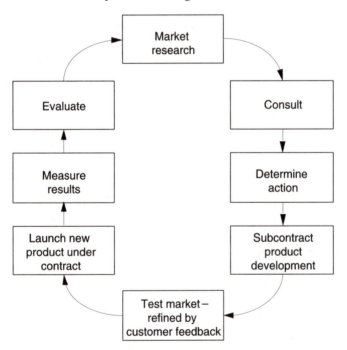

Figure 6.4 Surrey Training and Enterprise Council's development strategy
Source: Interview with Ian Barclay, Marketing Consultant, Surrey TEC, 4 July 1996.

Organisational learning in different countries

Hofstede's (1991) research highlights the significant differences that exist between different countries in terms of both organisational and commercial behaviour. Berger and Watts (1994) confirm that these differences are repeated in different countries' learning styles, although their analysis applies only to Europe.

Blanchard and Waghorn believe that 'Asian companies in general, and Japanese companies in particular, have been very adept at importing the concepts and competencies of their Western allies, but this isn't a one-way street' (Blanchard and Waghorn, 1997: 102). They attribute this to the importance of networks in Asian business, believing that membership of a network makes learning indispensable. However, Japanese and Asian companies have not been especially prominent among those companies famed for their organisational learning prowess. This may be due to a combination of the inherent Asian reluctance to trumpet one's own achievements, and the reluctance of Western researchers and consultants to study Asian companies in preference to taking up the opportunities for study available closer to home.

In their empirical study of strategic behaviour in US and Japanese companies, Sullivan and Nonaka (1986) tested Weick's (1969) theory that organisational learning should be governed by a theory of action. Weick and other early organisational learning theorists such as Argyris and Schön (1978) have argued that each organisation embodies a 'theory of action' that all organisation members must learn. According to the theory, competent managers create new information in order to control the level of uncertainty. In their survey of 75 American managers and 75 Japanese managers Sullivan and Nonaka found that Weick's prescription for a successful theory of action, namely variety amplification by senior managers and variety reduction by junior managers, does seem to characterise Japanese managers more than American managers. This seems to suggest that the concept of organisational learning (according to Weick's theory) as a explanation for management behaviour is more relevant and applicable to the Japanese style of management than to the American style of management. These differences in learning behaviour may also have important considerations for US–Japanese joint ventures.

The author's own survey of organisational learning practice showed that organisations in the US were ahead of their UK counterparts in terms of their knowledge of, and implementation of, organisational learning. Although all participating companies had offices in the South-east of England they were categorised according to the location of the ultimate parent company's Head Office. Table 6.2 shows the geographic distribution of the participating companies.

The cross-tabulation of the geographic origin of each organisation with the answers to the other questions yielded a number of interesting, and statistically significant, results. Looking at the prevalence of e-mail systems, employees in companies with a Head Office in the US or Europe were far more likely to have access to such systems (see Figure 6.5). This is supported by a similar, subsequent study, by Graham (1996: 4), which found that 81 per cent of North American companies had installed e-mail, compared with 73 per cent in the UK and 66 per cent in the Asia-Pacific region.

One possible explanation for the greater access to e-mail in North America and Europe is the higher level of technology possessed by overseas companies, particularly those from North America. Alternatively, overseas companies may place more emphasis on communication within the corporation and so are more likely to invest in an e-mail system in the hope of further stimulating such communication. A third possibility is that overseas companies must, by virtue of their participation in the study, be multinationals. Thus the need for international communications and the greater average size of these companies make the need for an e-mail system much stronger.

The next variable to yield a significant result when cross-tabulated with country of origin was the level of cross-functional working. This result was significant at the 1 per cent level. A high level of cross-functional working is perceived to be one of the key attributes of a learning organisation, and so this result is a significant indicator of differing organisational learning practices between regions.

Figure 6.6 shows the percentage of respondents from each region who gave answers in each category. The conclusion we can draw from this is that organisations with their home base in North America are more likely to exhibit high levels of cross-functional working than UK companies. The most likely explanation for this is simply that North American organisations place more emphasis on this area of management than their UK counterparts. It suggests, in turn, that organisational learning may be more relevant as an

Table 6.2 Geographic origin of participating organisations

United Kingdom	North America	Europe	Asia Pacific	Africa
94 (58.8%)	32 (20.0%)	28 (17.5%)	5 (3.1%)	1 (0.6%)

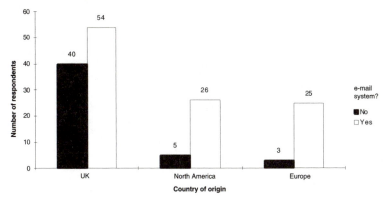

Figure 6.5   The prevalence of e-mail systems in different regions

explanation of the behaviour of North American companies than of the behaviour of UK companies.

Another difference between North American and UK companies was the different emphasis that they place on learning from others. As Figure 6.7 shows, when country of origin was cross-tabulated with the level of learning from others, North American companies had cultures which place greater emphasis on learning from others than those of UK companies. A possible reason for this difference between the two countries is the greater emphasis that US companies typically place on the benchmarking process, a key way of learning from other companies. Alternatively, or perhaps additionally, US companies are more likely to engage in strategic alliances, another valuable source of learning from others.

The overall conclusion that we can draw from the results of the survey carried out as part of this research is that North American companies are

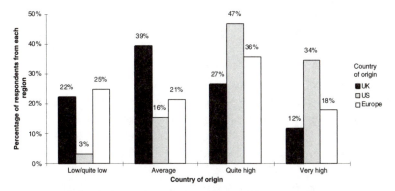

Figure 6.6 The level of cross-functional working in different regions

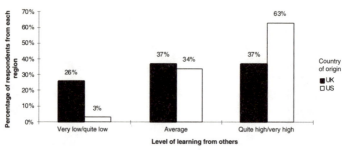

Figure 6.7 The level of learning from others in different regions

more advanced in their application of organisational learning practices than their UK counterparts. Thus organisational learning theory has greater relevance to the study of North American companies than to the study of UK companies. Graham's (1996) report produced similar, although perhaps less conclusive, results about the greater importance of organisational learning in North American companies.

Different countries seem to have adopted the ideas of organisational learning at different rates. Japanese and Asian companies, if Sullivan and Nonaka (1986) are to be believed, seem to have an instinctive grasp of organisational learning. North American companies, meanwhile, are undoubtedly more advanced in their application of organisational learning practices than their British and European competitors. We can hypothesise that British and European companies will continue to copy American management practices and so may begin to close the already quite narrow gap in favour of US companies.

The prescience of organisational learning

It is interesting to note that the two key management ideas of the day are almost diametrically opposed in their implications for people management. On the one hand there are the continuing trends in downsizing, delayering and outsourcing, while on the other hand we have the increased prominence of organisational learning. The first set of trends embodies an increasing movement towards treating employees as commodity items, to be replaced if unsuitable, relegated to an outside agency or eliminated entirely if possible. Organisational learning, in stark contrast, elevates employees to a central position in the organisation, with their skills and abilities vital to the organisation's survival and prosperity.

Part of the relevance of organisational learning at this moment in the development of management theory may derive from its use as a counter-point to downsizing and related ideas. A backlash is developing against some of the worst excesses of downsizing and re-engineering, and organisational learning is an alternative for disaffected managers to consider. Kim and Mauborgne (1997) argue that, after a decade of downsizing and increasingly intense competition, profitable growth is a tremendous challenge faced by many companies. Since the publication in 1993 of *Re-engineering the Corporation*, even Hammer and Champy have backtracked significantly in the face of the realisation that many of the improvements that were promised have not been realised. One of the main reasons for the failure of so many re-engineering initiatives has been the focus on tackling 'hard' issues, such as systems and processes, often at the expense of 'soft' issues, such as people, cultures, skills and values. Organisational learning explicitly addresses these issues, at a time when the need for initiatives focusing on 'soft' issues is apparent. Perhaps for this reason, organisational learning is seen as attractive by many employees and managers who have become only too aware of the potential threats to their jobs posed by re-engineering.

Paradoxically, organisational learning has risen to prominence at a time when rival ideas have also been in the ascendant. In some ways, this conflict – between the ideas of organisational learning, on the one hand, and re-engineering/downsizing, on the other – has worked to increase interest in organisational learning. Perhaps organisational learning and re-engineering should be considered in the context of Handy's (1994) 'Doughnut Principle', more commonly known as the core/periphery model. Organisational learning may be seen as a suitable way of managing those in the core of the organisation, while the periphery is more suited to re-engineering tech-niques. Organisational learning is thus particularly relevant in today's business environment, in a way that it would not have been in the past.

The relevance of organisational learning: a summary

The central message of this section has been that, while the relevance of organisational learning varies between different groups, there are no organi-sations for which organisational learning is entirely irrelevant, both as a source of management ideas and practices, and as a potential explanation for their behaviour. One situation in which organisational learning is likely to be particularly relevant is when the organisation is participating in a strategic alliance or joint venture. This situation is likely to offer an excellent opportu-nity to learn from the partner organisation, and organisational learning practices may help the organisation to derive maximum benefit from this opportunity.

Small organisations have both advantages and disadvantages compared to larger organisations when considering organisational learning. They benefit from less bureaucracy and greater flexibility, but are hampered by their lack of established training and development practices. In practice, while most examples of learning organisations are drawn from large companies, there is no reason why smaller companies should not benefit equally. Similarly, there is no evidence to suggest that organisational learning is more relevant to one industrial sector than another. Both service and manufacturing companies can, and do, apply organisational learning ideas. Public-sector organisations can also function effectively as learning organisations, although they have not generally been at the forefront of the application of organisational learning.

Finally, the author's own research suggests that organisational learning practices are more widespread in North America than in the UK. This conclusion is supported by other empirical studies and by anecdotal evidence. Japanese companies are also at the forefront of organisational learning, and some evidence suggests that their progress may be more advanced than that of North American companies.

Again, however, we return to the conclusion that organisational learning is, broadly speaking, equally relevant to all types of business, large and small, service and manufacturing, public and private, and British, American and Japanese. Part of this relevance derives from the timeliness of organisational learning and its suitability as a counterbalance to some of the commoditisation of employees inherent in management practices such as downsizing, outsourcing and re-engineering.

Conclusion

Excellent business performance is undoubtedly the result of a number of synergistic, and yet in many ways competing, factors. It goes without saying that excellent products are a prerequisite for success, but so are skilled, committed employees, a good marketing plan, a sound business strategy and good financial management. Even the strongest proponents of organisational learning would not claim it is the key to success in all these areas. The multiple causes of success mean that the exact reasons for success will always remain obscure and mysterious. The complex, multidimensional nature of success means that attempts to explain it must increasingly take into account more and more variables. In one sense organisational learning is thus attractive because it can be seen as wide-ranging and, in some ways, all-embracing. However, the difficulty of accurately defining organisational learning detracts from its usefulness as an explanation of organisational behaviour.

It is likely that organisational learning will continue to be redefined, by both academics and managers, in ways that make it more meaningful and useful. Managers still see organisational learning as a useful source of competitive advantage, and for as long as this attraction remains organisations will continue to implement organisational learning ideas. Academics are continually refining their understanding of organisational learning and seeking to use it as a way of explaining the way in which organisations behave. Their overall view of organisational learning is quite negative, largely because of the lack of clarity and vagueness present in much organisational learning theory. However, this lack of academic clarity does not necessarily result in the conclusion that organisational learning is neither useful nor relevant.

It is instructive at this point to recall our conclusion to Chapter 4. We demonstrated that, of the five case companies, three (3M, CCSB and Mayflower) could be described as genuinely successful. 3M and CCSB were the two companies which most closely fitted the ideal of the learning organisation. Mayflower, while grouped with Morgan Crucible and Siebe, was, of these three companies, the one which had made most progress in its attempts to become a learning organisation. Thus the three most successful case companies are the three which best fit the ideal of the learning organisation. While acknowledging that it would be dangerous to read too much into this information, especially given the caveats above concerning causality and the problem of counterfactual reasoning, this does suggest a link, albeit a somewhat tenuous one, between organisational learning and success. Thus, unlike many of the studies of organisational learning cited above, we do offer empirical evidence supporting organisational learning as a useful and relevant concept.

Thus our overall conclusion on the usefulness and relevance of organisational learning is broadly positive. Organisational learning is certainly not a panacea for all organisational ills, and neither is it the culmination of the search for a general theory of business success; a search which is in any case fundamentally flawed and ultimately doomed to failure. However, while there are clearly a number of problems and unanswered questions surrounding the issue of organisational learning, it does appear to offer real opportunities and benefits for organisations. As Andy McIntosh, Director of Group Personnel at Morgan Crucible, says: 'I think any organisation that sets out to be a learning organisation is one which inevitably has a competitive advantage.' The extent and sustainability of this competitive advantage is unclear, but it is difficult to avoid the conclusion that, *ceteris paribus*, an organisation which learns more effectively than its competitors will enjoy a concomitant advantage.

7 Organisational learning and organisational effectiveness – myth and reality

Introduction

We have endeavoured to answer the broad question 'How useful is the concept of organisational learning as a sustainable source of competitive advantage?' In short, does organisational learning lead to enhanced organisational effectiveness? The popular concepts of organisational learning and the learning organisation, and their role in organisational effectiveness, formed the concrete objects of discussion. The role and importance of organisational learning in the five case companies were analysed in great depth. The reasons behind the growth of organisational learning, the practice of organisational learning and the usefulness of organisational learning were all examined. Before we move on to a discussion of the main findings and implications for managers, a brief overview of the different chapters is warranted.

In Chapter 1 the topic of organisational learning as a whole was introduced. We noted the increasing popularity and importance of organisational learning. The goal of integrating management theory and practice was outlined. The major research issues were set out and the need for further research was established. It was argued that the need for further research was apparent both in the academic literature and in the minds of managers. The research questions developed for the project were set out and the structure of the book was outlined. The sources and methods used for the research were briefly summarised.

Chapter 2 presented an original analysis of the origins of organisational learning and of the driving forces or antecedents which have made the concept popular with both managers and academics. Six antecedents of organisational learning were identified, based on both the existing literature and interviews with managers in the case companies. The six antecedents are the shift in the relative importance of the factors of production away from capital towards labour, particularly intellectual labour; the increasing acceptance of knowledge as a prime source of competitive advantage; the increasingly rapid pace of change in the business environment; increasing dissatisfaction with the traditional command-and-control management paradigm; the increasingly competitive nature of global business; and the greater demands being placed on all businesses by customers. These antecedents formed the context within which organisational learning was evaluated in subsequent chapters. The discussion of the antecedents was followed by an explanation of the filters through which knowledge regarding organisational learning is communicated to senior managers. These filters represent important channels of communication, and we argued that the source of senior managers' information regarding organisational learning is an important determinant of the way it is implemented. In summary, Chapter 2 showed how top-management commitment to the creation of a learning organisation develops.

In Chapter 3 the way in which each of the five participating organisations approaches organisational learning was described and assessed. Each case study was unfolded in terms of three dimensions: strategy, structure and culture. This chapter introduced entirely new information drawn from interviews with managers and employees in the case companies. These case studies were used to create a comprehensive picture of how organisational learning is applied in a number of practical settings. This chapter highlighted the significant differences between the approaches adopted by each company. This, in turn, suggests that organisational learning is best viewed as a fairly loose construct.

In Chapter 4 we drew heavily on the case studies which were presented in Chapter 3 to establish a model of best practice in organisational learning. Chapter 4 was divided into two main parts, 'The characteristics of organisational learning' and 'The five case companies and best practice in comparative perspective'. In the first part a model was developed showing the key characteristics of organisational learning. 'Ideal' organisational behaviour was outlined in terms of each characteristic. The second part placed the five case companies in comparative perspective and assessed their respective attempts to achieve best practice. Comparative analysis of the key characteristics of organisational learning was followed by an integrative section comparing and contrasting the companies' approaches to organisational learning practice as a whole.

Chapter 5 looked at leadership and the role of senior management in the creation of a learning organisation. We concluded that effective leadership from senior managers is critical to the creation of a learning organisation. Using case studies of organisational learning, leadership and strategy in four of the case companies, we showed that leadership styles vary markedly across the sample. We argued that leadership roles have changed significantly in recent years, and predicted that they will continue to do so. We concluded that if leaders wish to create learning organisations they need to fulfil new roles to create shared vision and commitment, and design a team-based organisation.

Chapter 6, a key part of the book, directly addressed the main theme of organisational learning as a source of competitive advantage. We showed that the usefulness of organisational learning is determined by its ability to create meaningful benefits for companies that become learning organisations, while the relevance of organisational learning depends on its applicability in a variety of organisational settings.

Companies which have applied the concept of organisational learning were examined to determine whether they had gained meaningful benefits. The chapter progressed through individual learning, then through the conversion of individual learning to organisational learning, and finally to organisational learning itself. We explained the critical importance of showing that learning leads to new behaviours if we are to imply that organisational learning is useful. The barriers which often prevent or delay change were discussed and their importance was evaluated. Finally, we questioned whether the changed behaviour is necessarily superior, and whether changes can be measured or compared with what would otherwise have occurred. We concluded that it is very difficult to attribute specific benefits to organisational learning, but that it is possible, perhaps probable, that benefits do exist. Going further, the size and extent of these benefits is impossible to determine accurately.

Turning to look at the relevance of organisational learning, we questioned the implicit assumption made by many writers that organisational learning is equally applicable to all organisations. Organisational learning was considered in different situations, in large and small organisations, in different industries, in the public sector and in different countries. We also discussed the prescience of organisational learning, and argued that organisational learning is a timely counterpoint to the continuing trends in downsizing, delayering and outsourcing. The conclusion to this chapter outlined the view that the usefulness and relevance of organisational learning depend on how it is defined and on who is doing the defining. Managers tend to view organisational learning in terms of the group of management practices that it represents, which means it has limited, but still significant, usefulness as a guiding principle. Academics tend to define organisational learning far more tightly, making it valuable when explaining certain types of organisational behaviour, but limiting its value by reducing the field of vision.

Key findings

The main findings of this study are captured in the answers to the research questions that were set out in the introductory chapter. The first research question was concerned with the factors which have spurred the development of the learning organisation. We showed that there are six main antecedents of organisational learning. The confluence of circumstances through which these six factors co-exist has created a need for organisations to change and respond. This need for change can be seen as an opportunity, and many organisations have indeed taken this view. We also noted at this point the importance of the route by which ideas reach managers. There are essentially two routes: via academics or via managers and consultants. We showed that consultants tend to present a more positive view of organisational learning than academics. We suggested that a manager's view of organisational learning may depend crucially on how he or she first learnt of the concept. We showed that the three most important sources of information for managers on organisational learning were the work of Peter Senge, the *Harvard Business Review* and colleagues or other managers. Academic works were of relatively little importance. This means that most managers were first exposed to organisational learning in a positive setting, something which is likely to have influenced their long-term view of the concept.

The next two research goals were closely related and can be answered together. One goal was to develop a model of the characteristics of organisational learning and how they interrelate, while the other was to assess which of the nine characteristics are considered important by the case companies and why. A set of nine characteristics was developed, based on the case studies of the five participating companies and on an analysis of the wider literature on organisational learning. Three key characteristics of organisational learning were identified as a learning strategy, a flexible structure and a blame-free culture. A key aspect of organisational learning was found to be the combination of these characteristics. Organisations could not be seen as learning organisations unless they successfully achieved most or all of the nine characteristics; it was not enough to be very good in terms of only one or two characteristics. However, the characteristics form an aspirational model which managers can use as a window on what is possible in ideal conditions. Each of the five case companies had particular characteristics which it considered important and in which it performed well. 3M emphasised its blame-free culture, its vision, its expertise in knowledge creation and its supportive atmosphere. CCSB considered vision and supportive atmosphere to be particularly important characteristics. Mayflower focused on its quality programme, while Morgan Crucible highlighted flexible structure and quality as being important. At Siebe flexible structure, quality and team emphasis were considered particularly important characteristics. These differences of emphasis between the case companies were explained in terms of their different structures, histories and strategies. We concluded that the meaning and practice of organisational learning differ from company to company.

An examination of current best practice in organisational learning was called for in the next research question. Again, this is closely related to the previous questions. Best practice was mainly dealt with by using the five case companies as examples, although evidence was brought in from elsewhere when necessary. The markedly different approaches of the five case companies to organisational learning made an examination of best practice difficult. The use of the model of the characteristics of organisational learning detailed above gives one perspective on best practice. However, as this is designed as an aspirational model it is somewhat divorced from best practice. Corporate change of all types is necessarily improvisational in nature, and this may be particularly true of organisational learning. Thus a description of best practice risks becoming a nebulous management nostrum. It is perhaps best to emphasise again the elusive nature of organisational learning, and to highlight the importance of viewing organisational learning practice in terms of both meaning and content.

The next research goal was to investigate how businesses can become learning organisations. The characteristics of organisational learning give a model of what the organisation needs to achieve but do not show the steps that it needs to take to reach this goal. However, the characteristics do show that becoming a learning organisation requires not just that the company make organisational learning a strategic goal, but also that it make changes in structure and in culture. We also suggest that a useful first step is the creation of a single entity to oversee all organisational learning activities. Most important of all, we emphasise the role of senior management in creating the structures, processes and techniques needed in a learning organisation.

This leads us nicely to the next research goal: to evaluate the role of top management in creating learning organisations. In Chapter 5 we showed that effective leadership is crucial to the creation of learning organisations. This leadership can most readily come from senior managers, particularly as organisational learning is invariably introduced in a top-down, senior-management-led manner. We concluded that in order to create learning organisations senior managers would need to take on new leadership roles. These new roles should lead to the creation of commitment and shared vision, and to the building of a team-based organisation. These are the foundations on which organisational learning can then be practised.

The next research goal was to assess the usefulness of organisational learning as a means of building competitive advantage. In evaluating the usefulness of organisational learning, we first showed the progression from individual learning, through team learning, to organisational learning. We then argued that for organisational learning to be useful it has to lead to a demonstrable change in behaviour, and that this behaviour has to be superior to the previous behaviour (and, arguably, to alternative behaviours). We delineated the barriers to changes in behaviour, grouping them as political difficulties, problems of control and cultural issues. We showed that even if learning leads to a change in behaviour there are a number of important obstacles to the conclusion that it is a useful source of competitive advantage. To reach such a conclusion we would need to show that organisational learning leads to superior behaviour and performance. One obstacle is the problem of not knowing the behaviour and performance that would have occurred had the learning not taken place. Another difficulty is that of determining causality – whether organisational learning causes an otherwise ordinary company to become successful, or whether successful companies choose to become learning organisations. The third obstacle to concluding that organisational learning is useful is the difficulty inherent in measuring the benefits of organisational learning. Even if the learning has led to significant changes in behaviour, placing a value on these changes may be almost impossible. We offered a number of possible measures of the results of learning, but concluded that these were likely to be, at best, imperfect. Overall, then, the answer to this question has to be broadly positive – organisational learning can be useful as a means of building competitive advantage. We demonstrated in Chapter 4 that the case companies which most closely fitted the ideal of the learning organisation were also the most successful. There must be a strong possibility, even presumption, that organisational learning is a useful concept, but we acknowledge that this cannot be definitively proven.

Following closely from this question is the question of whether organisational learning is an appropriate and realistic response to changes in the business environment. We noted that the two key management ideas of the 1990s are almost diametrically opposed in their implications for people management. Downsizing, delayering, re-engineering and outsourcing, on the one hand, all imply an increasing trend towards treating employees as commodity items; organisational learning, on the other hand, implies the elevation of employees to a central position in the organisation. Thus organisational learning is likely to be particularly relevant at present as a counterpoint to the downsizing, re-engineering and related ideas, and as an expression of the backlash that has developed against such concepts.

The next research goal was to analyse whether organisational learning has any relevance for managers other than as an umbrella term for a disparate group of standard management practices. We offered two perspectives on this question. First, if organisational learning is tightly defined – as in 'organisations are seen as learning by encoding inferences from history into routines that guide behaviour' (Levitt and March, 1988: 320) – it is useful as an explanation of certain, limited, types of behaviour. In this sense, however, its usefulness will be largely confined to academic circles. Second, if organisational learning is more loosely defined, so as to be, in effect, an umbrella term, it may be highly useful as a guiding principle for managers, but of limited use as an explanation for particular examples of organisational behaviour. In conclusion, we can say that organisational learning can be more than just an umbrella term, but that this may reduce its practical relevance for managers. What is required is a widely accepted definition that encompasses both the guiding principle required by managers and the explanation of organisational behaviour required by academics. However, such a definition does not exist at present.

The final research goal was to assess the relevance of organisational learning for different groups and in different settings. Many writers have implicitly suggested that organisational learning is a concept that is equally applicable to all organisations. We argued that this was not necessarily the case and that it is unwise to generalise from a particular type of organisation in a particular context to all organisations in all contexts. We considered the relevance of organisational learning in different situations, for example in joint ventures or during new product development, in large and small organisations, in different industries, in the public sector and in different countries. The main conclusion here was that, while the relevance of organisational learning varies between different groups, there are no organisations for which organisational learning is entirely irrelevant, both as a source of management ideas and practices, and as a potential explanation for their behaviour.

We have now dealt with each of the research questions in turn. As was articulated in the introduction, the main research aim is *the evaluation of organisational learning as a source of competitive advantage.* In pursuit of this aim a number of points need to be made. Organisational learning is a highly attractive concept, particularly to managers, despite readily apparent problems of definition and application. Given this attractiveness, it would be easy to assume that since so many companies are trying to become learning organisations the concept must be a source of competitive advantage. However, this research shows that the question of whether organisational learning is a source of competitive advantage is much more complex than that.

Despite the breadth, even vagueness, of the concept, it is likely that learning is becoming (and will continue to become) an important aspect of the strategies of many companies. It is difficult to establish a causal link between organisational learning and competitive advantage. However, it is clear that knowledge – and, more specifically, the application of knowledge – is a key source of competitive advantage, as are the people within an organisation. Organisational learning prioritises the creation and acquisition of new knowledge, and emphasises the role of people in the creation and utilisation of that knowledge. In this sense, organisational learning represents an important route to competitive advantage.

Some of the above findings may seem like an argument against the value of organisational learning as a source of competitive advantage. However, that would be too simplistic an interpretation of the findings. The main argument is that organisational learning is a complex phenomenon, and that overly simplistic interpretations represent the biggest threat to its successful interpretation.

Links to other research

This book has exposed many of the significant problems inherent in much of the literature on organisational learning. Practitioner-oriented works, in particular, were exposed as inadequate and superficial accounts of organisational learning. They were shown to offer overly simplistic and overly prescriptive views of organisational life. Examples of such works include those by Braham (1995), Wick and Leon (1993), Marquardt (1996) and Tobin (1993). Organisational learning is often treated as a panacea capable of transforming any organisation into the epitome of business success. Fortunately, this view is balanced by the more realistic views of academics and more analytical consultants. Academic authors have been shown to be much more critical of what organisational learning can and cannot achieve. Thus a more balanced, rounded view of organisational learning is presented in the academic literature. We have drawn heavily on the work of academic authors such as Senge (1990a), Watkins and Marsick (1993) and Argyris (1996). This book supports the prevailing view among such works that organisational learning is a complex phenomenon. We reinforce this message by offering examples from the case companies. Indeed, we go further, detailing the specific nature of this complexity with reference to the many barriers to organisational learning, the different definitions and meanings attributed to organisational learning, and the problems of obtaining demonstrable results from organisational learning. The literature on organisational learning is almost totally bereft of meaningful empirical studies, and this is a serious shortcoming which detracts from the value of many studies in the area.

Overall, we have shown that the literature on organisational learning has a number of limitations. The practitioner-oriented literature is often superficial and fanciful, while the academic literature is limited both empirically and in terms of the complexity of its analysis. As we will see in the next section, one of the contributions of this book has been to address some of these limitations. Of course, this book is not entirely new or totally original. However, it reinforces, extends and evaluates important messages put forward by Senge, Argyris and others. It does so by a careful grounding of their suggestions in organisational reality, thus offering a counterweight to the largely simplistic practitioner-oriented literature on organisational learning.

The value of organisational learning

As we have seen, the value of organisational learning is very difficult to assess. However, one of the most important contributions of this book stems from the thoroughness with which it examines the concept of organisational learning. The case-study approach is common within the literature on organisational learning. However, most case studies contain little more than limited and selectively reported details. In fact, in some instances what is described as a case study turns out to be little more than a short anecdote about a particular organisation. This book faces up to the problem by offering genuinely detailed accounts of organisational learning within five major manufacturing companies. More generally, the lack of detailed empirical work on organisational learning is marked, and significantly detracts from the value of much of what has been written on the subject. In essence, the book marks a small yet significant step along the road towards developing a credible body of empirical work on organisational learning.

The holistic approach employed in carrying out the research for this book has allowed a more balanced view of organisational learning to be presented. Many works consider only certain aspects of organisational learning and its interaction with everyday management; some are purely academic, others emphatically practice-oriented. Some works are distinguishable by their focus on the results of organisational learning, and some by their focus on the mechanisms of organisational learning. In these circumstances the value of such works is limited by what they do not consider. By using a more wide-ranging, holistic approach we have drawn together the different strands of thinking on organisational learning. By engaging with both the academic literature and practising managers we have been able to gain a clearer insight into the realities of organisational learning and the pursuit of competitive advantage.

A key contribution of this book is to offer a realistic, albeit inconclusive, assessment of the usefulness of organisational learning as a source of competitive advantage. While it was ultimately impossible to assess definitively the usefulness of organisational learning, significant value can still result from the delineation of the process necessary to show such usefulness. We can only hope that further research will shed more light on this complex question.

The origins of organisational learning are clear. The rise to prominence of the concept has been driven by a coherent logic that is derived from managers' everyday experience. The successful description of the antecedents that have led to the espousal of organisational learning by so many consultants, and its adoption by so many managers, is a powerful aid to any assessment of organisational learning's contribution to enhanced effectiveness. While other studies have described forces behind the rise of organisational learning, they have not shown in such detail the confluence of circumstances that has led to the increased prominence of organisational learning. Nor have they shown the different roles of consultants, academics and peer pressure in the communication of management ideas.

As readers will be aware, there exists an ongoing debate on the role of senior managers in modern organisations. We showed that leaders must take on new roles if they are to create learning organisations. Many organisations already acknowledge the importance of vision, commitment and team-working, but this book shows that organisations must renew their emphasis on these factors, in practice as well as in rhetoric. These findings result from extensive interviews at board level in major companies and offer valuable insights for all senior managers engaged in running large organisations.

One limitation of this book is that no rules have been devised for managers to transform their companies into learning organisations. There are no neat models or rules for implementation which can be applied easily in a wide range of contexts and settings. The view of organisational learning presented here is less straightforward and more complex than those typically offered in consultancy reports and the popular management literature. However, I hope that this book will strike a chord with practising managers as well as with academics – purely because it conforms more closely with their own tacit understanding of organisational realities.

Finally, I hope that this book will be of value to all those interested in organisational learning: managers, consultants, academics and students. I hope to have demonstrated that there is indeed real value in the concept of organisational learning – it is, as one interviewee said, 'a great vision' (Jeff Skinner, Management Development Manager, 3M UK). Equally, however, I must acknowledge that further research is required to determine definitively both the usefulness of organisational learning and the best way of implementing the ideas explored here. I look forward to considering the answers of other researchers to the many questions which remain to be explored. I remain convinced that the only way to understand the complexities of corporate life and the influence of ideas as elusive as those associated with organisational learning is through rigorous intellectual analysis of contemporary management practice. As they say in the *X-Files*, the truth is out there.

Appendix 1
Interviewees

Interviewees at the main case companies

Company	Name	Position (with subsidiary company in parentheses)	Date interviewed
3M UK	Mike Adams	R&D Manager – Automotive Trades	18/02/1994
	Jan Conway	Manager, Employee Planning and Resourcing	15/08/1996
	Paul Davis	Human Resource Development Director (3M Europe)	16/07/1996
	Tony Griffiths	Manager, Corporate Marketing and Public Affairs	01/10/1996
	Kevin Hall	Silver Halide R&D Manager	02/06/1994
	Frank Hill	Customer Support Manager	09/07/1994
	Ben Holmes	Corporate Communications Executive	16/07/1996
	John Howells	Technical Director	04/01/1996 15/08/1996
	Ken Jackson	Director – Human Resources	16/11/1993 11/04/1994 05/06/1996
	Thomas Kendall	Marketing Operations Manager	05/01/1994
	David Meekison	Human Resource Development Manager	10/01/1995
	Liz Mosley	European Marketing Development Manager	09/06/1995
	John Mueller	Chairman and Chief Executive	18/08/1995 16/07/1996

Company	Name	Position (with subsidiary company in parentheses)	Date interviewed
	Ron Neal	Manager – Cash and Insurance Quality Manager – Finance and Technology	09/06/1994
	Jeff Skinner	Management Development Manager	21/10/1994
	Chris Varian	European Marketing Manager, Imaging	20/06/1995
	Richard Northrop	Vice-President, Europe (Imation)*	07/10/1996
	Lance Quantrill	Marketing Communications and Public Affairs Manager, North Europe and Nordic Region (Imation)*	07/10/1996
Coca-Cola and Schweppes Beverages Limited	Dick Charlton	Team Leader	12/10/1994
	Keith Dennis	Personnel Director	13/09/1994 14/11/1995 16/02/1996
	Richard Doyle	Human Resource Manager, Distribution and Logistics	24/10/1994
	Mike Hill	Team Leader	15/03/1995
	Jackie McGuire	Human Resource Manager, Corporate Services	20/10/1994
	Hilary Moos	Human Resource Manager, Frontline	24/10/1994
	Beverley Stratton	Human Resource Manager, Frontline	15/05/1995
	Brian Wileman	Plant Manager	12/10/1994
	Derek Williams	Managing Director	16/02/1996
The Mayflower Corporation plc	Mike Bryant	Managing Director (International Automotive Design)	18/09/1995
	Patrick Crutchley	Project Engineer	21/07/1994
	Mike Fell	Human Resource Director	26/04/1994 25/08/1994 22/04/1996

Company	Name	Position (with subsidiary company in parentheses)	Date interviewed
	John Fuller	Engineering Director	05/09/1995
	Andrew Powling	Business Planning Manager	23/01/1997
	John Simpson	Chief Executive	22/08/1995
The Morgan Crucible Company plc	Graham Bailey	General Manager – Lubrication (ROCOL)	14/10/1994
	Steve Chapman	General Manager – Technical Department (ROCOL)	08/07/1994
	Bruce Farmer	Group Managing Director	12/01/1995
	William Hopkins	Product Development Manager – Lubrication (ROCOL)	14/10/1994
	Andy McIntosh	Director of Group Personnel	28/04/1994 26/01/1995
	Don Neil	Managing Director (ROCOL)	08/07/1994
	Catherine Ripley	Product Development Manager – Safety Products (ROCOL)	14/10/1994
	Philip Wright	Managing Director (Morganite Thermal Ceramics)	07/12/1995
Siebe plc	Alan Barnard	Engineering Director (CompAir Hydrovane)	24/05/1996
	Richard Bradford	Vice-President – Human Resources	03/05/1994 18/10/1995
	Harry Craig	Special Projects Director (CompAir Hydrovane) Group Technology Manager (Siebe)	29/03/1995 12/07/1995
	Malcolm Quarterman	Managing Director (CompAir Hydrovane)	24/08/1994
	Paul Woodroofe	Engineering Services Co-ordinator (CompAir Hydrovane)	24/05/1996

Note: *Readers should note that Imation is now a separate company, although at the time of these interviews it was still part of 3M.

Interviewees at other companies

Company	Name	Position	Date interviewed
BMW	John Banovic	Manpower Development Director	17/08/1994
Civil Service College	Laurence Cranmer	Senior Lecturer	23/05/1994
Procter and Gamble	Richard Desmier	Product Development Manager	06/05/1994
	Phil Marchant	Research Scientist	06/05/1994
	Catherine Nelson	Advertising Brand Manager	09/08/1994
	Tim Penner	General Manager – UK and Ireland	25/04/1994
Surrey TEC	Ian Barclay	Marketing Consultant	04/07/1994
	Mike Essex	Head of Education	16/06/1994

Appendix 2
Participating organisations

The 600 Group Plc
The Automobile Association
ACI Europe (UK) Ltd
Air Products PLC
AKZO Chemicals Ltd
Alfred Dunhill Ltd
Allied Bakeries Ltd
Arjo Wiggins Appleton
Asea Brown Boveri
WS Atkins
A.T.S.
Autobar Ltd
Avco Trust Ltd
B + W Loudspeakers
BAA Heathrow
Bacon and Woodrow
BACS Ltd
Baker and McKenzie
Balfour Beatty
Bally UK Sales Ltd
Bank of England
Barclays Bank PLC
BASF PLC
Bass Plc
Bayer PLC
Bechtel Ltd

BET Plc
Blue Circle Industries
The BOC Group Plc
Robert Bosch Ltd
Bovis Construction
British Telecom
BUNZL/Moss Plastic Parts
BUPA
Campbell's (UK) Ltd
Caradon Plc
Cargill Plc
Carlsberg Tetley
Carlton TV
Channel Four TV
Chantrey Vellacott
The Cheese Company
Chubb Security Ltd
Colgate-Palmolive Ltd
Compass Services (UK)
Courtaulds Plc
CPC (UK) Ltd
Defence Research Agency
Del Monte Foods Int.
DHL International (UK) Ltd
Dow Chemical Company
Easams Ltd

Enterprise Oil Plc

Ericsson Ltd

Esso UK Plc

Eurodollar (UK) Ltd

Fiat Auto (UK) Ltd

Field Group Plc

First National Bank Chicago

Forbuoys Plc

Forte Plc

Friends' Provident Life

Fyffes Group Ltd

Gardner Merchant Ltd

Gestetner Management

Going Places

GPT Video Systems Ltd

Guiness Plc

Hacker Young

Hambros Bank Ltd

Harcros

Henkel Ltd

Hewlett-Packard

HFC Bank

Hill Samuel Bank Ltd

H. J. Heinz Company

Hoechst UK Ltd

Hogg Robinson Plc

ICL Plc

IKEA Ltd

Inchcape Plc

Instore

Intergraph (UK) Ltd

IPC Magazines Ltd

Independent Television News

Jamont UK Ltd

JLI Group PLC

Johnson Mathey Plc

Johnson Wax Ltd

KLM Royal Dutch Airlines

Kodak Ltd

Kone Lifts Ltd

KPMG Peat Marwick

Kuoni Travel Ltd

John Laing Plc

Legal and General

Leo Burnett Ltd

Life Sciences Int.

Liffe

Linnco Ltd

Lloyd's of London

Logica Plc

London Electricity Plc

London Int. Group

Manpower Plc

McGraw-Hill Int. (UK)

Merrill Lynch Europe

Modopaper UK Ltd

Moores Rowland

National Westminster Bank plc

Northern Telecom Europe

Odeon Cinema Ltd

Pannell Kerr Forster

George Payne & Co.

Penguin Books Ltd

Pioneer Hi-Fi (GB) Ltd

Price Waterhouse

Prudential Corporation

Rank Hovis Ltd

The Rank Organisation

Rank Xerox Ltd

Redland PLC

Ricardo Consulting

Royal Insurance

Ryder Plc

Ryman Ltd

J. Sainsbury Plc

Samsung Electronics

Sears Plc
Sedgwick Group Plc
Seiko UK Ltd
Smiths Industries
Smurfit UK
Sotheby's
Spelthorne Borough
Stoy Hayward
Sun Microsystems
Supasnaps Ltd
Superdrug Stores Plc
Surrey County Council
Swiss Bank Corporation
J. Walter Thompson
Toshiba Info. Systems
Total Oil Great Britain

Towry Law
Toyota (GB) Ltd
Trans World Airlines
UBS Phillips & Drew
Unichem Plc
Unisys Ltd
Van Leer (UK) Ltd
Vickers Plc
Vinamul Ltd
S. G. Warburg Group Plc
R Watson & Sons
Andrew Weir and Co. Ltd
Willis Corroon
George Wimpey Plc
WRC Plc
John Wyeth & Brother

References

Adair, J. (1984) *The Skills of Leadership*, Aldershot: Gower.

—— (1988) *Effective Leadership: A Modern Guide to Developing Leadership Skills*, London: Pan.

Albrecht, K. (1992) *The Only Thing That Matters: Bringing the Power of the Customer into the Centre of Your Business*, New York: Harper Business.

Argote, L. and McGrath, J. E. (1993) 'Group processes in organizations: continuity and change', in C. L. Cooper and I. T. Robertson (eds) *International Review of Industrial and Organizational Psychology*, New York: John Wiley.

Argyris, C. (1977) 'Double loop learning in organizations', *Harvard Business Review* 55(5), September–October.

—— (1990) *Overcoming Organizational Defenses: Facilitating Organizational Learning*, Boston, MA: Allyn & Bacon.

—— (1993) 'Education for leading-learning', *Organizational Dynamics* 21(3).

—— (1996) 'Towards a comprehensive theory of management', in B. Moingeon and A. Edmondson (eds) *Organizational Learning and Competitive Advantage*, London: Sage.

Argyris, C. and Schön, D. A. (1978) *Organizational Learning: A Theory of Action Perspective*, Reading, MA: Addison-Wesley.

—— (1983) 'Editorial', *Journal of Management Studies* 20(1): 3–5.

Ashton, D. (1988) 'Are business schools good learning institutions? Institutional values and their effects in management education', *Personnel Review* 17(4): 9–14.

August, O. (1996) 'Siebe ready to head out on the acquisition trail', *The Times*, 4 December.

Bacon, F. (1597) *Meditationes Sacre*.

Bain, N. (1995) *Successful Management*, London: Macmillan Business.

Barabba, V. P. and Zaltman, G. (1991) *Hearing the Voice of the Market: Competitive Advantage Through Creative Use of Market Information*, Boston, MA: Harvard Business School Press.

Barrow, M. (1995) 'Morgan Crucible reaps rewards', *The Times*, 12 September.

Bass, B. M. (1985) *Leadership and Performance Beyond Expectations*, New York: Free Press.

Bass, B. M. and Stogdill, R. M (1990) *Bass and Stogdill's Handbook of Leadership*, 3rd edn, New York: Free Press.

Bateman, T. S. and Zeithaml, C. P. (1993) *Management: Function and Strategy*, 2nd edn, Homewood, IL: Irwin.

Beer, M., Eisenstat, R. A. and Biggadike, E. R. (1996) 'Developing an organization capable of strategy implementation and reformulation: a preliminary test', in B. Moingeon and A. Edmondson (eds) *Organizational Learning and Competitive Advantage*, London: Sage.

Beer, M., Eisenstat, R. A. and Spector, B. (1990) *The Critical Path to Corporate Renewal*, Boston, MA: Harvard Business School Press.

Bennis, W. and Nanus, B. (1985) *Leaders: The Strategies for Taking Charge*, New York: Harper & Row.

Bennis, W., Parikh, J. and Lessem, R. (1994) *Beyond Leadership: Balancing Economics, Ethics and Ecology*, Cambridge, MA: Basil Blackwell.

Berger, M. and Watts, P. (1994) 'Management development in Europe', in C. Mabey and P. Iles (eds) *Managing Learning*, London: Routledge in association with the Open University.

Blanchard, K. and Waghorn, T. (1997) *Mission Possible: Becoming a World Class Organization While There's Still Time*, New York: McGraw-Hill.

Boisot, M. H. (1995) *Information Space: A Framework for Learning in Organizations, Institutions, and Cultures*, London: Routledge.

Bolling, G. F. (1996) *Leadership and Immensity*, Aldershot: Gower.

Boursiquot, M. (1996) 'New product development and Coca-Cola Schweppes Beverages', unpublished MBA dissertation, University of London.

Bowen, H. K., Clark, K. B., Holloway, C. A. and Wheelwright, S. C. (1994) *The Perpetual Enterprise Machine: Seven Keys to Corporate Renewal Through Successful Product and Process Development*, New York: Oxford University Press.

Braham, B. J. (1995) *Creating a Learning Organisation*, London: Kogan Page.

Browne, J. S. and Duguid, S. (1991) 'Organisational learning and communities of practice: toward a unified view of work, learning and innovation', *Organization Science* 2(1): 40–57.

Burns, J. M. (1978) *Leadership*, New York: Harper & Row.

Camillus, J. (1997) 'Shifting the strategic management paradigm', *European Management Journal* 15(1): 1–7.

Chakravarthy, B. S. (1982) 'Adaptation: a promising metaphor for strategic management', *Academy of Management Review*: 735–744.

Chandler, Jr, A. D. (1994) 'The functions of the HQ unit in the multibusiness firm', in R. P. Rumelt, D. E. Schendel and D. J. Teece (eds) *Fundamental Issues in Strategy: A Research Agenda*, Boston, MA: Harvard Business School Press.

Child, J. (1997) 'Strategic choice in the analysis of action, structure, organizations and environment: retrospect and prospect', *Organization Studies* 18(1): 43–76.

Clark, K. B. and Fujimoto, T. (1991) *Product Development Performance: Strategy, Organization, and Management in the World Auto Industry*, Boston, MA: Harvard Business School Press.

Collins, J. C. and Porras, J. I. (1996) *Built to Last: Successful Habits of Visionary Companies*, London: Century Business.

Conger, J. A. (1988) *The Charismatic Leader: Behind the Mystique of Exceptional Leadership*, San Francisco, CA: Jossey-Bass.

Coopey, J. (1996) 'Crucial gaps in "the learning organization": power, politics and ideology', in K. Starkey (ed.) *How Organizations Learn*, London: International Thomson Business Press.

Cotton, S. (1996) 'The organic growth of Morgan Crucible: strategic market planning and the European market for speciality chemicals', unpublished MBA dissertation, University of London.

Couchman, C. (1996) 'Mayflower Vehicle Systems: how sustainable is success?', unpublished MBA dissertation, University of London.

Covey, S. R. (1992) *The Seven Habits of Highly Effective People: Powerful Lessons in Personal Change*, London: Simon & Schuster.

Crainer, S. (1996) *Key Management Ideas: Thinking that Changed the Management World*, London: Pitman.

Critchley, B. and Casey, D. (1996) 'Second thoughts on teambuilding', in K. Starkey (ed.) *How Organizations Learn*, London: International Thomson Business Press.

Cyert, R. M. and March, J. G. (1963) *A Behavioural Theory of the Firm*, Englewood Cliffs, NJ: Prentice Hall.

Czeglédy, A. P. (1996) 'New directions for organizational learning in Eastern Europe', *Organization Studies* 17(2): 327–41.

Daft, R. L. and Weick, K. E. (1984) 'Towards a model of organizations as interpretation systems', *Academy of Management Review* 9: 284–95.

Davis, T. (1994) 'Benchmarks of customer satisfaction measurement: Honeywell, Toyota and Corning', *Planning Review* 22: 38–41.

De Geus, A. P. (1988) 'Planning as learning', *Harvard Business Review* 66(2), March–April: 70–4.

—— (1997) 'The living company', *Harvard Business Review* 75(2), March–April: 51–9.

Dench, S. (1993) 'Why do employers train?', *Employment Department Social Science Research Branch*, Working Paper No. 5, December.

Denton, J. and De Cock, C. (1997) '3M and Imation: demerger as a source of innovation', *Creativity and Innovation Management* 6(2), June: 73–88.

Derdak, T. (ed.) (1988) *International Directory of Company Histories*, Chicago, IL: St James Press.

Dibella, A. J., Nevis, E. C. and Gould, J. M. (1996) 'Understanding organisational learning capability', *Journal of Management Studies* 33(3), May: 361–79.

Dixon, N. (1992) 'Organisational learning: a review of the literature with implications for HRD professionals', *Human Resource Quarterly* 3(1).

Dodgson, M. (1993) 'Organisational learning: a review of some literatures', *Organisational Studies* 14(3): 375–94.

Drucker, P. F. (1969) *The Age of Discontinuity: Guidelines for Our Changing Society*, London: Heinemann.

—— (1992a) 'The new society of organisations', *Harvard Business Review* 70(5), September–October.

—— (1992b) *Managing for the Future: The 1990s and Beyond*, New York: Dutton.

—— (1993) *Post-capitalist Society*, Oxford: Butterworth-Heinemann.

Dumaine, B. (1990) 'Who needs a boss?', *Fortune* 7 May: 40–7.

—— (1989) 'What leaders of tomorrow see', *Fortune*, 3 July.

The Economist (1995) 'And then there were two', 18 November, 104–9.

Edmondson, A. C. (1996) 'Three faces of Eden: the persistence of competing theories and multiple diagnoses in organizational intervention research', *Human Relations* 49(5): 571–95.

Farkas, C. M. and Wetlaufer, S. (1996) 'The ways chief executive officers lead', *Harvard Business Review* 74(3), May–June: 110–22.

Fiol, C. M. and Lyles, M. A. (1985) 'Organizational learning', *Academy of Management Review* 10(4): 803–13.

Fogel, R. W. (1964) *Railroads and American Economic Growth: Essays in Econometric History*, Baltimore, MD: Johns Hopkins University Press.

Friedlander, F. (1983) 'Patterns of individual and organizational learning', in S. Srivastva and Associates (eds) *The Executive Mind: New Insights on Managerial Thought and Action*, San Francisco, CA: Jossey-Bass.

Frohman, A. L. (1997) 'Igniting organizational change from below: the power of personal initiative', *Organizational Dynamics*, winter: 39–53.

Garratt, B. (1987) *The Learning Organization: and the Need for Directors Who Think*, London: Fontana.

—— (1990) *Creating a Learning Organization: A Guide to Leadership, Learning and Development*, Cambridge: Director Books.

Garvin, D. A. (1993) 'Building a learning organisation', *Harvard Business Review* 71(4), July–August: 78–91.

Gervitz, D. (1984) *The New Entrepreneurs*, New York: Penguin.

Ghoshal, S. (1987) 'Global strategy: an organizing framework', *Strategic Management Journal* 8: 425–40.

Goffee, R. and Scase, R. (1995) *Corporate Realities: The Dynamics of Large and Small Organizations*, London: Routledge.

Graham, A. (1996) *The Learning Organisation: Managing Knowledge for Business Success*, New York: Economist Intelligence Unit.

Grant, R. M. (1996) 'Prospering in dynamically-competitive environments: organizational capability as knowledge integration', *Organization Science* 7(4), July–August: 375–87.

Griffith, V. (1995) 'Corporate fashion victim', *The Financial Times*, 12 April.

Haines S. G. and McCoy, K. (1995) *Sustaining High Performance: The Strategic Transformation to a Customer-focused Learning Organization*, Delray Beach, FL: St Lucie Press.

Hamel, G. (1991) 'Competition for competence and inter-party learning within international strategic alliances', *Strategic Management Journal* 12: 83–104.

Hamel, G. and Prahalad, C. K. (1994) *Competing for the Future: Breakthrough Strategies for Seizing Control of Your Industry and Creating the Markets of Tomorrow*, Boston, MA: Harvard Business School Press.

Hammer, M. and Champy, J. (1993) *Re-engineering the Corporation: A Manifesto for Business Revolution*, London: Nicholas Brealey.

Handy, C. B. (1989) *The Age of Unreason*, London: Business Books.

—— (1994) *The Empty Raincoat*, London: Hutchinson.

Hastings, C. (1993) *The New Organization: Growing the Culture of Organizational Networking*, London: McGraw-Hill.

Hayes, R. H., Wheelwright, S. C. and Clark, K. B. (1988) *Dynamic Manufacturing: Creating the Learning Organization*, New York: Free Press.

Hayward, A. (1996) 'The growth and development of the components division of the Japanese electrical and electronics industry, 1954–94', unpublished PhD dissertation, University of London.

Hedberg, B. (1981) 'How organizations learn and unlearn', in P. C. Nystrom and W. H. Starbuck (eds) *Handbook of Organization Design*, Oxford: Oxford University Press.

Heifetz, R. A. and Laurie, D. L. (1997) 'The work of leadership', *Harvard Business Review* 75(1), January–February: 124–34.

Heller, R. (1992) *The Superchiefs: The People, Principles and Practice of the New Management*, London: Mercury.

Hofstede, G. (1991) *Culture and Organizations: Software of the Mind*, Maidenhead: McGraw-Hill.

Huber, G. P. (1991) 'Organizational learning: the contributing processes and the literatures', *Organization Science* 2(1), February: 88–115.

Huczynski, A. A. (1993) *Management Gurus: What Makes Them and How to Become One*, London: Routledge.

Imai, K., Nonaka, I. and Takeuchi, H. (1985) 'Managing the new product development process: how Japanese companies learn and unlearn', in K. B. Clark, R. H. Hayes and C. Lorenz (eds) *The Uneasy Alliance*, Boston, MA: Harvard Business School Press.

Industrial Society, (1996) *The Industrial Society's Training Trends Survey*, London: Industrial Society.

Inkpen, A. (1995) *The Management of International Joint Ventures: An Organizational Learning Perspective*, London: Routledge.

Johannessen, J. and Hauan, A. (1994) 'Organizational unlearning', *Creativity and Innovation Management* 3(1), March: 43–53.

Jones, A. M. and Hendry, C. (1994) 'The learning organization: adult learning and organizational transformation', *British Journal of Management* 5: 153–62.

Kanter, R. M. (1989a) *When Giants Learn to Dance: Mastering the Challenges of Strategy, Management and Careers in the 1990s*, London: Simon & Schuster.

—— (1989b) 'The managerial work', *Harvard Business Review* 67(6), November–December: 85–92.

—— (1991) 'Transcending business boundaries: 12,000 world managers view change', *Harvard Business Review* 69(3), May–June.

—— (1994) 'Collaborative advantage: the art of alliances', *Harvard Business Review* 72(4), July–August: 96–108.

Kaplan, R. S. and Norton, D. P. (1992) 'The balanced scorecard: measures that drive performance', *Harvard Business Review* 70(1), January–February: 71–9.

Karash, R. (1996) 'Coaching and facilitating systems thinking', *The Systems Thinker* 7(5), June–July: 6–7.

Katzenbach, J. R. and Smith, D. K. (1993) *The Wisdom of Teams: Creating the High-performing Organization*, Boston, MA: Harvard Business School Press.

Kay, J. A. (1993) *Foundations of Corporate Success: How Business Strategies Add Value*, Oxford: Oxford University Press.

Kets De Vries, M. F. R. (1988) 'Prisoners of leadership', *Human Relations* 41(3): 261–80.

Kilmann, R. H. (1996) 'Management learning organizations: enhancing business education for the 21st century', *Management Learning* 27(2): 203–37.

Kim, W. C. and Mauborgne, R. (1997) 'Value innovation: the strategic logic of high growth', *Harvard Business Review* 75(1), January–February: 102–12.

Kotter, J. P. (1990) *A Force for Change: How Leadership Differs from Management*, New York: Free Press.

Kotter, J. P. and Heskett, J. L. (1992) *Corporate Culture and Performance*, New York: Free Press.

Leonard-Barton, D. (1995) *Wellsprings of Knowledge: Building and Sustaining the Sources of Innovation*, Boston, MA: Harvard Business School Press.

Lessem, R. (1991) *Total Quality Learning: Building a Learning Organization*, Oxford: Basil Blackwell.

Levitt, B. and March, J. G. (1988) 'Organizational learning', *Annual Review of Sociology* 14: 319–40.

Lewis, P. S., Goodman, S. H. and Fandt, P. M. (1994) *Management: Challenges in the 21st Century*, Minneapolis/St Paul, MN: West.

Leymann, H. (1989) 'Learning theories', in H. Leymann and H. Kornbluh (eds)

Socialization and Learning at Work: A New Approach to the Learning Process in the Workplace and Society, Aldershot: Gower.

Lundberg, C. C. (1996) 'Managing in a culture that values learning', in S. A. Cavaleri and D. S. Fearon (eds) *Managing in Organizations that Learn*, Cambridge, MA: Blackwell.

McGill, M. E., Slocum Jr., J. W. and Lei, D. (1992) 'Management practices in learning organizations', *Organizational Dynamics* 21(1), summer: 5–17.

Maira, A. and Scott-Morgan, P. (1996) *The Accelerating Organization: Embracing the Human Face of Change*, New York: McGraw-Hill.

Maisel, L. S. (1992) 'Performance measures: the balanced scorecard approach', *Journal of Cost Management*, summer.

Manz, C. C. and Sims Jr, H. P. (1995) *Business Without Bosses: How Self-managing Teams are Building High Performing Companies*, New York: John Wiley.

March, J. G. (1991) 'Exploration and exploitation in organizational learning', *Organization Science* 2(1), February: 71–87.

March, J. G. and Olsen, J. P. (1975) 'The university of the past: organizational learning under ambiguity', *European Journal of Political Renewal* 3: 141–71.

Marquardt, M. J. (1996) *Building the Learning Organisation: A Systems Approach to Quantum Improvement and Global Success*, New York: McGraw-Hill.

Marquardt, M. J. and Reynolds, A. (1994) *The Global Learning Organisation: Gaining Competitive Advantage through Continuous Learning*, Burr Ridge: Irwin.

Maslow, A. (1954) *Motivation and Personality*, New York: Harper & Row.

Mayo, A. and Lank, E. (1995) 'Changing the soil spurs new growth', *People Management*, 16 November: 26–8.

Meyer, C. (1993). *Fast Cycle Time*, New York: Free Press / Macmillan.

Miles, R. H. (1980) *Macro Organizational Behaviour*, Santa Monica, CA: Goodyear.

Miner, A. S. and Mezias, S. J. (1996) 'Ugly duckling no more: pasts and futures of organizational learning research', *Organization Science* 7(1), January–February: 88–99.

Mintzberg, H. (1983) *Structures in Five*, Englewood Cliffs, NJ: Prentice Hall.

—— (1994) *The Rise and Fall of Strategic Planning*, New York: Prentice Hall.

Moingeon, B. and Edmondson, A. (eds) (1996) *Organizational Learning and Competitive Advantage*, London: Sage.

Morgan, G. (1988) *Riding the Waves of Change: Developing Managerial Competencies for a Turbulent World*, San Francisco, CA: Jossey-Bass.

Mumford, A. (1994) 'Individual and organizational learning: the pursuit of change', in C. Mabey and P. Iles (eds) *Managing Learning*, London: Routledge in association with the Open University.

Nelson, R. R. and Winter, S. G. (1982) *An Evolutionary Theory of Economic Change*, Cambridge, MA: Harvard University Press.

Nonaka, I. (1991) 'The knowledge-creating company', *Harvard Business Review* 69(6), November–December: 96–104.

—— (1994) 'A dynamic theory of organizational knowledge creation', *Organization Science* 5(1): 14–37.

Nonaka, I. and Takeuchi, H. (1995) *The Knowledge-Creating Company: How Japanese Companies Create the Dynamics of Innovation*, New York: Oxford University Press.

Normann, R. (1985) 'Developing capabilities for organizational learning', in J. M. Pennings (ed.) *Organizational Strategy and Change*, San Francisco, CA: Jossey-Bass.

Oram, R. (1996) 'Cadbury sells UK soft drink plants', *The Financial Times*, 5 June.

Pascale, R.T. (1990) *Managing on the Edge*, London: Viking.

Pearn, M., Roderick, C. and Mulrooney, C. (1995) *Learning Organizations in Practice*, London: McGraw-Hill.

Pedler, M. and Aspinwall, K. (1990) *'Perfect plc'? The Purpose and Practice of Organizational Learning*, Maidenhead: McGraw-Hill.

Pedler, M., Boydell, T. and Burgoyne, J. (1988) *Learning Company Project Report*, Sheffield: Training Agency.

Pedler, M., Burgoyne, J. and Boydell, T. (1991) *The Learning Company: A Strategy for Sustainable Development*, Maidenhead: McGraw-Hill.

Peters, T. J. (1987) *Thriving on Chaos: Handbook for a Management Revolution,* New York: Alfred Knopf.

—— (1992) *Liberation Management: Necessary Disorganization for the Nanosecond Nineties*, New York: Alfred Knopf.

Peters, T. J. and Austin, N. K. (1985) *A Passion for Excellence: The Leadership Difference*, London: Collins.

Peters, T. J. and Waterman Jr, R. H. (1982) *In Search of Excellence: Lessons from America's Best-run Companies*, New York: Harper & Row.

Pettigrew, A. M. (1975) 'Strategic aspects of the management of special activity', *Personnel Review* 4.

—— (1985) *The Awakening Giant: Continuity and Change in ICI*, Oxford: Blackwell.

Pilkington, A. (1996a) *Transforming Rover: Renewal Against the Odds, 1981–94*, Bristol: Bristol Academic Press.

—— (1996b) 'Learning from joint venture: the Rover–Honda relationship', *Business History* 38(1), January: 90–114.

Porter, M. E. (1985) *Competitive Advantage: Creating and Sustaining Superior Performance*, New York: Free Press.

Powling, A. (1996) 'Mayflower PLC: the strategic way forward', unpublished MBA dissertation, University of London.

Preston, D., Smith, A., Buchanan, D. and Jordan, S. (1996) 'Symbols of the NHS: understanding the culture and communication processes of a general hospital', *Management Learning* 27(3): 343–57.

Quinn, J. B. (1992) *Intelligent Enterprise: A New Paradigm for a New Era: How Knowledge and Service Based Systems are Revolutionizing the Economy, All Industry Structures, and the Very Nature of Strategy and Organization*, New York: Free Press.

Quinn Mills, D. (1991) *Rebirth of the Corporation*, New York: John Wiley.

Rebello, K. and Schwartz, E. (1992) 'The magic of Microsoft', *Business Week*, 24 February: 60–4.

Roth, G. (1996) 'From individual and team learning to systems learning', in S. A. Cavaleri and D. S. Fearon (eds) *Managing in Organizations that Learn*, Cambridge, MA: Blackwell.

Sadler, P. (1995) *Managing Change*, London: Kogan Page.

Saggers, R. (1994) 'Training climbs the corporate agenda', *Personnel Management*, July: 40–5.

Sandelands, L. and Drazin, R. (1989) 'On the language of organizational theory', *Organization Studies* 10: 457–78.

Sandelands, L. and Srivatsan, V. (1993) 'The problem of experience in the study of organizations', *Organization Studies* 14.

Schein, E. H. (1985) *Organizational Culture and Leadership*, San Francisco, CA: Jossey-Bass.

—— (1993) 'How can organizations learn faster? The challenge of entering the green room', *Sloan Management Review* 35, winter: 85–92.

Senge, P. M. (1990a) *The Fifth Discipline: The Art and Practice of the Learning Organization*, New York: Doubleday.

—— (1990b) 'The leader's new work: building learning organisations', *Sloan Management Review* 32, fall: 7–23.

Senge, P. M., Roberts, C., Ross, R. B., Smith, B. J. and Kleiner, A. (1994) *The Fifth Discipline Fieldbook: Strategies and Tools for Building a Learning Organization*, London: Nicholas Brealey.

Shrivastava, P. (1983) 'A typology of organizational learning systems', *Journal of Management Studies* 20(1): 7–28.

Sillince, J. A. A. (1995) 'Extending the cognitive approach to strategic change in organisations: some theory', *British Journal of Management* 6: 59–76.

—— (1996) 'A model of social, emotional and symbolic aspects of computer-mediated communication within organizations', *Computer-supported Cooperative Work* 4(2): 1–31.

Stalk Jr, G. and Hout, T. M. (1990) *Competing Against Time*, New York: Free Press.

Stata, R. (1989) 'Organisational learning: the key to management innovation', *Sloan Management Review* 31, spring: 63–74.

Stewart, T. A. (1996) '3M fights back', *Fortune*, 5 February.

Sullivan, J. J. and Nonaka, I. (1986) 'The application of organizational learning theory to Japanese and American management', *Journal of International Business Studies*, fall: 127–47.

Syrett, M. and Hogg, C. (eds) (1992) *Frontiers of Leadership: An Essential Reader*, Oxford: Basil Blackwell.

Thomas, A. B. (1993) *Controversies in Management*, London: Routledge.

Thurbin, P. J. (1994) *Implementing the Learning Organisation: The 17-Day Programme*, London: Pitman.

Tobin, D. R. (1993) *Re-educating the Corporation: Foundations for the Learning Organisation*, Essex Junction: Omneo.

Toffler, A. (1970) *Future Shock*, London: Bodley Head.

Tushman, M. and Nadler, D. (1996) 'Organizing for innovation', in K. Starkey (ed.) *How Organizations Learn*, London: International Thomson Business Press.

Ulrich, D., Jick, T. and Von Glinow, M. A. (1993) 'High impact learning: building and diffusing learning capability', *Organizational Dynamics*, autumn: 52–66.

Vaill, P. B. (1989) *Managing as a Performing Art: New Ideas for a World of Chaotic Change*, San Francisco, CA: Jossey-Bass.

—— (1996) *Learning as a Way of Being: Strategies for Survival in a World of Permanent White Water*, San Francisco, CA: Jossey-Bass.

von Krogh, G. and Roos, J. (1995) *Organizational Epistemology*, London: Macmillan.

von Krogh, G. and Roos, J. (eds) (1996) *Managing Knowledge: Perspectives on Cooperation and Competition*, London: Sage.

Watkins, K. E. and Marsick, V. J. (1993) *Sculpting the Learning Organization: Lessons in the Art and Science of Systemic Change*, San Francisco, CA: Jossey-Bass.

Weick, K. E. (1969) *The Social Psychology of Organizing*, Reading, MA: Addison-Wesley.

Weick, K. E. and Westley, F. (1996) 'Organizational learning: affirming an oxymoron', in S. R. Clegg, C. Hardy and W. R. Nord (eds) *Handbook of Organization Studies*, London: Sage.

Whipp, R., Rosenfeld, R. and Pettigrew, A. (1989) 'Culture and competitiveness: evidence from two mature UK industries', *Journal of Management Studies* 26: 561–85.

Whiteley, R. C. (1991) *The Customer Driven Company: Moving from Talk to Action*, London: Business Books.

Wick, C. W. and Leon, L. S. (1993) *The Learning Edge: How Smart Managers and Smart Companies Stay Ahead*, New York: McGraw-Hill.

Wittgenstein, L. (1990) *Tractatus Logico-philosophicus*, trans. C. K. Ogden, London: Routledge.

Zeithaml, V., Parasuraman, A. and Berry, L. (1990) *Delivering Quality Service*, New York: Free Press.

Zuboff, S. (1988) *In the Age of the Smart Machine: The Future of Work and Power*, New York: Basic Books.

Index